LISBON &
CENTRAL
PORTUGAL

REGIONS OF PORTUGAL
Algarve and Southern Portugal
Lisbon and Central Portugal
Northern Portugal

REGIONS OF FRANCE
Series Editor: Arthur Eperon

Auvergne and the Massif Central
Brittany
Champagne-Ardennes and Burgundy
The Dordogne and Lot
Languedoc and Roussillon
The Loire Valley
Normandy, Picardy and Pas de Calais
Paris
Provence and the Côte d'Azur
The Rhône Valley and Savoy
South West France

Also:
Alsace: the complete guide

REGIONS OF ITALY
Series Editor: John Julius Norwich

Florence and Tuscany
Naples and Campania
Umbria, the Marches and San Marino
Venice and Northeastern Italy

LISBON & CENTRAL PORTUGAL

Brian and Eileen Anderson

A & C BLACK • LONDON

© 1997 Brian and Eileen Anderson

Photographs © Brian and Eileen Anderson
Maps and plans drawn by Robert Smith
© A&C Black (Publishers) Ltd

Published by A & C Black (Publishers)
Ltd, 35 Bedford Row, London WC1R 4JH.

ISBN 0–7136–4147–9

A CIP catalogue record for this book is
available from the British Library

The authors and the publishers have done
their best to ensure the accuracy of all the
information in this guide. They can accept
no responsibility for any loss, injury or
inconvenience sustained by any traveller as
a result of information or advice contained
in this book.

The publishers invite readers to write in
with comments, suggestions and corrections
for the next edition of the guide. Writers of
the most informative letters will be awarded
a free Regional Guide of their choice.

Printed and bound in Singapore by Imago.

To Bob Callow for his friendship and conversation.

Acknowledgements

Perhaps the last thing we expected in central Portugal was to be infected: infected with the enthusiasm of people like Mario Machado of the Sintra Tourist Office, Angelina Barbosa of the Serra da Estrela Natural Park and Letitia Frazer, resident of Portalegre, who shared with us their deep love and knowledge of the country. Meeting them were highlights in a very rewarding tour, but many tourist offices also rendered us valuable assistance and our thanks in particular go to Cristina Bessa at Coimbra, Ana Isabel Correira at Setúbal and João Andrade Santos at Évora. Frederiko Knebull at Sintra is also owed our thanks for his kindness and hospitality, likewise João Manuel V de Castro Ribeiro, director of the Buçaco Palace Hotel, who took the time and trouble to show us around. Pilar Peireira of the Portuguese National Tourist Office has lent us considerable support over the years we have been writing about Portugal and thanking her has become something of a ritual but it is none the less sincere.

CONTENTS

Maps and plans

1. INTRODUCTION

Here, in Portugal's central region, lies the country's cultural and intellectual heart. The area is littered with magnificent palaces, churches and monasteries, many built on the wealth generated from its golden age of discovery. It might be as well to warn of sensory turbulence ahead although there is no way to prepare for the cultural assault in store, from the richness of Sintra's Pena Palace to the austerity of tiny Capuchos monastery nearby. Portugal is the custodian of some of Europe's finest medieval monuments, including the monasteries of Jerónimos, built to commemorate Vasco da Gama's voyage to India in 1497; elegant Alcobaça housing the tombs of Portugal's most famous lovers, Dom Pedro I and Inês da Castro; Batalha, built after victory at the battle of Aljubarrota; and the Convent of Christ at Tomar, founded by the Order of the Knights Templar.

Historic towns and villages are equally demanding of time and attention. Atmospheric Coimbra on the banks of the Rio Mondego, dominated by its university, is a magnet for visitors, but it is hard to press its claims higher than those of Évora, a cultural centre favoured by two dynasties of Portuguese kings and now recognised by UNESCO as a World Heritage site. On a lesser scale but even more evocative are the picturesque old walled towns which dot the region, including Óbidos, Marvão and Castelo de Vide. Top of the list for most visitors to the region, however, are Lisbon and nearby Sintra. Built on seven hills, Lisbon can be hard on the legs but there are always the colourful trams on hand to assist. There is nothing lacking here in culture or atmosphere and the city will absorb as much time as can be spared from a holiday.

If the faintest strains of 'Over the hills and far away' can sometimes be imagined, they are evoked by the many reminders that Sir Arthur Wellesley, later the Duke of Wellington, brilliantly mustered a powerful line of defence here against Napoleon's French forces in the Peninsular War: castles seem to dominate the skyline with each new turn of the road. But there were castles here before, for Portugal is a country which, after an uncertain birth, felt that a strong defence was necessary to secure its continuing existence. Many of the castles are open for inspection, some large, some small and each with its own special atmosphere. Romantics will probably head for Almourol castle, located on an island in the River Tagus (Tejo), or Monsaraz near Évora, but there are many to equal them.

Beach lovers are spoilt for choice. The coast line of central Portugal seems to be endlessly ribboned with fine silver sand, easily justifying its name 'Costa de Prata' (the Silver Coast). Most beaches have good depth and space with only the more popular beaches becoming crowded in high season. Although the Atlantic is not the warmest or calmest of seas, it is warm enough in the summer months to tempt swimmers into action, and when the Atlantic is particularly restless in the spring and autumn it is much loved by surfers.

In character, Central Portugal shows a distinct division between east and west. On the face of it, the western half seems to have all the advantages. It has the coast with all its glorious beaches along with the larger towns and major monuments, but there is a sense of escape in moving east – escape from the traffic and the people into the peace and quiet of the countryside. Walkers and country lovers will appreciate the Natural Park of Serra da Estrela in Portugal's highest mountain range, and for big skies and rolling country head south into Alentejo.

All these aspects of Portugal are explored throughout this book which covers the area from south of the Douro to an imaginary line drawn between Setúbal and Évora. The chapters describe a clockwise tour of the region starting in Lisbon then moving in stages to Sintra, Aljubarrota, Coimbra, Serra da Estrela, Portalegre, Évora and Setúbal, each of which was used as a base to explore the surrounding area.

Geography and Geology

Sand and dunes dominate the littoral region, much of it stabilised by pine plantations. This is especially evident in Costa Azul, south of Lisbon, which is nothing more than a huge sand bank, and again along many of the coasts in the centre of the region. Inland there is a diversity of landform, hilly in parts but with no significantly high mountains until Serra da Estrela is encountered. This is the highest mountain range in Portugal reaching an elevation of 1993m at Torre. Extensive undulating plains take over in the south, especially in Alentejo, and give the region a unique character.

One of the most striking features of this central region is the Tagus valley. The River Tagus, rising in Spain, takes a south-westerly course through the whole of Portugal, culminating in a huge watery estuary at Lisbon. Its waters are further swollen by the River Zêzere flowing south from the Serra da Estrela. The Tagus leaves in its wake a swathe of fertile alluvial land which cuts deep into the peninsula. Only the Mondego river which rises in the region of Serra da Estrela and joins the Atlantic at Figueira da Foz is wholly Portuguese.

Matching the diversity of landform is the diversity of geology. Granite dominates in many areas inland and particularly in the Serra da Estrela which are old-fold mountains believed to have arisen during Hercynian folding in the late Palaeozoic, some 300 million years ago. Granite tors and boulders are seen scattered throughout, as they are in other granite regions, sometimes assuming weird and wonderful shapes. The outstanding examples are often

Candy-striped beach tents and huts are a feature along parts of the Silver Coast

given descriptive names but not all are instantly recognisable without applying a liberal dose of imagination. Limestone mountains are found in Serra da Arrábida and again in Serra dos Candeeiros, near Porto de Mós. This latter mountain range is remarkable for a number of huge caves discovered in the region. Marble deposits too are scattered about and are quarried in some regions, especially around Estremoz in Alentejo and Pero Pinheiro just north of Sintra.

Climate

Central Portugal is a meeting point of three different climatic influences. It is very much under the influence of Atlantic weather patterns and moist westerlies, which penetrate deep into the country before yielding to drier continental influences in the east and Mediterranean climatic conditions in the south. Winter is mild and wet in the coastal regions and colder and drier inland. Rainfall patterns vary also from north to south. Except for Serra da Estrela, the north-west generally receives the highest rainfall with Porto averaging around 1290mm annually compared to 725mm in Lisbon, and almost all of it falling between November and March. The highest rainfall is reserved for the mountains of Serra da Estrela which receive a massive 2365mm annually, much of it falling as snow on the higher ground from December through to March. Mild winter temperatures are enjoyed in coastal areas with insignificant variation from north to south. Mean temperature in January is around 10.2°C. The olive tree, a good indicator of a Mediterranean climate, grows

3

throughout the region (except for the Serra da Estrela) suggesting that minimum winter temperatures are rarely low enough to create a serious frost.

Summers are long, hot and dry with temperatures kept down in coastal regions by the cool westerlies. The mean July temperature in Lisbon is around 21.1° C, very similar to conditions in Porto. Temperatures increase steadily moving inland towards the centre of the peninsula and, in Alentejo for example, maximum temperatures frequently reach 40° C in the height of summer. Rainfall is generally low throughout the whole of summer and Lisbon expects around 95 rain-free days each year, which is rather more than Porto. Drought periods are even longer inland.

When to Go

In spite of the risk of rain, Costa Lisboa attracts a surprising number of visitors in winter, especially from January onwards. The days are mild and, when the sun shines, it can be extremely pleasant. Portugal is on GMT and like Britain advances its clocks one hour for summer at the end of March. It returns to GMT at the end of September, one month ahead of Britain.

April starts the main tourist season when temperatures are on the rise and the days gradually lengthening. Showers are still possible but, with the country-side sparkling under its new green coat and the wild flowers at their best, this is one of the loveliest times of the year. May sees the summer season taking control, with showers now less likely and temperatures climbing steadily. Summer temperatures are high but pleasantly moderated by the westerlies, so that they rarely reach the burningly high temperatures of the interior.

Spring is possibly the best time for touring inland regions, especially Alentejo which is at its most alluring under a cloak of green and with the storks busy nesting. Summer heat burns this landscape to a dull, dusty brown and reduces breathtaking spring landscapes to the very ordinary. Travel writers are often polarised in their opinions of Alentejana landscapes; some are totally captivated whilst others describe them as boring. To make a fair judgement Alentejo needs to be seen in both spring and high summer, but those uncomfortable in extreme heat should avoid the main summer period.

High season in Serra da Estrela is in winter, from December through until the end of March when skiing is in progress. Snow depths average around 2m but good snow is only reliable between January and March: hotel prices are at their highest throughout this period. Snow lies around the upper levels until early summer. Most of the rain, or snow, falls between October and May often with low cloud obscuring the mountain tops. Summers are dry and surprisingly warm even at higher altitudes. Late May is probably the earliest time for summer visitors to contemplate, although cool temperatures can still be expected. June through until September is the best time for reliable weather but, as in all mountain areas, brief thunderstorms are not unusual.

September is a delightful month to visit the region. It introduces the 'season of mellow fruitfulness' – particularly apt in central Portugal which is largely dedicated to farming. The weather continues fine, warm and dry and it is a delight to see the harvests being gathered from the fields, especially the grape picking. This activity starts in late August in the hotter regions and continues throughout September, progressively later at higher altitudes. October is a variable month and brings an increasing risk of showers although temperatures remain pleasantly warm. This month also sees a steady decline in the number of visitors, especially towards the end of the month which marks the close of the main tourist season.

Flora and Fauna

The climatic types – Atlantic, Continental and Mediterranean – which produce a marked gradation of climate across the country also influence the flora and its distribution patterns. Serra da Estrela is a distinct meeting point of these climatic influences and there are easily observed differences in the vegetation on crossing the mountains east to west or north to south (see the feature on page 175 for more details).

Exclusively Western Atlantic species, such as some of the *Erica* heaths, green lavender, *Lavendula viridis* and gorse (*Ulex* species), are only observed on the far western side of the region, but they may sometimes be found with typically Mediterranean species like cistus. Otherwise there is a spread of plant communities throughout.

Dominant pine species are the maritime pine, *Pinus pinaster*, and the stone or umbrella pine, *P. pinea*, but these are complemented by broadleaved trees such as the ubiquitous sweet chestnut, *Castanea sativa*, and oaks such as the Pyrenean oak, *Quercus pyrenaica*. Evergreen oaks such as the cork oak, *Quercus suber*, and the holm oak, *Q. ilex* are especially common in the south of the region, notably in Alentejo. The olive grows throughout, with the exception of the upper levels of Serra da Estrela, and citrus fruits, mainly oranges and lemons, thrive best in the western half of the region.

There are two regions of particular interest to botanists, the limestone hills of Serra da Arrábida and the granite heights of Serra da Estrela, both of which are described in detail in the appropriate chapters. Another limestone area worth investigation is the Serra dos Candeeiros, now protected as a Natural Park, which has received less intensive study.

Most of the region's fauna today comprises small mammals like rabbit, fox, gennet and the Egyptian mongoose, although there are still plenty of wild boar (*Sus scrofa eastillianus)* around, especially in the south. The male can be dangerous, but is rarely encountered in the daytime as wild boar are nocturnal. Wolves occur nowhere in the region, not even in the wilds of Serra da Estrela, being apparently restricted to the wilder parts north of the River Douro.

Parts of Central Portugal offer a feast for bird-spotters. The huge estuary of the River Tagus, on which Lisbon stands, attracts birds throughout the year, but is especially good in winter when it is estimated that some 40,000 wading birds visit. A large part of the estuary is now protected as a nature reserve. This is the place to see avocet, *Recurvirosta avosetta*, which are present in great numbers as are black-tailed godwit, *Limosa limosa*. Other species easy to spot include the bar-tailed godwit, *Limosa lapponica*, the grey plover, *Pluvialis squatarola*, the ringed plover, *Charadrius hiaticula*, and the redshank, *Tringa totanus*. The Sado estuary just south of Setúbal is also good for wading birds and likewise enjoys the status of a nature reserve. Much of the area surrounding this reserve is good for spotting little egrets, *Egretta garzetta*, and white storks, *Ciconia ciconia*. One church tower here was noticed adorned with at least seven large storks' nests.

Perhaps the most varied avifauna is reserved for Alentejo. Although small birds like corn bunting, *Emberiza calandra*, and stonechats, *Saxicola torquata*, present themselves at every turn of the road, it is the raptors which usually command attention. With luck it is possible to see booted eagles, *Heiraeatus pennatus*, red kites, *Milvus milvus*, and black-shouldered kites, *Elanus caeruleus*, amongst others.

Green Issues

There is a growing awareness of green issues on a national scale and a recognition of the need for conservation and protection of areas of outstanding beauty or special interest. Although the country has only one national park, the Peneda-Gêres National Park in the north, it has other areas which are protected as natural or nature parks. These are areas of great natural beauty which are already well populated and perhaps farmed. Their designation as natural parks is an attempt to preserve the countryside and the culture without imposing the stricter regulations of national parks.

Green consciousness amongst the general public is still low although bottle banks for recycling are starting to appear. Litter remains one of the biggest problems and the one most noticed by visitors. At least, unleaded petrol is now freely available throughout the region.

2. HISTORY

Before the Romans

Much of the early history is speculative. There are plenty of archaeological sites scattered throughout Portugal indicating early occupation but there seems to be no evidence of organised communities until the *castro* culture emerged in the second millennium BC. The idea of defended settlements built on strategic hilltops suited the Celts who arrived around 700–600 BC. These warring tribes adapted and refined the system to allow their people to conduct primitive farming and goatherding close to a safe refuge. Later the Romans took over some of these *castros* which may explain why there are so many well-preserved examples to be seen.

Whilst the Celts were taking refuge in the wild northern mountains, other tribes like the Phoenicians traded from coastal regions in the south exploiting metals mined inland. They were joined by the Greeks around the 6th century BC and by the Carthaginians, who played a dominant role until the arrival of the Romans.

The Romans

As a consequence of the Second Punic War (218–202 BC), the Iberian peninsula as a whole passed to the control of the Romans and Portugal as it is known today simply became part of Hispania Ulterior. It was not an easy war for the Romans. Attacking from the south, they had little trouble in colonising coastal areas but met serious resistance when attempting to capture the interior. Major resistance came from the Lusitani who lived north of the Tagus. Portugal's first legendary hero, **Viriatus**, emerged from the bitter fighting which continued for almost two centuries. Thought to have hailed from the village of Folgosinho, near Linhares in the Serra da Estrela, he led resistance cleverly and held up the Roman advance until he was finally assassinated in 139 BC by three of his followers who had been bribed by the Romans. Within two years the legions of Decimus Junius Brutus had swept through and taken control.

Using Olisipo (Lisbon) as his capital, it was **Julius Caesar** in 60 BC who set about integrating the peninsula into the Roman Empire. Colonies were established at Ebora (Évora), Scallabis (Santarém), Pax Julia (Beja), Myrtilis

(Mértola) and Bracara Augusta (Braga), although, with a few exceptions, little remains to excite the present day visitor. This page of history is not entirely closed since the 400 years of Roman rule has left lasting legacies in the Portuguese language, the legal system, roads and bridges and large scale farming of wheat, barley and the now ubiquitous vine. Towards the end of the Romans' rule Christianity was established with important bishoprics at Évora and Braga. In the early 5th century, with the Romans in decline, waves of **barbarians** swept through Spain and Portugal from beyond the Pyrenees. First the Vandals settled in Galicia, then the Alani in Lusitani with the Suevi taking up the region between the Minho and the Douro. It was the Suevi who mixed most readily with the Hispano-Roman population and the Suevi who soon became the dominant force. Before the end of the 5th century the Visigoths had established a tenuous rule over most of the peninsula which they managed to maintain for almost a century.

The Moors

The arrival in the south in 711 of the Moors from Africa seriously challenged the Visigothic rule. They overran Spain quickly and moved steadily north-wards into Portugal pushing Christianity north of the Douro, an area which was never really conquered by the Muslims. Southern Portugal became part of Spain and was known by the Moors as **Al-Garb** (the West) which evolved eventually into the modern name of Algarve. They established a capital at Shelb, now Silves, and set about ruling with a great deal of tolerance, respecting the rights of the Christians and the Jews to practise their own religions. Social order brought considerable advances: the Moors allowed small-holders to rent land owned by the state, encouraged work to improve irrigation techniques introduced by the Romans, and introduced new crops including oranges, lemons and cotton. Centuries of harmony gradually decayed with the decentralisation of rule and the arrival at the end of the 11th century of more militant Muslim groups like the Almoravids.

The Birth of a Nation

The victory of the Christians at the **Battle of Covadonga** in the Asturias in 718 is regarded as the start of the long struggle for liberation from the Moors. From that small start the Muslims were pushed back slowly but steadily from León and Galicia southwards. Porto was taken in 868, Coimbra in 878 and raids were mounted against Lisbon by 955. South of the Douro there was no real consolidation of territory throughout this period and the land remained a fluctuating battle ground. Towards the end of the 9th century, the country that was to become Portugal started to emerge with the consolidation of the lands between the Lima and the Minho. This territory was called Portucale after its capital city. Although under the command of the kingdom of León, the region was stabilised by a dynasty of *duces* beginning with Gonçalo Mendes, but the incipient nation suffered control by division before its status as a country was finally accepted in the 11th century.

Towards a Kingdom

Alfonso VI succeeded his father, Ferdinand I of León, in 1065 and by 1073 had declared himself emperor of the kingdoms of León, Castile, Galicia and Portucale. His call for crusaders to help fight the Almoravids brought, amongst others, Raymond of Burgundy and his cousin Henry who both married daughters of Alfonso, Henry marrying the illegitimate Teresa. Henry took charge of the County of Portucale and worked steadily towards confirming the autonomy of the state of Portugal, work carried on by Teresa after Henry's death around 1112 when she became regent for her son, Afonso Henriques.

After the death of Alfonso VI a war of succession broke out and the mantle of emperor was assumed by **Alfonso VII**, son of Raymond and Urraca. Teresa's attempts to maintain Portugal's independence eventually failed when her armies fell and she accepted the dominance of Alfonso VII in 1127. This inspired Teresa's 18-year-old son, **Afonso Henriques** (1128/39–85), to rebellion and over the next decade and a half he constantly vied with his cousin for control of Portugal. The Treaty of Zamora, signed between them in 1143, made Afonso Henriques the first King of Portugal. Not feeling entirely secure, Afonso sought recognition from Pope Lucius II but this was not forthcoming, since the Pope favoured a policy of supporting Iberian union as representing the best hope of holding back the Muslim tide. Later, in 1179, Pope Alexander III finally granted recognition to the 70-year-old Afonso Henriques in exchange for a yearly tribute and other privileges.

The First Dynasty, House of Burgundy

Afonso Henriques I, o Conquistador (the Conqueror)	1128/39–1185
Sancho I, o Pavoador (the Resettler)	1185–1211
Afonso II, o Gordo (the Fat)	1211–1223
Sancho II	1223–1248
Afonso III	1248–1279
Dinis, o Lavrador (the Husbandman)	1279–1325
Afonso IV, o Bravo (the Brave)	1325–1357
Pedro I, o Justiceiro (the Justicer)	1357–1367
Fernando, o Formoso (the Beautiful)	1367–1383

Evicting the Moors

In his determination to establish Portugal and his kingdom, Afonso Henriques enlisted the help of crusaders to fight against the Moors. Santarém and Lisbon were both taken in 1147 and joined with his emerging nation. Lisbon was taken by siege with the help of the English, French, Flemish and German crusaders who were passing through on their way to the Holy Land. Fighting for Christianity alone proved not persuasive enough but the offer of loot and land grants secured their services. The Reconquista was eventually backed by the Church, convinced by the argument that chasing out the Muslims here was just as important as fighting the infidel in the Holy Land. The Knights Templar and the Hospitallers lent their support and became extremely wealthy and powerful as a consequence of land grants.

Afonso Henriques fought his last battle in 1170 at Badajoz. Fernando II of León, concerned that land retaken from the Moors was in effect expanding Portugal instead of his own kingdom, joined forces with the powerful Almohads. Afonso Henriques broke a leg in the midst of the battle and was captured. He secured his release only by yielding land and castles to his enemy.

The **final victory** was still over a century away. Again with the help of passing crusaders, Sancho I invaded western Algarve and captured the capital Silves in 1189 but lost it, together with much of the area south of the Tagus, the following year in what proved to be the last great campaign of the Moors led by al-Mansur. Steady expansion under Sancho II and his successor Afonso III led to the recapture of territory in Alentejo and eastern Algarve until, in 1249, western Algarve too had been recovered and the Portuguese kingdom, endorsed by the **Treaty of Alcañices** in 1297, took its ultimate shape.

Organising a New Kingdom

New territories were divided between the Church, the Templars and other religious orders, and the most powerful nobles. Most of the population of 400,000 lived in the north so some internal recolonisation programmes were introduced to protect the new areas. There were problems of a social order too; the northerners with their Celtic genes had the arrogance of conquering invaders whilst the southerners had learnt gentler ways from a more settled existence under the rule of the Moors. An increase in social mobility amongst the lower classes did much to weld the divergent cultures but never completely so, even to this day.

Some moves towards democracy started when the kings of the Burgundian line recognised the need for popular and financial support. They began to consult with the nobles and clergy and later the wealthy merchants and townsmen, and this was formalised into the **Cortes** (parliament), first held in Coimbra in 1211. In the 1254 Cortes at Leiria, the king conceded the right of municipal representation in fiscal matters, an important concession since the king only called a Cortes when he needed to raise taxes. The Church was doing well with its extensive lands, freedom from taxation and right to collect its own taxes from the population; rather too well, in fact, and its increasing power was soon felt as a threat by the monarchy. Afonso II generally failed in his attempts to curb its power as did Sancho II, who was ultimately excommunicated and dethroned in 1245.

The reign of **Dom Dinis** (1279–1325) proved significant in consolidating Portugal's independence and putting the monarchy firmly in control. Dinis was far-sighted in his reforms which were extensive and affected all walks of life. For security he financed the building of 50 castles along the frontier and started negotiations with Spain which eventually led to the 1297 Treaty of Alcañices by which Spain acknowledged Portugal's borders. He introduced agricultural reforms to produce export quantities of wine, olive oil, grain and dried fruit, and created afforestation schemes. He encouraged music and poetry and gave Lisbon a university in 1290 which was transferred to Coimbra in 1308. The Templars, in decline in Europe, were reorganised as the Order of Christ (of which Henry the Navigator was later to become a Grand Master). They were responsible to the king rather than the Pope, and this forced the Church to accept a larger degree of state control.

Afonso IV (1325–57), who succeeded Dinis, had a much less happy reign. The Black Death struck in 1348–49 and decimated the population, especially in the urban centres. It became a burden throughout the rest of his reign, indeed over the next century, as the pestilence returned again and again. Labour problems arose through migration to towns, leaving insufficient agricultural workers to fill the nation's breadbasket and creating inflationary pressures and stagnation. Fears of Castilian domination persisted, not helped by continual intermarriage between the two royal families. But Portugal was bent on independence. Fear of a Castilian heir through his son's love affair with Inês de Castro, first a mistress and later his wife, was enough for Afonso to arrange her brutal murder (see feature page 124).

Just two years later, in 1357, **Pedro I** came to the throne after the death of his father and one of his first acts was to seek out the murderers of Inês to extract his revenge. Peaceful coexistence with Castile continued throughout his reign as the country started to recover from the ravages of the plague, but the growing power of the nobles and the emerging bourgeoisie were to create social unrest in the reign of his son **Fernando I** (1367–83). Alienating his subjects by his marriage to Leonor Teles and engaging the country in a series of unpopular wars against the Castilians, Fernando also failed to produce a male heir and in 1383 the House of Burgundy came to an untidy end. Power passed to his widow Leonor but not for long as their daughter Beatriz, at the age of 12, had recently married the widowed Juan I, King of Castile. By the terms of the marriage contract Beatriz, with her husband, would succeed to rule Portugal. Following the death of her father, Juan insisted that Beatriz be proclaimed queen and entered Portugal to take authority from Leonor. Although this move received support from the nobles, it incited the middle classes to riot and throw their weight behind the claims of João, the Grand

11

Master of the Order of Avis and illegitimate son of King Pedro, who became regent. It started two years of war with Castile, finally settled with the **Battle of Aljubarrota** (1385) which resulted in a decisive victory for João, backed by a force of English archers, against overwhelming odds. Later that year João was crowned at Coimbra to become **João I**, the first king of the House of Avis, and the great abbey of Batalha was ordered to commemorate his victory. Relations with England were sealed through the Treaty of Windsor of 1386 and by João's marriage to Philippa of Lancaster, daughter of John of Gaunt, the following year.

The new dynasty was much like the old, except that the mercantile classes gained political representation. Skirmishes with Castile continued until peace was finally made in 1411. It was during this period that Portugal started to look overseas to solve problems at home, and the proximity of North Africa made it a natural target for overseas expansion.

Second Dynasty: House of Avis

João I, de Boa Memoria (of Good Memory)	1385–1433
Duarte, o Elequente (the Eloquent)	1433–1438
Afonso V, o Africano (the African)	1438–1481
João II, o Principe Perfeito (the Perfect Prince)	1481–1495
Manuel I, o Venturoso (the Fortunate)	1495–1521
João III, o Piedoso (the Merciful)	1521–1557
Sebastião, o Desejado (the Awaited)	1557–1578
Henrique, o Casto (the Pure)	1578–1580

Building an Empire

João's main contribution to the building of a new empire was in fathering some brilliant children. One of these, Pedro, travelled widely sending home maps and works of geography, and another, **Henry the Navigator** (1394–1460) played a very significant early role. He founded a school of navigation at Sagres in Algarve and used his power and wealth to staff it with the cream of Europe's cartographers, astronomers and navigators. During his lifetime Madeira (1419), the Azores (1427) and the Cape Verde Islands (1457) were all discovered and colonised and the west coast of Africa explored. Following the death of Henry the Navigator, who is also featured on page 129, there was a lull in the process of exploration.

Duarte (1433–38) succeeded João I but died after only five years on the throne, some say from grief over the fate of his younger brother delivered as a hostage to the Muslims following an ill-fated expedition against Tangier in 1437. His son, **Afonso V** (1438–81), was too young to rule without a regent so Pedro, Duke of Coimbra, stepped forward with the support of the populace to press his claim against that of Queen Leonor, Duarte's widow. Events

The Age of Discovery

Portugal's explorations started haphazardly and were variously motivated. Outflanking the Muslims and spreading the Christian faith lent a crusading element and respectability to their excursions, but there were other issues like the need for gold which was in short supply throughout Europe, and the need to stabilise currency and support commerce. Maritime trade was of growing importance too and there was the unending search to discover the earthly paradise of Prester John. The existence of this legendary priest and ruler of a vast Christian empire somewhere in the middle of Africa was a deeply held belief that stretched all the way back to Rome. The Pope granted Portugal the sole right to explore and colonise Africa except for those parts ruled by Prester John.

However faltering or dubiously motivated in the beginning, Portuguese sailors developed skills of seamanship superior to any in Europe and rapidly became intrepid explorers. A number of epic voyages took place around the dawning of the 16th century. Vasco da Gama sailed to India and back again (1497–99), Pedro Alvares Cabral discovered Brazil (1500) and, from 1519 to 1522 Ferdinand Magellan, ignoring pleas from his Portuguese masters, led the first navigation of the globe under the sponsorship of the Spanish. The Spanish too were taking to the seas creating fresh dispute between the two nations but, with Papal intervention, the **Treaty of Tordesillas** (1494) divided the world between them at an imaginary line 370 leagues west of the Cape Verdes. This gave Portugal the as yet undiscovered Orient and the key to great wealth.

Opening new trade routes brought with it enormous wealth and not just in gold. Spices from the East, cinnamon, cloves and peppers, grain, sugar and dyestuffs from Morocco and slaves from Africa activated the merchants and stimulated the development of key overseas trading posts, not always achieved without battles. On a more humble scale, one product from their discovery of Newfoundland, *bacalhau*, (dried, salted cod), became virtually part of the staple diet and remains so even today.

This period of Portugal's history produced some epic heroes, a stable economy but no lasting wealth. Only the monarchy, taking a royal fifth from all trade revenues, benefited but even its wealth had no permanency.

took a dramatic turn when Afonso came of age and turned to the parties who opposed Pedro. In the subsequent battle of Alfarobeira in 1449 Pedro lost his life. Two uncles who had proved trusted advisers, Fernão, the Duke of Bragança, and Henry the Navigator, were both rewarded with a large share of independent power. Afonso is remembered most for his crusading in North Africa which gave him the epithet of o Africano.

Overseas exploration became important again under **João II** (1481–95) especially when, in 1487, Bartolomeu Dias finally made it around the southern tip of Africa which he christened 'the Cape of Good Hope'. João started to assert more royal power over the nobles, particularly with regard to land ownership. A conspiracy gathered against the king but the perpetrators were quickly discovered and rapidly dispatched. In 1483 the Duke of Bragança, head of a family whose estate covered a third of the kingdom, was executed and his lands recovered by the crown, and the following year the Queen's brother, the Duke of Viseu, was treated in a similar way.

Dom Manuel I (1495–1521), who succeeded João, continued to centralise power in the crown. However, he appeased the nobles by restoring their estates although not their political power. It was an enlightened reign in which a postal service was instituted, the taxation of the districts was regulated and exercise of justice was brought under royal control. Manuel presided over Portugal's greatest period of exploration and enjoyed the wealth flowing from it. The exuberance of this age led to the development of a new architectural style involving twisted forms in the columns, ribs and corbels which later became known as Manueline (featured on page 128).

However, Portugal's hitherto lenient attitude towards its Jewish minority was gathering resentment amongst the people of the country.

An Age of Decline

João III (1521–57) continued Manuel's policies of establishing royal authority and expanding trade. Literature was flowing from the printing presses and the humanistic influences of Europe were making a noticeable impression. Colleges were established and the university at Lisbon was moved permanently to Coimbra in 1537. Permitting the establishment of the Inquisition was a turning point that led Portugal into decline. Slowly and steadily a whole entrepreneurial class was snuffed out, robbing the country of the engine to drive the huge commercial empire it had striven so hard to build. Humanism and the Inquisition proved incompatible bedfellows and it was the Inquisition which gained the ascendancy.

Stability still held with the ascension of the young **Dom Sebastião** in 1557 and it was during his reign (1572) that Luís de Camões published his epic *The Lusiads*, which was to achieve lasting fame. Strains in the economy were showing which became overpowering around the 1570s when increasing competition, falling prices, foreign debts and a drop in productivity signalled a serious decline.

Sebastião, an unstable and idealistic king, yearned for a crusade against the Moors in North Africa and when he sensed the time was right he emptied his coffers to equip an 18,000-strong force. It sailed to Morocco from Algarve in 1578 but met a superior force at Alcácer-Quibir and was effec-

The Jews and the Inquisition

As physicians, astronomers, bankers, money lenders and tax collectors, the Jews had lived in Portugal for a thousand years or more without gathering any great resentment. Their influence was growing and it was the Jews who opened Portugal's first printing presses with their first eleven books all in Hebrew. Complaints against the Jews raised in the Cortes in 1490 indicated changing attitudes, and events in Spain were to further compound their difficulties.

Some 60,000 Jews expelled from Spain in 1462 were allowed to settle peacefully in Portugal. Unfortunately for the Jews, Dom Manuel was forced to take a hardened attitude against them as a condition of his marriage to Princess Isabela of Spain just four years later. There was a considerable reluctance on the part of the king to order the expulsion of such a valuable sector of the community, so he offered the option of baptism as an alternative to expulsion. Some Jews did leave for the Netherlands but many were baptised as `New Christians', accepting assurances there would be a twenty-year period of grace before their new faith was tested. New Christians and Old Christians intermarried freely but this was to offer no protection for the Jewish heritage.

Dom João III in 1536 eventually persuaded the Pope of the need to introduce the Inquisition, in spite of the fact that there was no disunity threatening the faith in Portugal. Intended as a tool of the monarchy, it quickly took on a life and force of its own with the inquisitor-generals responding directly to the Pope. The main target was the New Christians and thousands were tortured, left to rot in prison cells or burnt at the stake as the Inquisition became nothing other than a reign of terror, until it was finally suppressed in 1820.

Small Jewish communities still exist in Portugal and there are traces of Jewish quarters in the towns where they first settled including Viana do Castelo, Bragança, Lamego, Guarda and Castelo de Vide. The latter houses the oldest synagogue in Portugal, founded in the 13th century, hidden away down a small side street. In Tomar too there is a 14th-century synagogue which now contains a museum named after Abraham Zacuto. A brilliant astronomer and mathematician, it was Zacuto who first published *Almanac Perpetuum*, in Hebrew, which enabled mariners to calculate latitude at sea by declination of the sun. He was amongst those who declined to convert at the bidding of Dom Manuel and left the country.

tively annihilated. Around 8000 were left dead on the battlefield including the king and many young nobles, and most of the rest were taken prisoner, with only a hundred or so escaping capture.

Cardinal Henrique, an elderly uncle of the dead king, assumed control and further weakened the country by paying ruinous ransoms for the release of prisoners. He died after only two years in power leaving no male heirs. King Philip II of Spain invaded and was installed as King **Filipe I** of Portugal in 1581.

The Castilian Usurpers

Although this rule was initially unpopular, the union with Spain brought short-term advantages to the economy. Spanish wheat helped to feed the people and the Spanish helped to guard the Portuguese empire. Filipe started well by observing Portuguese autonomy and leaving control of the Cortes and the judicial system entirely with the Portuguese, while promising that the Portuguese language would remain and that their empire overseas would still be ruled by Portugal. Apart from the first two years, the whole of the Castilian reign was conducted from Spain.

During this period the balance of power was tilting from Spain to northern Europe. The year 1588 witnessed the failure of the Spanish Armada which was supported by boats built in Lisbon and crewed by Portuguese. Portuguese ports were closed to English ships, and the seizure of 50 Dutch ships in Lisbon by Filipe in 1594 brought a Dutch retaliation aimed at the Portuguese in India. By 1602, with both the English and the Dutch established in India, the Portuguese monopoly was broken. Much of their maritime empire was under threat with the country no longer powerful enough to mount a robust defence.

Third Dynasty: the Hapsburgs	
Filipe I, o Prudente (the Prudent)	1581–1598
Filipe II, o Pio (the Pious)	1598–1621
Filipe III, o Grande (the Grand)	1621–1640

Filipe II (1598–1621), not as diplomatic as his father, started to advance the power of Spain by appointing Spaniards to the Council of Portugal in Madrid. Although he still retained favour with the Cortes, seeds of resistance were sown amongst the populace. In 1621 **Filipe III** succeeded to the throne but his reign continued to erode and undermine the union. Portugal was drawn into Spain's 30-year war with France and its troops were pressed into battle to quell an uprising in Catalonia. 1 December 1640 dawned as any other but on this day Spanish rule was effectively overthrown, creating a landmark in Portuguese history remembered to this day as a national holiday. A group of conspirators stormed the palace in Lisbon to depose the Duchess of Mantua, governor of Portugal, and install as king the Duke of Bragança, head of one of the oldest families in Portugal and reluctant leader of the uprising.

The House of Bragança

The Duke of Bragança was crowned **João IV** (1640–56), and with Spain seriously distracted on other fronts there was no immediate opposition. Dom João focused his efforts on rebuilding the country, placing its independence beyond doubt and gaining recognition abroad. England agreed to renew the old alliance of 1386 and treaties were signed with Charles I (1642) and Oliver Cromwell (1654). Later, in 1662, the alliance was strengthened by the marriage of Charles II to Catherine of Bragança. Although skirmishes with Spain waxed and waned, and taxes were raised to fairly high levels, it was a quietly successful reign which also saw the emphasis in trade swing from India to Brazil.

Consolidation continued under Luisa, the Spanish wife of João IV, acting as regent for her son, **Afonso VI**, and a peace treaty was signed with Holland. Young Afonso, just 13 years old, was a problematic child associating with street gangs and criminal elements. His mother was deposed as regent by the Count of Costelho Melhor who promptly married off Afonso to a French Princess, Marie-Françoise. The count himself became subject of a conspiracy and fled, whereupon Marie-Françoise entered a convent and asked for an annulment of her marriage on the grounds that it had never been consummated. This was agreed by Cortes and the princess promptly married Afonso's younger brother Pedro, who assumed the role of regent.

Luisa's third child, Catherine, was married to Charles II in 1662 to give Portugal another treaty of alliance with England, who provided forces to help fight off the Spanish at Évora. The treaty gave England in turn a handsome dowry and trading rights in all Portuguese territories, Tangiers and Bombay. Spain, on the other hand, now seriously weakened, finally agreed peace in the Treaty of Lisbon of 1668.

Remarkably, all Luisa's three children ascended to a throne, Afonso and Pedro as kings of Portugal and Catherine as queen of England.

Pedro acted as regent for his brother from 1668 until he was crowned King **Pedro II** in 1683. Economic problems beset the country throughout this period reflecting a decline in maritime commerce, the loss of the spice trade and greater competition in the sugar trade. Agriculture at home was not so productive and wheat shortages continued, so efforts were directed towards increasing manufacturing output to solve the difficulties. Tariff-protected glass and textile industries were developed, exports boosted and the import of luxury goods controlled, and all this, together with concessions from the English for Portuguese wines (Methuen Treaty, 1703), did much to stabilise the economy. However, the discovery of gold in Brazil poured in new wealth and the growing new industries instantly faltered.

When **João V** succeeded Pedro II in 1706 he had Brazilian gold to spend. The Crown's revenues soared as it took one fifth of all the revenues, and the money was spent on building palaces, churches and monasteries, including the vast monastery-church at Mafra which virtually bankrupted the monarchy. Scholarship also flourished under the king's patronage and, with his concern for the poor, João became known as o Magnanimo. Palaces were also built to house João's bastard sons, three of them from nuns.

José (1750–77), Dom João's successor, was genial and easygoing. He shared his father's love of the arts, particularly opera, and was happy to leave the affairs of state in the capable hands of his minister, the **Marquês de Pombal**. Pombal was to go down in history as one of Portugal's greatest statesmen, admired by some but reviled and hated by others. His was an oppressive, dictatorial rule, exercised by using the royal prerogative rather than his own personal power.

It was church as usual for the people of Lisbon on All Saints' Day, 1 November 1755, when a terrifying and furious **earthquake** hit the town. Buildings collapsed and fires from the many church candles added further devastation. After nine days of raging fires the heart of the city was reduced to ashes. Much of the surrounding country was also seriously affected as shock waves spread as far as France in the north and Algarve to the south, yet the north of the country escaped serious damage. The Jesuits laid the blame for this divine retribution entirely on Pombal. After the king survived an assassination attempt, Pombal declared the Jesuits and certain nobles responsible and took his revenge with executions and the disbandment of the Jesuit movement in 1759. Granted emergency powers by the king, Pombal set about rebuilding Lisbon on a simple grid plan, with houses in a neo-classical style.

Oppressive though Pombal's regime was, his policies helped to reform Portugal's economy and lay the foundation of the modern Portuguese state. Towards the end of King José's life, Pombal plotted to force the heir apparent, Maria, to renounce her rights to the throne in favour of her son, José, who was a disciple of Pombal. He failed, and on her accession, **Maria** (1777–1816) tried Pombal for crimes against the state and confined him to his estates.

A pious woman, Maria revived many of the religious elements of government but left Pombal's economic reforms undisturbed. Roads and canals were built, agricultural methods improved and industry, including textiles, was again supported. Slowly and steadily Portugal made economic progress until the French Revolution of 1789 reverberated around Europe. Maria, deeply disturbed by the loss of loved ones – including her eldest son to smallpox after she had forbidden vaccination – and other events, suffered hallucinations and slipped towards insanity. In 1791 she was declared insane and her son, João, took over as regent until his mother died in 1816, when he was crowned **King João VI** (1816–26).

The Era of Napoleon

In 1807 Napoleon delivered an ultimatum that Portugal declare war on Britain and close its ports to British shipping. Since Portugal was dependent for half her trade on Britain and on British sea power to protect her trade routes, there was little option but to reject Napoleon and face the inevitable

Fourth Dynasty: House of Bragança

João IV, o Restaurador (the Restorer)	1640–1656
Afonso VI, o Vitrioso (the Victorious)	1656–1683
Pedro II, o Pacifico (the Peace Lover) regent from 1668	1683–1706
João V, o Magnanimo (the Magnanimous)	1706–1750
José, o Reformador (the Reformer)	1750–1777
Maria I, a Piedosa (the Merciful)	1777–1816
João VI, o Clemente (the Merciful)	1816–1826
Pedro IV, o Libertador (the Liberator)	1826 (abdicated)
Miguel, o Usurpador (the Usurper)	1828–1834
Maria II, a Educadora (the Educator)	1834–1853
Pedro V, o Esperancoso (the Hopeful)	1853–1861
Luís, o Popular (the Popular)	1861–1889
Carlos, o Martirizado (the Martyr)	1889–1908
Manuel II, o Desventuroso (the Unfortunate)	1908–1910

war. The monarchy immediately slipped off to Brazil to set up court there as the French, under General Junot, entered Lisbon. The Portuguese invoked the alliance with Britain and an expeditionary force commanded by the brilliant tactician Sir Arthur Wellesley (later the Duke of Wellington) quickly defeated the French. In all, there were three waves of French attacks in the Peninsular War, all repelled, but it left the country fatally weakened. The French failed to pay the agreed compensation and another Anglo-Portuguese treaty, this one in 1810, gave Britain the right to trade freely with Brazil, eliminating Portugal's lucrative middleman's role. Brazil itself was proclaimed a kingdom in 1815.

From 1808 to 1821, Portugal effectively became a British protectorate governed by Marshal **William Beresford**. He ruled with a heavy hand which brought about bitter resentment. Liberal ideas introduced from France were spread by secret societies including the Masonic order of which Lisbon had 13 groups. A plot was hatched to dispose of Beresford but it was discovered and 12 conspirators were executed in October 1817. In 1820, Beresford, alarmed at the growing strength of the liberals in Spain and the support spilling over the border, went to Brazil to request more powers from the king. In his absence the liberals rose to seize power and João VI was forced to return from Brazil, but he was too late to resist the new liberal ideologies.

Constitutional Wrangles

A new constitution was adopted in 1822 which assured the establishment of broad voting rights, no special prerogatives for nobles or clergy, a liberal Cortes more truly representing the people, and the end of the Inquisition. On a divergent course from the king, the queen remained firmly against its adoption and used ill health as an excuse to avoid becoming a signatory.

In the same year, Crown Prince Pedro, who had remained in Brazil, was stirred by attempts at home to restrict Brazilian autonomy and promptly declared Brazil independent. Portugal had troubles enough at home with an uprising to restore absolute monarchy by the anti-liberals headed by Miguel, the queen's youngest son, and backed by the queen. They won a victory and the constitution was suspended in 1824. This almost destabilised the monarchy and left the king no option but to send his son Miguel into exile.

By 1825 Portugal had conceded and recognised Brazil as an independent empire with Pedro as Emperor of Brazil. On João's death the following year, the Regency council declared **Pedro IV** king. He hardly knew Portugal, or his younger brother Miguel, but he had conceived a plan to settle all the problems. He proposed a new compromise constitution in which a chamber of deputies was partly elected and partly nominated, with an upper house of hereditary peers. Pedro IV then abdicated on condition that Miguel marry Maria, his seven-year-old daughter, and rule as her regent under the new constitution. **Miguel** happily agreed, returned to Portugal, swore his oath of loyalty and promptly abolished the constitution. He recalled the old Cortes and, in 1828, proclaimed himself king. Maria, still in transit when the news reached her, diverted to England. The Azores, out in the Atlantic, were not in favour of accepting Miguel so declared Pedro regent in the name of his daughter. Pedro abdicated his Brazilian empire to establish his daughter's claim to the throne and promptly set sail for the Azores where he made his base. The 'War of Two Brothers' led to capitulation by Miguel and in 1834 he was back in exile. Pedro died in the same year and his 15-year-old daughter took the throne as **Maria II.**

The Decline of a Monarchy

At 16, Maria married the Duke of Leuchtenburg but he died soon after his arrival in Lisbon. A year later she married the German Duke Ferdinand of Saxe-Coburg-Gotha, had eleven children and died, still only 36, giving birth to her twelfth. Her reign was to witness the birth of political parties.

Disputes still continued over the **constitution**. Some favoured the charter introduced by Pedro II, strongly supported by Maria herself, whilst the liberals wanted a return to the constitution of 1822. The liberals themselves failed to present a unified view and soon divided into conservatives and progressives, the latter calling themselves the Septembrists after their revolutionary victory of September 1836 brought them to power. Their first demand was the restoration of the 1822 constitution but in 1838 they adopted a more moderate version. The so-called Chartists made a return in 1842 and, under Costa Cabral, restored the Charter of 1826. It proved a firm government which re-established free trade and set Portugal on a track back towards prosperity. Cabral foundered on a relatively minor issue but one which struck at the very heart of age-old custom. He declared that burials inside church were unhygienic and must stop. Devout women from the north were outraged and one in particular, Maria da Fonte, became the symbol of unrest which grew into a national rebellion in 1846. Feeling personally threatened, Cabral fled in disguise to Spain. Civil war seemed imminent, but English and French intervention steadied the unrest and restored Costa Cabral. In 1851 Cabral was ousted for good by another Chartist, Saldanha.

Maria II died in childbirth in 1853 and her husband, Duke Ferdinand of Saxe-Coburg-Gotha, ruled as regent for the next two years until their son, Pedro V, came of age. His was a brief reign and he died in 1861 to be succeeded by his brother Luís, who became king at 23. **Dom Luís** (1861–89) was generally judged a popular king – but then he left politics to the politicians and concentrated on things he did best, like translating Shakespeare and playing the cello. Two sons were born from his marriage to Maria Pia, daughter of Victor Emmanuel of Savoy who later became king of Italy.

Although Dom Luís' was a popular and peaceful reign, Portugal continued to lag behind the rest of Europe. An improved infrastructure encouraged foreign investment but the growth of industry was slow. Portugal was tenacious in holding on to its colonial claims and territories in Africa but these too were a burden on the country's finances.

Carlos succeeded Luís in 1889 and inherited a **crisis**. In 1887 the Portuguese announced their intention to bring all the lands between the Angolan and Mozambican coasts under their control. This brought them into conflict with British interests and in 1890 Lord Salisbury issued an ultimatum: Portugal was to withdraw from that territory. There was no compromise on offer and the old alliance was at stake so Portugal had little option but to concede. The Progressist government fell, the Regenerators formed a government and fell, and a coalition government failed. Crisis followed crisis but Portugal was broke and forced to declare itself bankrupt.

The real threat to the establishment of the monarchy came from **Republicanism**, a radical and nationalist movement arising from the middle and lower classes. This movement attacked the government for its corruption and inefficiency and the pendulum of power started to swing in their favour with the collapse of the governing parties in the crisis of the 1890s.

Carlos, still dreaming of restoring the empire, could do little about growing Republicanism, socialism and trade unionism. Struggling to maintain some sort of control, he appointed **João Franco** as Prime Minister in 1906 and endowed him with dictatorial powers. Franco promptly dismissed the Cortes and ruled by decree, but this had the effect of driving more liberals over to the Republican movement. Demonstrations against his dictatorship frequently ended in violence. An attempted Repulican revolt in 1908 was followed by the assassination of the king and the crown prince. The Republicans denied involvement yet it benefited their cause.

Portugal's last king, **Manuel II** ascended the throne in 1908. His attempts to appease the Republicans proved futile and the monarchy was violently overthrown on 5 October 1910. Dom Manuel, the Unfortunate, went into exile in England where he died in 1932.

The Republic

It can hardly be said that the Republicans grasped their opportunity with both hands. It is true that they won an overwhelming victory in 1911 with strong support from the urban and rural poor, but they promptly disenfranchised much of their support by introducing electoral laws based on literacy. Unrealistically high hopes of the Republican supporters never materialised and there were further measures which alienated support, like the Law of Separation passed by parliament in an attempt to divide the Church from the State and gain control of the Catholic Church. Weak economic factors, cyclical revival of the monarchists and general political turmoil brought about 45 changes of government in the years up to 1926.

The Salazar Dictatorship

A bloodless coup on 28 May 1926 overthrew the Democratic government and put the military in control. Portugal's first Republic was at an end. There was an instant jostling for power from which **General Óscar Carmona** emerged as president.

One of Carmona's first acts was to invite the well-known professor of economics from Coimbra University, **António de Oliveira Salazar**, to take the post of finance minister, but Salazar quickly resigned when he realised his control was too limited. In 1928, with the country's finances in an even worse mess, Salazar was reappointed, this time with full powers, to put the economy in order. Now he had complete control over government and departmental expenses and, by using strict monetarist policies, he brought the budget into balance for the first time in many years. In 1932 he was appointed Prime Minister, a position which he held until an accident with a deck chair in 1968 brought on a stroke.

In 1933 a new political constitution converted the military dictatorship into an authoritarian, nationalistic and pro-Catholic regime. A special police force kept vigilant guard against subversive activities and censorship was rigid, especially over journalism. Salazar had no appetite for party politics so he permitted just one party, the National Union, but it was without power. Numerous coup attempts were put down but Salazar's leadership was never seriously threatened and he continued to govern as a virtual dictator. Improvements in the infrastructure included bridges over the Tejo, Douro and other important waterways, new roads and hospitals, while the country's economy in general grew steadily.

Portugal remained formally neutral throughout the Spanish Civil War but sent an unofficial army of some magnitude to aid Franco's Nationalist forces. Although Salazar and his ministers were admirers of Germany, Portugal remained neutral again in World War II. Under pressure to sell the metal wolfram to the Germans, the Portuguese achieved a balancing act by allowing Britain the use of a base on the Azores and in giving generous credit.

Refugees flooded into neutral Portugal including the rich and the famous, and also spies of all nationalities. There was no doubt where the sympathies of the ordinary people lay and the allied victory was widely celebrated throughout the country.

Following the end of the war, Salazar called free elections allowing a role for a newly formed liberal party, the Movement of Democratic Unity. It was the first legal opposition party permitted under Salazar's rule. Some election-eering was permitted in the month preceding elections but the disenchant-ment of the new party was immediate when they were listed by the police as dissidents. Portugal's strategic location proved more important than her record on democracy when membership of the North Atlantic Treaty Organisation was mooted, and she joined in 1949.

By 1960, **events in the colonies** were causing concern to Portugal, espe-cially the violent uprising in Angola in 1961. It proved the spark to ignite war across all of Portugal's African colonies. Portugal reacted by crushing the revolts and, without offering concessions, tried to appease the people by speeding up economic reforms. The colony of Goa was lost, seized by India in 1961. Greater military involvement in the colonies, now renamed 'Overseas Provinces', was draining the country's finances. Salazar's tight control of the nation's purse strings had ensured the country was free from national debt but, at the same time, had no foreign investment. With the tasteful conversion of some of the country's historic buildings into *pousadas*, tourism was playing a more important role and bringing in a new source of wealth, but not enough; by 1965 Salazar, on his 76th birthday, agreed to allow foreign investment.

Revolution

A deck chair accident in 1968 brought Salazar's active term in office to a close. Acting Prime Minister **Marcelo Caetano** had the vision but not the strength to introduce reforms at home and solve the colonial problems over-seas. His limited liberal changes only stimulated demand for further democ-ratisation. The clandestine Communist party, which had been in existence for around 20 years, gained ground and military unrest led to the formation of the **Armed Forces Movement** (MFA) in 1973. In February 1974, the ageing General António de Spínola, a former member of government, published *Portugal and the Future,* a comprehensive critique of the country and its prob-lems. The solution proffered was a **military coup**. After a couple of abortive attempts, it happened bloodlessly on 25 April 1974. The populace was euphoric sensing the end of a long nightmare.

The following day Spínola announced a **Junta of National Salvation** comprising seven military officers, co-ordinating committees and a council of state. Censorship was immediately abolished and elections promised. On 15 May, Spínola was inaugurated as president and a provisional government formed from a coalition of Communists, Socialists and Centrists led by

Adelino da Palma Carlos with socialist Mário Soares as foreign secretary. Discontent festered with waves of strikes, shortages and general unrest which brought Carlos' resignation. Colonel Vasco Gonçalves, military governor of Lisbon, took over. Spínola himself, opposed to early decolonisation, consented to the independence of Guinea in 1974 but was reluctant to hand over Angola. He was pushed aside as president in 1974 and succeeded by General Costa Gomes who lasted for two years. Decolonisation did continue, with Mozambique and the Cape Verde islands going peacefully but Angola and East Timor only after civil wars.

Towards Democracy

Elections for a constituent assembly on 25 April attracted almost 92 per cent of the registered voters and was won by the Socialists and Centrists, but it did not bring stability. In the two years after the revolution the Portuguese had six governments and in the following two years, between July 1976 and July 1978, they elected ten. By 1976 the economy was in poor shape, banks and insurance companies had been nationalised and giant monopolies taken over by the workers. A new constitution attempted to uphold democracy and socialism while giving greater powers to the president. Elections of 1976 favoured General Eanes as president who appointed **Mário Soares** as Prime Minister.

The next decade brought no greater stability since elections invariably failed to give any party overall majority, at least until 1987. Mário Soares held office as prime minister three times in that politically volatile period. In 1986 the presidential elections were narrowly won on the second round by Mário Soares who became the first civilian head of state in 60 years.

In 1986 Portugal entered the European Community which initiated changes greater than at any time since the revolution. Funds poured in to help modernise the infrastructure and, with increased foreign investment, the country enjoyed a sustained period of economic growth. Today there is a new wealth about with many now enjoying a good standard of living, but this prosperity masks a deep poverty still experienced in parts of the countryside.

3. TOURING THE REGION

National Tourist Offices

Useful information leaflets are usually available on just about all areas of Portugal, as are brochures on the *pousadas*. Enquiries should be made to:

UK
Portuguese National Tourist Office, 22/25A Sackville Street, London W1X 1DE. Tel: 0171 494 1441.

USA
Portuguese National Tourist Office, 590 Fifth Avenue, New York, NY 10036-4704. Tel: 212 354 4403/4/5/6/7/8.

Canada
Portuguese National Tourist Office, 60 Bloor Street West, Suite 1005, Toronto, Ontario M4W 3B8. Tel: 416 921 7376.
Other enquiries not directly connected with the promotion of tourism, such as visa applications, should be directed to the Embassy or consulate.

Passport Requirements

A valid passport allows entry for EU nationals for a period of 90 days and for North American citizens for a period of 60 days. To extend this period it is necessary to apply before the time expires to the Foreigners' Registration Service, Rua Conselheiro José Silvestre Ribeiro, 22, 1600 Lisbon.

Embassies and Consulates

Consular help is available in emergency situations and is largely advisory. The following indicates some areas in which they can help but it does not fully define the powers of the office:

- in the event of a lost or stolen passport they can issue an emergency one
- help with problems over lost or stolen money or tickets but only by contacting relatives or friends at your request to ask for financial assistance
- advise on details of transferring funds
- encash a cheque supported by a banker's card but only in an emergency
- make a loan to cover repatriation expenses but only as a last resort
- arrange for the next of kin to be informed following an accident or death and advise on procedures
- act for nationals arrested or imprisoned to inform relatives
- provide a list of local interpreters, English-speaking doctors and solicitors
- give guidance on organisations experienced in tracing missing people

Useful addresses in this context are:

British Embassy,
35–37 Rua São Domingos à Lapa,
Lisbon.
Tel: 01 661 191

British Consulate,
3072 Avenida da Boa Vista,
Porto.
Tel: 02 684 789

British Consulate,
21 Rua de Santa Isabel,
Portimão, 826-3°
Algarve.
Tel: 082 23 071

British Consulate,
4 Rua General Humberto Delgardo,
Vila Real de Santo António,
Algarve.
Tel: 081 43 729

British Consulate,
Quinta de Santa Maria,
Estrada de Tavereve 3080,
Figueira da Foz.
Tel: 033 22 235

United States Embassy,
Avenida das Forças Armadas,
Lisbon.
Tel: 01 726 6600

United States Consulate,
Rua do Júlio Dinis,
Porto.
Tel: 02 63 094

Canadian Embassy,
2 Rua de Rosa Araújo,
Lisbon.
Tel: 01 562 547 or 563 821

Getting There

Lisbon is the country's main airport and well served by scheduled flights between all major countries. There is also a full programme of charter flights from Britain and other European countries throughout the summer months. Only a very few continue throughout the winter.

Personal transport is essential to fully explore this central region and the easiest way is to book a **fly-drive** package, although many motorists drive down from Britain using the ferry services either to Santander or Bilbao. There is a wide choice of routes from these ports, either through Portugal or Spain.

By Air

TAP, the Portuguese national airline runs scheduled flights between London Heathrow and Porto, Lisbon and Faro; similar services are also offered by *British Airways*. In North America *TAP* operates services to Lisbon from New York, Boston, Los Angeles and Toronto. Some American carriers also offer direct flights to Portugal and other Spanish cities which may be equally convenient on a fly-drive holiday.

Charter flights from the UK especially to Faro and Lisbon, vastly outnumber scheduled services and offer the most economical way to travel. If a seat only is required then these can be booked through a travel agent. *TAP* and some tour operators sometimes offer fly-drive holidays but it is just as convenient, and often more economical, to book a car in the UK before departure. All the major car hire companies are present in Portugal and can arrange **car hire** before departure but the most competitive of these is *Transhire* (Tel: 0171 978 1922, Fax: 0171 978 1797) which operate through *Auto Jardim*, a leading car hire company in Portugal with offices at all airports. Portugal is one of the cheaper countries in Europe for car hire.

The cheapest flights available are often those to Faro in Algarve and this opportunity should not be discounted too quickly for it is a convenient and quick entry point into Alentejo which is less than 3 hours' driving. It is just as convenient to follow the tours in this book starting in Alentejo as any other entry point.

Charter flights including a **package holiday** offer such good value that visitors from North America sometimes find it more economical to fly to Britain to take advantage of them. There are many tour operators listing holidays in Portugal, especially Algarve, but travel agents mostly deal with a limited number of tour operators and may not be able to offer the destination required. All of them have directories and, on request, will check which operators do offer the preferred destination although it may be necessary to book elsewhere.

By Ferry

Car ferries link the south coast of England with ports in northern Spain which are convenient for Portugal. There are no services directly to Portugal itself. *Brittany Ferries* offer services between Plymouth and Santander in northern Spain while *P&O* operate ferries from Southampton to Bilbão. The choice of which route to follow from Spain into Portugal will be dictated by the intended destination. Since the borders are now open, crossing between Spain and Portugal offers no problems. Facilities for money exchange and refreshments exist only at major crossing points. *Brittany Ferries* also offer inclusive holidays which can be booked through travel agents.

Travel in Portugal

By Car

The Portuguese drive on the right. Main roads are generally well surfaced and there is an increasing network of motorways, some of which are toll roads. Minor roads are mostly reasonable but potholes can be a danger. Road markings have improved considerably in recent years making driving much safer but there is a need to keep a watchful eye on the local drivers who lack awareness of others and have a compulsion to overtake any vehicle in front without necessarily waiting for an opportune moment. Warning signs, especially temporary ones, are not necessarily in English so words to look out for are *perigo* = danger; *desvio* = diversion, *obras* = road works and *lombas* which is a ridge in the road to calm traffic flow. As far as road maps are concerned, *Hildebrand's Travel Map*, 1:400,000 series, is reasonably accurate (few maps are particularly accurate for the web of minor roads) and, available in Portugal, the *Turinta* maps are fairly good.

Drivers must be over the age of 18, seat belts are compulsory and speed limits for cars without trailers are 60kph (37mph) in built up areas, 90kph (55mph) in rural areas and 120kph (75mph) on motorways. Certain items of equipment are obligatory and these include a fire extinguisher, a warning triangle in case of breakdown or accident, a spare set of light bulbs and a small first aid kit. If the car is a right-hand drive then headlight deflectors must also be fitted.

Police checks are frequent and drivers must be able to produce their passport, driver's licence and papers relevant to the vehicle or face a heavy fine.

In the event of an accident it is essential to call the police before the vehicle is moved. Emergency SOS telephones (orange coloured) are available along main roads for reporting accidents and emergencies. Otherwise the emergency telephone number nationwide is 115.

Petrol stations are plentiful along main routes, although it pays to fill up before leaving if a route is chosen following minor roads. Unleaded petrol (*sem chumbo*) is freely available and major credit cards are accepted at main petrol stations although a small surcharge is sometimes levied.

Thanks to massive EU funding, new motorways are being laid around the country at a speed which is leaving the map-makers years behind. This does cause considerable problems to motorists unfamiliar with the region, for these potentially useful roads are badly signposted for destinations and the access points undivulged. Even more frustrating is that these fast roads are usually empty. Some, but not all, of the motorways are toll roads, like the IP1 from Lisbon to Porto and parts of the same road from Lisbon down to Algarve, and the sign 'Portagem' warns of pay boxes ahead. The network of minor roads throughout the region and the countless hamlets is too challenging for most road map publishers who tend to settle for the easier option of showing just the more important roads. Many of the smaller roads are well surfaced, good to drive and lead through rustic areas which are often more interesting

Despite tourism, Cascais still retains its image as a fishing village

than the main road routes. Even with a good map a compass is handy for these roads as they wind and twist so much that it is easy to lose orientation.

By Train

There is an extensive rail network in Portugal connecting most of the major towns. Long-distance services by *rapido* trains are excellent. They are fast and comfortable usually offering restaurant and refreshment facilities. The *directo* trains stop rather more frequently whilst the *tranvia* service is primarily local and stops at every lamppost. Main services are listed in the *Thomas Cook Continental Timetable*, available both in the UK and USA, and other timetables can be picked up locally. Tickets must be purchased before boarding.

By Bus

Comfortable express buses, some with toilet and refreshment facilities, connect most major towns to Lisbon and Porto. Until recently they carried the *RN* logo but privatisation has replaced Rodoviária Nacional by at least nine new companies, so the operating company varies with the region. In spite of this division, it remains an integrated nationwide service and the various regions work in harmony. Timetables are available locally and tickets must be obtained before boarding. There is also a good network of local buses which operate reliably to a timetable.

Accommodation

Lisbon and the Estoril coast has plenty of accommodation in all grades and finding a suitable place out of season should present no problems. The situation is different in high season, from July through until September, when the independent traveller is best advised to make prior bookings. Outside the Lisbon area there are relatively few hotels and similar establishments; although the demand for them is much less, the same advice is offered for high season: try to book in advance.

Other forms of accommodation, like *pousadas* and manor houses, now called *solares*, which predominate in the north of the country, also have a reasonable presence in the central region.

State-run *pousadas* are mostly located in outstanding beauty spots and often in buildings of great historical interest, like a converted castle or monastery. They are the equivalent of the Spanish *paradores* and represent the flagship of luxury accommodation. Unfortunately, these state-run establishments do not always meet the high standards intended and the warm welcome and personalised service are not always evident but, as always, some succeed more than others. They are priced according to three categories from B, lowest, through C to CH which are the most expensive. Bookings are made through *ENATUR*, a central agency, on Av. Santa Joana a Princesa, 10-1700 Lisbon, telephone 01 848 1221. There are 12 in the southern region but only two in Algarve.

Solares de Portugal

These houses are classified into three distinct groups: *casa antigas, quintas* and *herdades,* and *casa rusticas.*

Casa antigas are elegant manor houses and country estates mostly originating from the 17th and 18th centuries. They are furnished with period furniture and may contain valued works of art.

Quintas and **herdades** are agricultural farms and estates with a rural setting and atmosphere. These often have their own distinctive architectural style which is rather grand and their estates are enclosed by high walls.

Casa Rusticas are generally of a simpler architectural style and located in the heart of the country or within a farm.

Very few are in town locations, most are well off the beaten track and personal transport is essential. Booking conditions specify a minimum of three nights and there is no high and low season, with prices for January and August exactly the same.

Bookings can be made directly or through *ANTER*, Associação Nacional de Turismo, Quinta da Campo, Valado dos Frades, 2450 Nazaré, telephone 062 577 7135, who specialise in rural tourism, and *TURIHAB*, Praça da Republica, 4990 Ponte de Lima, telephone 058 741672.

Apart from hotels, there are *albergarias* and *estalagems*, both of which are described as inns. **Albergarias** offer a four-star comfort whereas the

Estalagems may be four or five star. Both seem indistinguishable from hotels. A *residencial* slots in somewhere between a hotel and a *pensão* and offers one- to four-star accommodation. Some hotels prefer to operate as *residencials* as do some pensions. **Pensions** form the lowest stratum and can be a mixed bag, best sorted out by actual inspection.

Crime and Theft

Portugal is normally a safe destination and a relatively crime-free country but recently there has been a rise in non-violent crime, particularly involving theft from car boots. Motorists are strongly advised to leave nothing on display in the car nor to leave valuables locked in the boot and not to let their car out of sight if it is loaded with luggage. Some areas are worse in this respect than others and the Lisbon region is one of the worst.

Otherwise, it is wise to protect valuables, including camera, with as much care as at home and not make it easy for any casual thief. All losses must be reported to the police, especially if an insurance claim is anticipated. In towns seek out the PSP (Policia de Segurança Pública) who deal with tourist incidents, but in rural areas this function is taken over by the GNR (Guarda National Rebulicana) who normally carry out traffic responsibilities and police the motorways. The chances of finding an English-speaking policeman are only fair. Old-fashioned courtesy and respect goes a long way in Portugal in all walks of life and is particularly recommended in dealing with the police.

Disabled Travellers

Portugal is only slowly coming to terms with the needs of the disabled and only the more recently built hotels offer anything like good facilities. Airports and main stations have generally adapted toilet facilities and there are specially reserved spaces in most towns for disabled motorists. Local tourist offices (addresses at the end of each chapter) can sometimes supply a list of wheelchair accessible hotels and campsites, but the Institute for the Promotion of Tourism, Rua Alexandre Herculano 51, 1200 Lisbon, publishes a list of hotels which are more suitable to wheelchair users. Ramps for crossing roads are still in short supply as are pavements outside main towns. A claim of provision for the disabled in hotel listings may be nothing more than a ramp at the door, so it is important to check the facilities provided in some detail.

Money Matters

Most towns of any size have a bank where money can be changed, either from bank notes, travellers' cheques or eurocheques. Bank hours are from 8.30am to 3pm during weekdays. Exchange bureaux can also be found in popular tourist areas. In addition there is a growing network of automatic teller machines called *Multibanco* which dispense cash 24 hours a day and can be used with a wide selection of cards, including Visa, Eurocheque, Eurocard and American Express. There is a daily limit of 40,000 escudos.

Museums and Galleries

In general, museums are closed on a Monday and, like the rest of Portugal, closed for a couple of hours midday. Although not closing officially until 12.30pm, last entry is usually 12noon and is strictly enforced.

Public Holidays

Since virtually every town has one or more religious festivals it sometimes seems that the country is on permanent holiday but the list of National Holidays celebrated nationwide is appreciably shorter. Easter is consistent with the rest of western Europe, and the holidays associated with it include Shrove Tuesday and Good Friday. Corpus Christi, late May or early June, is another variable holiday but the remainder are fixed as follows:

1 January	New Year's Day	5 October	Republic Day
25 April	Liberation Day	1 November	All Saints
1 May	May Day	1 December	Independence Day
10 June	Camões Day	8 December	Immaculate Conception
15 August	Assumption	25 December	Christmas Day

Restaurant Closing Days

Most eating places close on at least one day each week. Rather surprisingly, popular closing days are clustered around weekend, especially Friday, Saturday and Sunday, and in some places there is a very limited selection on these days. The closing day is usually posted on the door and it pays to take note of this at favoured restaurants.

Sport

Portugal is a haven for golfers, especially Algarve which is well endowed with **golf** courses and where the climate allows the sport to be enjoyed the whole year round. Lisbon too is good for golf and there are six courses in the immediate vicinity with a further five courses within comfortable driving distance. New courses seem to be opening steadily in other parts and the latest addition is near Ponte de Lima. **Tennis** facilities are mostly associated with hotels, some of which allow public access, but also there are clubs which open their courts to non-members. Similarly horse riding stables are usually to be found in centres of tourism. There is plenty of opportunity for **walking** but officially marked trails are found only in the Serra da Estrela. Some holiday companies lead organised walks, but the best guides are three books published by Sunflower books, *Landscapes of Algarve, Landscapes of Costa Verde* and *Landscapes of Sintra, Estoril & Cascais*, all by the authors of this book, which detail long and short walks.

Hunting – mainly for wild boar, partridge and pheasant – is a new growth area, and reserves and lodges are on the steady increase. Further details can be obtained from the Federação Portuguesa de Tiro com Armas de Caça, Avenida Jœlio Dinis, 10-4° Esq°, 1200 Lisboa.

There are plenty of opportunities for water sports in the main resort areas, conditions for surfing are often good, especially on the west coast, but there are also good spots for windsurfing. Sailing too is popular, with marinas spread around the coast, the majority in the south.

Particular details of facilities are listed at the end of each chapter, as appropriate.

Tax Free Shopping

Visitors from outside the European Union can take advantage of the tax free system by shopping at any of the 1500 shops which display the tax free logo. A receipt must be obtained for which a reimbursement of tax will be made at the airport on departure, either in cash or by credit if a credit card was used in the first instance.

4. FOOD AND WINE

Some of the huge kitchens in the older manor houses tell how the Portuguese discovered the art of good eating and lavish entertainment many centuries ago. As a nation of explorers, their great seafarers brought back more than gold and metals, they brought back pepper and spices of which cinnamon was the real prize. It is often said one boatload of cinnamon raised enough money to pay for an entire expedition to India. Vasco da Gama brought curry powder for the kitchen and this continues to find frequent use though rarely in overpowering quantities, being used to add a background oriental flavour to a wide range of soups and stews. The hot chilli pepper so successfully cultivated in Angola is another favourite of Portuguese chefs but it turns up under its African name of piri-piri, and is frequently used as a sauce mixed in oil and vinegar. It is these hints of other cultures – the taste of Africa, the smell of the Orient – which brings a uniqueness to the Portuguese cuisine.

Like the French, the Portuguese are devoted to their food and will happily drive long distances to their favourite restaurant or to try out a friend's recommendation. On the whole, they have farmer-size appetites which is reflected in massive portions, and some restaurants list half portions (*meia dose*) on the menu which are more or less half price. Where there is an option, the half dose is normally adequate and, in any case, there is always the opportunity of ordering another portion, or even something different, if it is not enough. The size of the portions do vary and tend to be smaller – actually not so much smaller as normal size – in regions like Algarve which cater more for tourists.

Soup

A meal starts invariably with soup and, for the Portuguese, may also end with a soup. One of the specialities of the north but equally popular throughout the country is *caldo verde*, a jade-green soup rich with potatoes, garlic, shreds of green cabbage and olive oil with a slice of a spicy sausage lurking at the bottom. Although it originated in the Minho, just about every region of Portugal is prepared to call this soup its own and it does vary around the country. The cabbage used is a non-heading variety with tender leaves which are taken from the plant as desired leaving a progressively longer bare stalk, rather like a Brussels sprout plant with all the sprouts removed. Cutting the cabbage is the secret to *caldo verde* soup. A stack of cabbage leaves is rolled into a cigar shape and then cut from the end into extremely fine shreds, the

Coffee and Cakes

The Portuguese are renowned for genteel afternoon tea, a custom which Catherine of Bragança introduced to the English. Visitors are unlikely to see any evidence of this but are certain to witness the Portuguese calling in to a local café during the morning for a quick coffee and cake. The larger shops act as a gathering place for those happy to while away the hours, morning, noon or night. No matter where it is bought, the coffee is always excellent, which is perhaps not too surprising for a country which once ranked some of the great coffee producing countries, like Brazil, Angola and Timor, amongst its colonies. **Coffee** is served in a bewildering variety of ways. The Portuguese mainly prefer a *bica*, a small strong coffee, which is good for a quick fix of caffeine but hardly slakes a thirst. Worse still, the small cup is only half full, so for a full cup ask for a *cheio* which simply means full. Milk lovers can ask for a *pingo* which will bring a small strong coffee with a drop (*pingo*) of milk, but for a larger coffee ask for a *meia de leite* which is usually a normal cup size, half of strong coffee filled up with hot frothed up milk. In tourist areas, *café com leite* is well understood and it usually produces a white coffee, but if less milk is preferred then *só pouco leite* added to the order should result in a less milky coffee. To be sure to get a large cup the word *grande* can be added to the order. Terms for coffee tend to be very local and do not always apply in other parts of the country. On one occasion, a request for *meia de leite*, literally 'half of milk', which works well in the north, produced a cup of milk and a cup of coffee in another part of the country where *café com leite* is more normally used. Two more coffees which are invariably on the list are *galão*, weak, milky coffee served in a glass and *galão direita* which is half milk, half coffee served in a glass. Other descriptions of coffee may appear on the menu but these are mainly alternative names of the types described.

Tea drinkers should beware that many of the shops make tea very badly often trying to brew it from hot rather than boiling water. If there is an opportunity, head for a tea shop for the best brew and where herbal teas may also be available. *Chá* will bring tea, *chá com leite* will bring tea with milk and *chá com limão* a refreshing tea with lemon.

Few coffee shops sell coffee without selling **cakes** (*bolos*). There are a number of specialities in the central region which are mentioned in the appropriate chapter. Available everywhere are rice cakes (*arroz*), a light sponge which is not usually too sweet, *bolo da rocha*, a delicious bun with a coconut top and filled with custard, and coconut cakes, (*cocos*). Doughnuts are mostly filled with custard, but for something plainer try the *palmier* which look like butterfly wings. *Pão de ló*, a light sponge cake, is another popular choice which, although baked as a large ring, is sold in slices.

On Lisbon's doorstep, Cascais is a popular tourist venue

finer the shreds the better the colour of the soup, and these shreds are added at the last minute with minimum cooking before the soup is served. There is another soup frequently on the menu which has achieved widespread popularity, **açorda à Alentejana** or Alentejo bread soup. It is more than a soup, it is a meal in itself. Coriander, salt and garlic are ground to a paste, let down with olive oil and poured into boiling water. Bread is added, sometimes in pieces or sometimes whole slices, and one or two eggs are dropped in. Even the Portuguese may struggle to start and finish a meal with this soup. Most commonly served in tourist regions is the simple but delicious vegetable soup, **sopa de legumes** and fish soup, **sopa de peixe.**

Bacalhau

Fish and meat dishes appear on the menu in almost equal ratio. Surrounded by sea, fresh fish is constantly available, but it is the dried salted cod, **bacalhau**, which has become the national dish. Looking more like pieces of board, it is distinctly unappetising and smelly in the dry state and it advertises itself strongly as you pass a shop selling it. As early as the 16th century sailors learnt to salt cod at sea and sun dry it for the long journey home. It dries down to thin, stiff slabs which can be safely kept for months and reconstituted by soaking in water. Almost since Columbus discovered America, Newfoundland's Grand Banks have been the traditional fishing ground for cod, and it has provided catches enough to be a source of cheap food which has served the tables of the poor particularly well. The over-fished Grand Banks no longer yield enough to meet the nation's demands and it has become necessary to import *bacalhau* from Norway at a price which the poor can now hardly afford.

Bacalhau à bràs

This is one of the most popular *bacalhau* dishes and the one most likely to be found on menus throughout the country. It also has the advantage of being one of the easiest dishes to prepare. Take around 500g of *bacalhau,* cut into 5cm squares and soak in water for 24 hours, then remove all scales and bones. Prepare an equal weight of potatoes by peeling and slicing them thinly for quick cooking and chop one good-sized onion. Warm some olive oil in a frying pan, add a crushed clove of garlic to be removed when browned, and fry the cod, onions and potatoes together. When cooked add six well beaten eggs and fry just a little longer until the eggs are cooked.

The Portuguese claim at least 365 ways to prepare *bacalhau,* one for every day of the year. All the recipes start by soaking the cod in water for 24 to 48 hours with frequent changes of water to remove the salt. Afterwards the cod is usually boiled gently until soft then mixed with potatoes in some form, covered with a cheese sauce and baked in the oven. Only the more popular recipes appear on restaurant menus; these include *bacalhau à bràs*, with egg, onion and thinly sliced fried potatoes, and *bacalhau à gomes de sá*, a casserole dish with onions and sliced potatoes then garnished with black olives and hard boiled eggs. Restaurants boasting regional cuisine in Algarve usually list a *bacalhau* dish but it normally does not find too much favour with tourists and is absent from most menus. In Alentejo it remains very popular.

Some fish items on the menu are easily recognised like *truta* and *sardinhas* but others are less obvious:

atum	tuna	*pargo*	bream
carapau	mackerel	*ipescada*	hake
eirós	eels	*robalo*	bass
espadarte	sword fish	*salmão*	salmon
lampreia	lamprey	*salmonete*	red mullet
linguado	sole	*solha*	plaice

Sardines

One speciality above all others which has to be tried is fresh sardines. They are grilled over charcoal, sometimes in the street outside the restaurant, and traditionally served with boiled potatoes. Local sardines are in season from June to October, which is the best time to buy them, but they are available all year round although the Portuguese claim they are too bony to eat between November and April. They are barbecued at just about every outdoor fair or celebration throughout the country.

The Cataplana

A speciality introduced by the Arabs and particularly popular in Algarve is the *cataplana*. This traditional seafood dish has a place on menus throughout the country, particularly in the larger restaurants. The *cataplana* is a hinged metal pan with a long handle which can be thrust into the fire. A close-fitting heavy lid retains the steam so that the pan behaves a little like a pressure cooker which can be safely shaken and turned over whilst the food is cooking. In the modern version, the *cataplana* is without a handle. There are various recipes in which clams feature prominently, but one of the most popular uses clams, pork, onions, herbs and white wine. Often the *cataplana* is brought to the table so that diners can enjoy the rich aroma released when opened.

Pork

Pork figures strongly on the meat menu and with good reason, for the meat is truly tender and succulent. Pigs in Portugal live the high life on a diet of acorns and chestnuts, with probably a few truffles thrown in, and are highly prized for the production of **presunto**, smoked ham. Pork is also used in endless garlicky sausages which are popular with the locals. **Chouriço** is a dark sausage, around 15cm long and 2.5cm thick, which is made from cured pork and spiced with garlic and paprika. **Murcela** is a blood sausage and one commonly used to add to *caldo verde* soup. **Linguica** is like *chouriço* but slimmer, while **alheira** is a fresh sausage made from pork. Thin slices of ham are used in a number of recipes in which they may be used to wrap around fish or chicken. Alentejo and pork are virtually synonymous and it features strongly on menus there, often running to several dishes.

Other Meat Dishes

Steak turns up mostly as **bife à Portuguesa** which is either grilled or cooked with a port wine sauce. *Cabrito*, kid, is also very popular with the Portuguese; it finds its way onto most menus in some dish or other and is usually excellent. Recipes for roast kid often read like Mrs Beeton ...kill the kid, cleanse and hang it in the cellar, while still warm wash well with water and salt... this is followed by frequent painting with a garlicky seasoning while still hanging before it reaches the oven two days later. Both chicken (*frango*) and turkey (*peru*) appear on the menu, generally served simply, although the locals prefer chicken with piri-piri sauce. Turkey is usually served as steaks.

Vegetables

Vegetables abound on local markets – and they are good quality vegetables too. There is just about everything imaginable, from carrots, through cauliflower to turnips, leeks or whatever is in season. None of these show up on the dinner plate in the restaurant, however, unless *cozido* is ordered. The recipe featured here shows how the vegetables are used and the quantities that the Portuguese eat.

Salads are sometimes served with the meal in place of vegetables and rice is rarely absent from the plate in restaurants where locals eat.

Portuguese *Cozido*

These quantities are for six people! Boil 500g of beef in water using a large pan and, a little while later, add half a chicken and season with salt. Cook in a separate pan, 300g ham, 500g salted pigs' ears, 500g fresh bacon, 500g salted pork ribs, one meat sausage and one blood sausage. Add no salt since the meat is already salted. To the beef pan add now the vegetables comprising two good green cabbages, one white cabbage and three large carrots, but tie the vegetables with white thread so that they can easily be removed. After 30 minutes, boil six halved potatoes separately until partly cooked and transfer to the beef pan followed by all the meat, now cooked, from the other pan. The *cozido* is ready as soon as the potatoes have finished cooking. Carefully remove the vegetables, place all the meat, suitably cut, onto a serving dish and decorate with the vegetables after removing all the threads.

The stock from the large pan can later be used to make soup by adding cooked, small white beans and small noodles.

Desserts

The Portuguese have a sweet tooth so there is certain to be a sweet trolley hovering at the end of the main course or a *sobremesa* list on the menu. Eggs and sugar are used in abundance to produce the fantasies so loved by the Portuguese. Fantasies they are too judging by some of the descriptive and colourful names, like *barriga de freiras* (nun's belly) and *papos de anjo* (angel's breasts). Two sweets ever present on the menu are **arroz doce**, a cold rice pudding liberally sprinkled with cinnamon and usually very sweet, and the ubiquitous **pudim de flan**, which is none other than crème caramel of which the Portuguese are extraordinarily fond. The calorie count is so high for most sweets that the energy released is best measured on the Richter scale; check out some of the recipes featured here.

Nun's Thighs and All That

There is an endless selection of recipes for sweets but they have two things in common, a huge quantity of sugar and countless eggs in some form.

Leite Pudim (Custard Cream)

Beat up eight egg yolks with 250g sugar and the rind of one lemon over 20 minutes. Blend two tablespoons of cornflower into one litre of milk, beat well and add to the egg yolk mixture. Heat to bring to the boil while stirring constantly, remove the lemon rind and pour into a dish. Before serving, sprinkle the surface with sugar and place under a grill to caramelise the surface.

Viana Pie

A fairly large tray is needed for this Swiss roll type sweet. Beat 10 egg yolks with 200g sugar and add grated lemon (or orange rind), beat the whites stiffly and add to the dough and sift in 170g flour. Beat lightly and bake on a tray lined with paper. Do not overbake otherwise it becomes difficult to roll. To make the filling, boil 100g sugar to a soft syrup, add the whisked yolks of four eggs and heat until the mixture comes to the boil.

Take the cake from the tray and place on a sugared surface, spread the egg filling and roll carefully.

Rabanadas Minhotas

These are essentially cooked bread slices which can be eaten for breakfast or at any time of the day.

Boil a little red Vinho Verde wine with sugar and cinnamon and dip slices of bread into the mixture until well soaked. Dip the bread next into beaten egg and fry in olive oil. Sprinkle with sugar and cinnamon before eating.

Egg cigars (speciality from Arcos de Valdevez)

Make the filling by boiling 250g sugar with a little water until the syrup reaches the thread stage and adding 250g ground almonds, eight egg yolks, a tablespoon of butter and the rind of a lemon.

Dampen some round filo pastry sheets with egg white, add the filling and roll into cigar shapes. Deep fry and coat with sugar before eating.

Cheese

If the puddings are all too sweet there is always the cheese which is some-times put on the table with olives to provide nibbles at the start of a meal. The pick of Portugal's limited cheeses, which are mostly expensive to buy in the shops, is the Brie-like *queijo da Serra* made strictly from the milk of sheep grazing on the mountains of Serra da Estrela. *Serpa*, cured in caves and brushed regularly with an olive oil/paprika mixture, is from Alentejo and equally delicious but much stronger after ageing. Tangy and creamy *azeitão*, from the Arrábida peninsula across the Tagus south of Lisbon is another of the more famous cheeses, as is *beja*, a semi-hard cheese again from Alentejo. For the calorie counters there is always *queijos frescos*, which is an uncured soft cheese rather like cottage cheese.

Wines

Port

Port wine is Portugal's most eminent ambassador. It has had a place on the dinner tables of Europe and beyond for more than three centuries, and is a household name. But there is no better place to drink port than in Portugal. The full range of styles is quite bewildering but the chief variables are the ageing process and the age. All ports start in casks for two years but after that they are either matured in wood or in bottles and may be a single vintage or a blend of different years. Some of the major styles are:

Ruby port: this is made for drinking as soon as it is bottled, which is usually after about three years in wood. This full-bodied fruity wine of good ruby colour is still the biggest selling port wine. More sophisticated `Reserve' and `Vintage Character' rubies are also made. Both of these are aged longer in the casks, usually to around four or more years, and the Vintage Character may be from selected harvests from different years, but the wine will not continue to improve in the bottle.

White port: made and fortified in exactly the same way as ruby but from white grapes. It may be sweet or dry but the modern tendency is for dry or extra dry. Taylors produced the first white port, Chip Dry, in 1935 and it is still one of the best, great as an apéritif, chilled.

Crusted: this starts life earmarked as vintage but it does not meet the stan-dards so is blended and aged for at least three years in a cask and two years in a bottle. During bottle storage it throws a deposit, or crust, and needs to be decanted before drinking.

Tawny: usually made from grapes from the lower Douro which are less heavily pigmented. It is matured in wood for much longer than the ruby so that the wine loses its red colour and acquires a brownish tawny colour. Smooth and mellow, the tawnies are very popular, especially the older ones. There are strict regulations controlling the labelling of port wines and a date on the label is not permitted except for exceptional wines of a single harvest under certain conditions. Even though they start life as blends, good quality tawnies can, with special approval from the Port Wine Institute, show their age as 10, 20, 30 or over 40 years old.

All the above wines are blends of several years but the following are only from single years and sometimes from particular *quintas* (estates). The wines are allowed to carry the date on the label.

Single Quinta: this is an unblended wine usually from a single harvest. It is vintage in character but without the full depth and character and it usually requires long ageing in the bottle to reach perfection.

Vintage: this is the flagship of the port wine industry. Hopes are raised for a vintage in years when the climate has been favourable and the harvest good, but they remain no more than hopes at that stage. Only after two years in the cask is a decision made and, if declared a vintage, the wine is bottled straight away. When mature it has a different quality to the cask-aged ports. Vintage declarations are not taken lightly and reflect the individuality of each of the port houses. The Douro has such a multitude of vineyard sites with different grape varieties and different micro-climates that declared vintages are not universal but mostly quite specific to a particular manufacturer. The larger port houses which have a wider variety of farms have more chance of producing a vintage than the smaller firms. Vintage ports take some years to reach their optimum and they do not all mature at the same rate. Cockburn's declare their 1963 vintage as drinking well and one of their finest vintages of recent times, that of 1970, as ready soon, while the 1975 vintage is said to be light but of good quality and just ready.

Late Bottled Vintage: is port of a single year, aged in wood for 4–6 years and filtered before bottling to prevent crusting.

The Port Wine Institute is the controlling body which guarantees that standards are maintained. The Institute has a bar in Lisbon where port wines can be tried by the glass. Nearly every port wine made is on the menu listed by style and by manufacturer, so it is a great place to sample the various ports (except the expensive vintages) without having to buy full bottles.

Something like 83 million litres of port are consumed annually, most of it in Europe with France drinking the lion's share. The UK has fallen down the league table of port consumption to be overtaken by Portugal itself. The USA is a small market taking only around 1.5 per cent of the annual production, but it is strongly biased to premium styles.

Vinho Verde and Douro Wines

Apart from port, Portugal has many very fine wines to offer in addition to the well known Mateus rosé, as well as some very ordinary ones. There are some excellent labels which have only a very local and limited distribution. **Quinta da Pacheca**, in Alto Douro, is an excellent red Douro wine but only rarely can it be found in shops or in restaurants away from the region where it is made. At least there is a sense of adventure in trying different wines with a chance of some rewarding discoveries.

The country has a number of regions of demarcation, two of them – Vinho Verde and the Douro – in the northern area. Although **Vinho Verde** translates as green wine it really means young or fresh wine and is usually listed separately on the wine list in restaurants; the other wines are listed under *Vinhos maduros*, or mature wines, which means everything other than the Vinho Verdes. *Garrafeira* on the wine label means that the wine has been aged for a minimum of two years in the barrel and one in the bottle, but often much longer, whilst *Reservas* spend even longer in the wood.

Douro wines are made from grapes grown in the Alto Douro in areas generally away from the river. The land close to the River Douro is prized for the port wine grapes. Even away from the river it is the same impossibly dry and impoverished stony soil which looks as though it will not sustain any sort of plant growth. This region produces some very fine and exciting wines including one of the country's best red wines, **Barca Velha**, made in limited quantity. Some of the best years which are still around are '81, '82, '83 and '84. Quinta do Cotto produces dense fruity wines which are well worth searching out and laying down.

The area of demarcation for Vinho Verde is quite extensive and covers much of the region outside the Douro. In fact the only region north of the Douro which is not dedicated to vineyards is the higher part of Trás-os-Montes. White Vinho Verdes are stimulatingly acidic and refreshing – ideal for picnics. With so many small producers in the north, the list of labels is endless but the Ponte de Lima whites have a good reputation. The white made from a single grape variety, the *loureiro* grape, and called by that name, is especially worth trying. Casa de Sezim, which is one of the more comfortable manor houses in the Solares scheme, is another small producer with a good reputation.

Bairrada and Dão Wines

Two demarcated areas south of the River Douro produce good wine: the Bairrada wines come from an area south of Porto, and the Dão wines from the region south of the Alto Douro. The mountainous Dão region is served by a river of the same name which filters down to the sea through Coimbra. The **Dão wines** built up a good reputation in the past but they have not advanced in quality in recent years as other regions have, notably Alentejo. With considerable capital investment in new stainless steel plant and new technology, winemaking in Portugal is in a mobile phase which is advancing some of the newer wines over old favourites. A new high-tech Sogrape plant in Viseu is producing some worthwhile Grão Vasco wines, both white and red.

Bairrada wines are made in the area south of Porto stretching all the way down to Coimbra. Although wine manufacture has been in hand here as long as most other areas of Portugal, it was recognised as a demarcated region only as recently as 1979. Vineyards are dominated by the *baga* grape and make good red wines which take some years to reach maturity. It pays to buy the *garrafeiras* and the older the better. The last years of the 1970s from '75 onwards are all worth buying. Guests at the Palace Hotel in Buçaco Forest and the nearby Curia Palace Hotel have the opportunity to try their legendary red wine, Buçaco, which is unavailable outside this chain of hotels. Much of the white wine of this region is converted to a sparkling wine by the champagne method.

Colares, Carcavelos, Bucelos and Setúbal Wines

Nearer to Lisbon there are four small demarcated areas: Colares (see feature) and Carcavelos, both very small, with the slightly larger Bucelos, all on the north side of the Tagus, and the Setúbal vineyards on the south. With the expansion of the holiday resorts of Estoril and Cascais south of Lisbon, the Carcavelos area is under threat – small and getting smaller. It produces a Madeira-style sweet apéritif or dessert wine of around 19 per cent strength, but it is difficult to find. Look for the Quinta do Barão label. Some 24km (15 miles) north of Lisbon lies the Bucelos wine area centred on the Trancão river. Predominantly two white grape varieties, *arinto* and *esgana cão*, are grown on the clay slopes and floor of the river valley. These produce reliable wines of moderate strength, 11–12 per cent, which are clean and dry with a slight acidity. As in the other small areas here, production is in the hands of one main producer, Camillio Alves, and the label to look for is Caves Velhas.

South of the Tagus is Setúbal which produces another of Portugal's distinctive and famous wines. This is the sweet and perfumed **Muscatel de Setúbal.** The vines are grown around the villages of Palmela and Azeitão – Setúbal muscles in on the name only because it is the nearest port. The crushed grapes are fermented in cement vats and arrested by the addition of grape brandy at the required sugar level, the same technique as used in the production of port wine. The secret of this wine lies in the next stage, when it is transferred to fresh cement vats and lightly crushed grapes and skins are added to impart to the wine the signature of the muscatel grape with its delightful aroma. After pressing again, the wine is held in casks until ready for bottling. This highly aromatic dessert wine is usually available in two ages, six and 20 years old. First one to try is Fonseca's Muscatel de Setúbal.

Algarve and Alentejo Wines

The final area of demarcation is in **Algarve** which has been growing vines since the time of the Romans, but its wines have no great reputation. Some 31 new areas throughout Portugal are seeking recognition and were accepted in 1990 as IPRs (Indicacões de Proveniência Regulamentada) on six years' probation for official wine region status (DOC). Both Lagos and Lagoa in Algarve are amongst the new applicants.

Colares Wines

Colares, near Sintra, produces one of the best and most distinctive wines in Portugal from vineyards which are not just unique, but defy belief. The practice is by no means new – it can be traced back as far as 1154. Vines are planted into clay but to reach the clay it is first necessary to dig through a depth of sand which may be as much as 10m. Digging a trench so deep through sand is not without danger, and it was commonplace for workers to cover their heads with a wicker basket while excavating at depth to give them protection and air to breath should the trench collapse. Once planted, the vines are encouraged to produce lateral shoots which are pegged down at intervals and allowed to root, thus producing a whole row of seemingly individual vines. As the vines start to grow the sand is slowly replaced until, eventually, the vines reach normal surface level. Once above ground, the vines are grown along wire strainers without achieving any great height, and the vineyards are protected by high fences of fine netting to prevent the Atlantic winds from disturbing the sand. One unexpected and invaluable advantage of this method was that the depth and density of the sand gave protection to the vine roots from the ravages of the phylloxera beetle which decimated the vineyards of Europe last century. This beetle operates by burrowing through the soil and feeding from the rootstock which eventually sickens the vine. It was introduced from the United States during viticultural exchanges and, oddly enough, the solution to the problem also came from the States in the form of more rugged root stocks which had proved immune to the scourge. European vines were then universally grafted onto these rootstocks. Colares still uses the original pre-phylloxera vines. The red wines are generally better than the whites but must be matured in oak casks for several years, at least 10, before reaching their best. The one to try is the award-winning **Colares Chita** which is a very quaffable, aromatic and fruity red wine.

Alentejo is currently the rising star in the wine world. Although it has only IPR regions, there has been considerable investment in new plant and it is already producing some of the country's most exciting wines which are eclipsing better known names. Areas worth trying include Redondo, Reguengos and Vidigueira.

Brandy

To accompany coffee at the end of a meal there is always the local brandy-like **aguardente** made from distilled wine or the **bagaceira** distilled from the alcoholic left-overs after winemaking. Two brandies which are popularly found on the shelves are Macieira and Croft's, neither of which is particularly expensive making them rather good value for money. One of the well regarded *aguardentes* is Aliança Velha, found in most shops selling spirits and also worth a try.

Water

Water usually has a place on the dining table and bottled water may be offered as carbonated (*com gas*) or natural (*sem gas*). One of the really outstanding bottled waters is from Carvalhelhos.

5. LISBON

A vibrant, modern city, Lisbon (Lisboa) outwardly exudes a suave image with an underlying bubbly effervescence where local colour goes hand in hand with culture. There is some truth in the old adage that whilst Coimbra sings, Braga prays and Porto works, Lisbon shows off. Here is a city offering just about something for everyone, from a wealth of cultural delights to the more down to earth pursuits of shopping and eating. Lisbon's **Bairro Alto** is famed for its nightlife, especially *fado*, where even hardened night owls will require reserves of stamina to keep up with the locals.

Like Rome, Lisbon was founded on seven hills but visitors today will be hard pressed to pinpoint their location. Rampant development has fanned out to blur their outlines so that they meld seamlessly with similar surrounding undulations. There is no difficulty in locating the hub of the old city as ruined **St Jorge's castle** (Castelo São Jorge) which stands sentinel on the most prominant peak around. Bustling and colourful **Alfama** clings tenaciously to the steep hillside beneath the castle, its downward tumble halted by the level and orderly **Baixa** below. Much of the original building in this area was destroyed in the 1755 earthquake. Fortunately, the much hated Marquês de Pombal (see pages 63–64) was on hand to save the city from hotchpotch redevelopment. Not renowned for letting the grass grow under his feet, figuratively speaking, he set in motion a grand plan to build a new and more aesthetically pleasing city. This is seen to best effect in the grid layout of the Baixa which is a major shopping area. The Baixa links Alfama with the Chiado and Bairro Alto districts which offer yet more shopping and *tascas* for those in search of a reasonably priced lunch shared with the locals.

The founding of Lisbon stretches back into the mists of time where fact becomes entangled with more colourful myth and legend. Whilst on one of his many voyages, Ulysses (Odysseus) is said to have put ashore here, hence a neat explanation of the name it was known by when the Romans arrived, Olisipo. The story is further embellished to include his seduction of the nymph Calypso who, heartbroken at his callous desertion of her, turned herself into a serpent whose coils became the seven hills on which the city was founded. Early chroniclers were not immune from flights of fancy either; they actually recorded the date of its foundation as 3259 BC, by Elishah, grandson of the biblical Abraham. In reality, the geographical position of the city, protective hills, abundant water, plentiful seafood and a safe anchorage has attracted settlers from the time of the prehistoric *castro* cultures and earlier.

The castle of São Jorge dominates the old city and provides a commanding viewpoint

Around 1200 BC those intrepid traders the Phoenicians arrived. Attracted to the natural harbour in the estuary of the Tagus (Tejo), well secluded from the rages of the Atlantic, the Phoenicians stayed to develop a port which they called Alis Ubbo (Serene Port). This provided a safe anchorage for shipping, involved in trade between the Mediterranean and northern Europe, along an otherwise unprotected stretch of coastline. The hill on which St Jorge's castle now sits became their settlement of the same name, a name which has evolved through the ages to the present-day Lisboa (Lisbon).

Greek and Carthaginian traders also recognised the strategic and commercial advantages enjoyed by the inhabitants of Alis Ubbo, so the sole tenure of the Phoenician settlers was relatively short-lived. The Greeks arrived in the 6th century BC and were closely followed by the more dominant Carthaginians, c 535 BC, who were in turn ousted by the invincible might of the Romans when they suffered defeat at their hands in the Second Punic War (218–202 BC). This victory strengthened the Romans' hold on the Iberian Peninsula and, in 205 BC, Olisipo (Lisbon) became a part of the province of Lusitania. Rumblings of unrest amongst the Lusitani manifested itself in a protracted uprising, begun in 154 BC, which only subsided when the Lusitanian leader, Viriatus, was murdered in 139 BC by three of his followers who had been bribed by the Romans. Viriatus later became a national hero although his efforts to oust the Romans were in vain. In 137 BC the Consul Decimus Junius Brutus tightened the Roman yoke and made Olisipo a 'capital' from where he sallied forth to quell unrest in the north.

Incorporated into the Roman Empire by Julius Caesar in 60 BC, Olisipo was raised to the rank of *municipium* and renamed Felicitas Julia. It served as a major administrative centre for the farthest flung westerly outpost of the Empire from where roads radiated to other important towns. Besides building roads the Romans fortified the castle, constructed public buildings and temples, the remains of which have been discovered beneath subsequent layers of habitation, and also laid the foundations of the Portuguese language. Fruit, olives, fish and salt were important economically but the city did not develop its potential as a maritime centre during that time.

The decline of the Roman Empire saw Lisbon abandoned and left to fend for itself. For 300 years, from AD 409, a succession of Germanic barbarian tribes, the Alans, Swabians (Suevi) and Visigoths, occupied the city until the arrival of the Moors.

Early in the 8th century the Moors began their conquest of the Iberian peninsula (711) and occupied Lisbon, whose name they changed from the Visigothic Olissibona to Al Usbuna. A prolonged period of stability ensued allowing the city to prosper and become wealthy.

In 1147 Dom (King) Afonso Henriques, the first king of the newly formed Portuguese nation, captured Lisbon from the Moors, and the capital, then located at Guimarães in the north, was moved further south to Coimbra. By the time Afonso III was on the throne (1248–79), only small pockets of Moorish resistance remained in Portugal and some time around 1260 the capital was moved south yet again to a Lisbon now considered safe from Moorish attack.

Lisbon reasserted itself once more into its role as a capital city but development was hampered by devastating bouts of the Black Death plague in the 14th and 15th centuries. A university was established in Lisbon by Dom Dinis in 1290 but transferred to Coimbra in 1308. Political wrangling between the Church and the Crown caused the university to be moved back and forth between the two cities a number of times, until it was settled back in Coimbra in 1537. It was to be 1911 before a university was finally established in the capital. Fortunes changed at the end of this period with the advent of the Age of Discoveries and subsequent overseas expansion. The city became a centre of trade and the wealthiest city in Europe, a position it enjoyed for more than a century.

A dose of Spanish rule between the years 1580 to 1640 suppressed earlier enterprise but the discovery of Brazilian gold in 1690 changed the fortunes of Lisbon yet again. Unfortunately, the lavish building projects and gold decoration from this era were mostly destroyed in the massive earthquake of 1755. Like the mythical Phoenix the city rose again from the ashes, thanks to the efforts of the Marquês de Pombal which can be seen to this day.

Since that time Lisbon has witnessed the demise of the monarchy and the repressive restrictions of dictatorship under Salazar. A peaceful revolution in 1974 heralded the eventual emergence of a democracy. Today, young *Lisboetas* take democracy for granted and Lisbon is once again shaping itself into a city of stature within the European Union.

Those with little time to spare can capture the essence of Lisbon in a couple of hectic days, whilst city lovers will find more than enough to fill a longer stay. If time is at a premium, the city centre is relatively compact with the main areas of interest easily accessible. Hills and cobbled streets are a predominant feature of Lisbon so comfortable footwear is essential, but non-walkers need not despair – there are ways and means of avoiding excessive physical exertion. Trams regularly trundle their way up the steep inclines of medieval Alfama and out to Belém. Bairro Alto is accessed by an unusual *elevador* (lift) from the Baixa and a funicular also ascends behind Rossio station from the Praça dos Restauradores. Belvederes (*miradouros* or view-points) are also a feature of this hilly city and provide a good excuse to pause for breath whilst admiring the views. Shoppers can enjoy life on the level in the Baixa or carry on shopping in Chiado en route up to Bairro Alto. There is plenty to absorb the culture vultures too, with **St Jorge's Castle**, the **Cathedral** (Sé) and the **Carmo monastery** for starters. If charging up and down narrow streets and shopping become too much, there is ample opportunity to opt out and let the world go by at one of the numerous pavement cafés. Another option is to escape to the restful ambience of the **Edward VII Park** or into the nearby **Botanical Gardens**. Away from the centre but not to be missed, **Belém**, lies seaward along the river beyond the high-level bridge over the Tagus. Belém is the location of the striking **Mosteiro dos Jerónimos** (Jerónimos monastery), a clutch of museums, including the **Museu Nacional de Arqueologia e Etnologia**, and the **Torre de Belém**. Nowadays the riverside here is a quiet backwater, but the Discoveries Monument (Padrão dos Descobrimentos) stands testimony to a time five centuries ago when Belém witnessed the departure of the early explorers, such as Bartolomeu Dias in 1487, from its shore.

Lisbon, like most major cities, is invariably choked with traffic and has limited parking. Excellent, cheap and frequent trains connect from Cascais and Sintra and are probably a better bet even than taxis to avoid traffic jams. The bridge south over the Tagus becomes congested at peak times but this will hopefully be eased with the opening of a second bridge further upstream, close to the airport by the 'Expo' site. A metro line, at present being extended, eases movement to the north of the centre, and there are of course trams, buses and taxis.

Arriving by train

Visitors from Sintra arrive at **Rossio** station which lies at the central hub of the city. Passengers spill out onto the 4th floor of this 19th-century neo-Manueline building, at Bairro Alto level, which is enough to disorientate strangers. Take the escalator down through the lower floors for the Baixa area, emerging onto Praça dos Restauradores. A right turn here will lead to Rossio Square but tourist information (Turismo) is located a short distance to the left, towards Avenida da Liberdade, on the left. Trains from Cascais end at **Cais do Sodré** station down by the waterfront near Praça do Comércio but there is soon to be a Metro link between the two stations. Long distance travellers from Porto (Oporto) or Spain arrive further east along the riverside at the

Santa Apolónia station, a taxi or bus ride away from the centre. The station for trains south to Algarve and Évora is at Barreiro, a ferry ride across the Tagus from Terreiro do Paço by the Praça do Comércio.

Getting around the city

The map distributed to tourists who venture into Turismo is adequate for locating high spots and good for Metro routes, but a more detailed scale is necessary for city forays. Most sights can be easily visited on foot but, because of the city's size and the hilly nature of the terrain, some use of public transport will be necessary especially to reach farther flung outposts. Books of tickets are the best bet for frequent travel on the bus, tram or Metro and these can be purchased from *CARRIS* kiosks. A weekly tourist pass for all municipal transport, including the *elevador* and funiculars, can be obtained from the main *CARRIS* ticket office beneath the Santa Justa *elevador*. The City Council has introduced a new card, the '*Lisboacard*', which gives visitors unrestricted travel on all public transport, buses, trams, lifts and the Metro. It also includes free entry into 26 museums, monuments and other places of interest plus a 10 to 50 per cent discount on some other tourist attractions. Cards are available in Lisbon for one, two or three days and cost roughly half-price for children between the ages of five and eleven. Under fives go free of charge but there is a restriction of two children per adult in this bracket. This offer will probably only benefit the most avid and energetic sightseer. Coach tours of the city and nearby sights can be booked from ticket kiosks; the main pick-up point is at the southern end of Eduardo VII Park in Praça Marquês de Pombal.

Bus/Tram

Buses and trams provide a frequent service. A route map is available from ticket kiosks but these are like gold and usually in short supply. Maps of routes and bus times can normally be found at bus shelters. Special buses, *Aerobuses*, run at 20-minute intervals from 7am until 9pm between Cais do Sodré, via Praça dos Restauradores (Rossio station), to the Portela International Airport. Tickets are validated in the machine on entering a bus or tram. A city tour by vintage tram runs from the Praça do Comércio in summer.

Car

Moving around the city by car is a nightmare of traffic congestion and lack of parking, making use of a car more of a hindrance than a help. It might pay to delay picking up a hire car if staying over in the city for a few days.

Elevators

High parts of the city can be quickly reached by *Elevadors* (elevators or lifts). A true lift is the **Elevador de Santa Justa**, a prominent landmark, which rises up from the Baixa to the Chiado district and ruined Carmo monastery. Others, also called *elevadors* are really funiculars, **Elevador da Glória** heading up

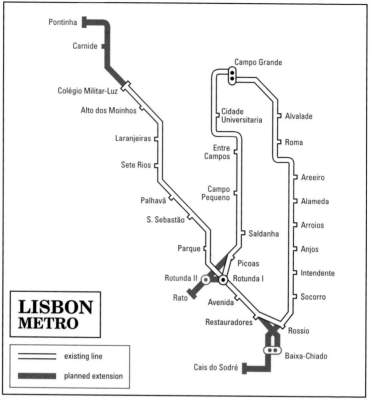

LISBON
METRO

existing line

planned extension

Calçada da Glória from Praça dos Restauradores to the São Pedro de Alcântara belvedere (Bairro Alto); **Elevador da Bica**, from Rua de São Paulo near the Santa Caterina belvedere (up behind the Mercado da Ribeira near Cais do Sodré) to just west of Praça Luís de Camões and the lesser known **Elevador do Lavra**, which runs from Largo da Anunciada, located on the right behind Avenida da Liberdade just uphill after leaving Praça dos Restauradores, to the Torel Belvedere.

Metro

At present, the Metro system serves the city north of Rossio Square. The main section is a narrow loop up through Campo Grande whilst a single line shoots north-west from Rotunda (Praça Marquês de Pombal) to Colégio Militar (Military College). The system is at present being extended to include a line south to Cais do Sodré railway station, via a new station at Baixo-Chiado, and there will be connections from Rotunda to Rato and Pontinha beyond the Colégio Militar. A large M indicates a metro entrance. Tickets are one price for any journey and are marginally cheaper bought from the machine than from the ticket kiosk. They have to be validated in machines at the entrance to the platform.

Taxis

Lisbon's black and green or beige taxis provide an inexpensive means of getting around, especially if four are sharing. The fare is metered within the city limits so charges are fairly straightforward but, for journeys beyond this boundary, fix a price beforehand. Drivers are allowed to make additional charges for heavy luggage and night-time journeys. A ten per cent tip is usual.

Ferries

Regular ferries ply daily between the city and the communities south of the river, known locally as the Outra Banda. Terreiro do Paço (Praça do Comércio) is the departure point for passengers to Cacilhas (where a bus connects with the statue of Cristo-Rei, Christ the King), Seixal, Barreiro (for trains south) and Montijo. A car ferry to Cacilhas leaves from the nearby Cais do Sodré. Crossings from Belém connect with buses at Trafaria and Porto Brandão for the *Lisboetas* seaside playground at Costa Caparica.

Baixa and the heart of the city

For a first flavour of Lisbon, as good a place as any to start exploring is the Pombaline centre of Baixa. The area slopes gently down from the city's heart, Rossio, to the Praça do Comércio by the riverside, its 18th-century neoclassical buildings arranged in a grid making navigation easy. Just to the northwest lies Praça dos Restauradores where passengers from Rossio station emerge and where 'Turismo' is located in the 18th-century Palácio Foz.

Rossio

Rossio or, to give it its formal name, Praça de Dom Pedro IV has been at the hub of city activity since the 13th century. Until the 18th century, this large open space variously witnessed bullfights, carnivals, parades and public executions, especially the dreaded Inquisition's *autos-da-fé* when real or imagined heretics met an agonising end by burning. Today, the square is a swirl of continuous movement watched over by a statue of Dom Pedro IV (1826) which is flanked by two large fountains brought from Paris in 1890. The statue was originally of Emperor Maximilian of Mexico and was acquired by the city fathers, at a knock-down price, when Maximilian was assassinated whilst the statue was en route from Marseilles to Mexico. A little bodging here and there and the statue has been passed off as a questionable likeness ever since. Shops, cafés, kiosks, peddlers, shoeshiners and colourful flower sellers all contribute to the kaleidoscope of activity in the square. Two of the most popular cafés in the area, the *Pasterlaria Suiça* and *Nicola*, are well placed to sit and watch the world go by. At its northern end, the square is presided over by the **Teatro Nacional** (Dona Maria II Theatre), built by the Italian Fortunato Lodi between 1842 and 1846. Its interior was destroyed by fire in 1964 but has since been restored. A building with a less illustrious

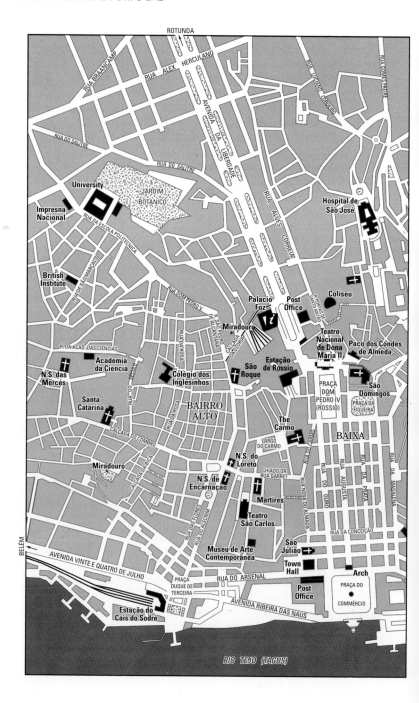

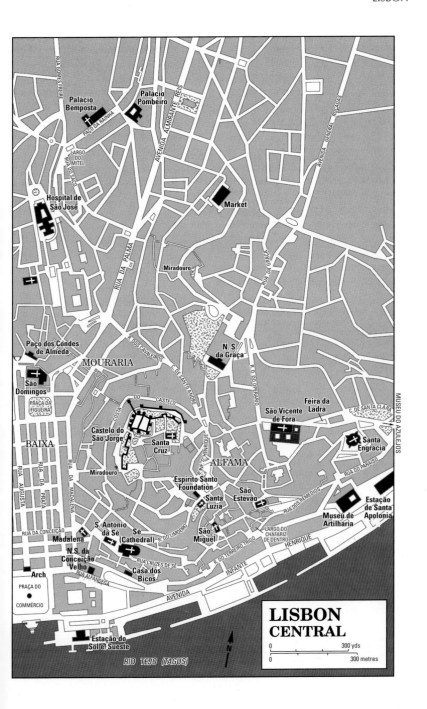

RIO TEJO (TAGUS)

LISBON
CENTRAL

| 0 | | 300 yds |
| 0 | | 300 metres |

purpose once occupied part of the theatre site, the Paço dos Estãos (1449). Used as a collection point for the expulsion from the country of Portuguese Jews (1497), it became even more iniquitous on being made the headquarters of the Inquisition in 1571, so its destruction by fire in 1836 was probably seen as just retribution. Those in search of shops with a touch of old Lisbon will find a diversion along pedestrianised Rua das Portas de Santo Antão, north of the theatre, an unexpected treat.

On the northern edge of Largo de São Domingos, to the east of the Teatro Nacional, is the **Paço dos Condes de Almada** (Palace of the Counts of Almada). It was here, in 1640, the 'Restauradores' conspired to overthrow the Spanish occupation of Portugal. The Church of São Domingos, in the southeast corner, was were the Inquisition passed sentence on their victims. Rebuilt after the 1755 earthquake, it was ravaged by fire in 1959 but has been reroofed and rendered serviceable. A little further south from here, parallel with Rossio, is the smaller Praça da Figueira (Figtree Square) with its statue of Dom João I.

South through the Baixa (lower town)

A uniform grid of streets stretches down to the triumphal arch leading into Praço do Comércio by the riverside. Constructed to the Marquês de Pombal's grand design after the 1755 earthquake, the streets reflect in their names the various trades to which they were allotted then, but notably less so today. The three main streets are the pedestrianised Rua Augusta, leading directly to the arch, either side of which lie the Rua Aurea, better known as the Rua do Oura (gold), and Rua da Prata (silver). All these are criss-crossed by a network of smaller streets, most of which are pedestrianised. Shops of all descriptions can be found in this area and a stroll down Rua Augusta is an entertainment in itself. At busy times this street positively pulses with a motley mix of business personnel, ardent shoppers and sightseers, where street entertainers and street traders constantly vie for attention.

Praça do Comércio

Rua Augusta spills out into Praça do Comércio through the imposing triumphal **Arch of Rua Augusta**, constructed at the end of the 19th century. Statues of Viriato, Nuno Alvares Pereira, Vasco da Gama and the Marquês de Pombal, historical figures in Portuguese history, grace the façade of the arch whose bulk emphasises the elegance of the surrounding 18th-century pink 'Pombaline' neoclassical arcades. Portugal's Stock Exchange, or *Bolsa,* is housed in the buildings on the eastern side of the square and the post office in those to the west. The earlier name of the square, Terreiro do Paço (Palace Terrace), is still used and comes from the time before 1755 when the 16th-century royal palace *da Ribeira* ('riverside') stood on the site. Centre stage is the bronze equestrian **statue of Dom José I** (1750–77), which gives the square its English name of 'Black Horse Square'. Sculpted by Machado de Castro in

1775, the statue commemorates Dom José's assistance after the city's destruction in 1755. A medallion of Pombal on the same statue was removed, and hidden by the sculptor, after Pombal's fall from grace in 1777 but was recovered and replaced in 1833. On the waterfront east of the square, ferries leave to cross the Tagus and it was from the central marble steps, in April 1662, that Catherine of Braganza embarked for England and her marriage to Charles II. Unfortunately, the present volume of traffic and the square's function as an unsightly car park diminish its grandeur and visual appeal.

From the north-east corner of the square, a short walk leads along Rua Alfándega to the church of **Nossa Senhora da Conceição Velha** with its notable Manueline doorway. Manuel himself ordered the building of this church (1495–1521) on the site of the synagogue, when the Jews were expelled from the country. A little further along on the left is the unusual **Casa dos Bicos** (16th century), whose front elevation is interspersed with distinctive pyramidal stones. The house, built by Brás de Albequerque, started life as a four-storey palace. It was destroyed in 1755 and, using old engravings as a guide, rebuilt as faithfully as possible to the original in 1983.

Leaving the square to the north-west along Rua do Arsenal, pass the spot close to the post office where, on 1 February 1908, King Carlos I and his heir Luís Felipe were assassinated. Not much further down on the right is the Praça do Munícipio with its 18th-century *pelourinho* (pillory). This is overlooked by the Câmara Municipal (Town Hall), built between 1865 and 1875, from where Portugal was declared a Republic on 5 October 1910. Continue along the road to reach the Praça Duque da Terceira and the Cais do Sodré station, just beyond which is Lisbon's main market, **Mercado da Ribeira**. The amazing array of produce sold here is something not to be missed by visitors in search of local colour.

Alfama and points east

Probably the most evocative district of the city, Alfama, is the old Moorish area between the castle and the river. This veritable maze of winding alleys and narrow lanes (*becos*), where caged birds trill from balconies draped with sun-dried washing, has survived the ravages of earthquakes because of its rocky foundation; a delight to wander but keep a tight hold on valuables which could prove easy targets for thieves.

To view the sights of the area go east along Rua da Conceição and start to rise up past the church of Madalena (1783). An alternative is to take a No. 28 Graça tram up to the Portas do Sol. This leaves a short final haul up to the castle and downhill walk to other sights. The Romanesque façade of the Sé (cathedral) looming close ahead takes attention away from the small church of **Santo António da Sé**, originating under Dom João II but rebuilt in 1767, on the left. Constructed around the room where Santo António or St Anthony of Padua (1195–1231) was born, the church (Museu Antoniano) is a magnet to his many devotees and depicts the life story of the saint. He started life as

Fernando de Bulhoês, changed his name on becoming a Franciscan monk, and acquired the Padua appendage after spending time in Italy. Alfama really swings every 12 and 13 June, its gaily festooned streets attracting hordes of *Lisboates* who come to celebrate the feast of their adopted patron saint, Santo António, the protector of love and marriage. His festival coincides with the time of the summer solstice and attendant ancient rites of fertility. Such is his popularity, the old city gates even had niches to hold his statue. By comparison, the relatively unknown official patron saint, São Vicente (St Vincent), of Spanish origin, has been unable to make it into the popularity stakes in quite the same way.

Remnants of the **Roman city** have been coming to light during rebuilding work. Besides a Roman *cryptoporticus* (*Termas Romanas, c* AD 1) under the Baixo at the Junction of Rua da Conceição and Rua da Prata, which can only be visited once a year, scant remains can be viewed of a Roman Theatre on Rua de São Mamede. Part of an inscription has been found dedicating the orchestra to Nero, which suggests a building date similar to that of the *cryptoporticus*.

The Sé (Cathedral)

More impressive from a distance than on closer inspection, the Sé is in sore need of sympathetic renovation. Its best feature is probably the two Romanesque bell towers, their austerity mellowed by a large central rose window. These steely towers have witnessed their fair share of history, especially in 1388 when the then incumbent, Bishop Martinho Anes, raised the passions of the local populace with his Spanish sympathies and was flung from the north tower. The cathedral was built on the orders of Dom Afonso Henriques for his first bishop, the English Gilbert of Hastings, soon after the capture of Lisbon in 1147. Stories that it was built on the site of a mosque have been refuted, but present extensive excavations in the cloisters may throw more light on its earlier history. Subsequent rebuilding and repairs, after earthquakes in the 14th century and 1755, have resulted in a mishmash of styles which leave the cathedral lacking in character. To the left on entry is the font where Santo António was baptised in 1195 and, a little further along, a nativity scene by the sculptor Joaquim Machado de Castro, but these do little to relieve the dull barrel-vaulted interior. In the chancel, originally built during his reign and restored in the late 18th century, lie the tombs of Dom Afonso IV and his wife Dona Brites. Afonso was instrumental in the murder of the Galician, Inês de Castro, his son Pedro's mistress, afraid that her Spanish connections might influence the throne when Pedro succeeded. Their love story has become legend and their tombs in Alcobaça Abbey a focus of romantic pilgrimage.

A small payment admits visitors to the **cloisters** which are approached along a Gothic ambulatory lined with chapels. The chapels contain the 14th-century tombs of Lopo Fernandes Pacheco, who had a hand in rebuilding work on the cathedral at that time, and of his wife; also that of the first

Trams still trundle the old city routes, as shown here, passing the front of the cathedral

archbishop, João Anes, who died in 1440. Archaeological excavations have transformed the open central area into something resembling a building site, demanding closer inspection. A purpose-built walkway allows visitors a bird's-eye view of the fascinating, substantial foundations of earlier building on the site. The remains of São Vicente are kept in a casket amongst other sacred objects in the sacristy, off the south transept. His remains were brought to Lisbon for safe-keeping in 1173, on the orders of Afonso Henriques, from Cabo de São Vicente in Algarve. Legend relates how the remains arrived in Algarve on a ship from Spain, guided by ravens, after the saint's martyrdom at Valencia. Ravens again accompanied the ship transporting his remains from Algarve to Lisbon and they figure in Lisbon's coat of arms to this day. The more probable story of the saint's arrival in Portugal is that citizens of Valencia, escaping persecution by the Caliph of Córdova, arrived in Algarve with the remains and built a stone chapel to house them at Cabo de São Vicente, which was later enlarged by the Visigoths.

Continue the uphill push into Rua do Limoeiro, past intriguing antique shops and buildings which were once the resplendent palaces of Limoeiro ('lemon tree') and Aljube, the archbishop's palace, reduced in later life to the ignominious roles of prisons for men and women respectively. It was from the royal palace of Limoeiro in 1383 that João, Master of Avis, the illegitimate son of Pedro I, was proclaimed regent after slaying Andeiro, the Galician knight and lover of the scheming widow of Dom Fernando, Leonor Teles, which heralded the end of the House of Burgundy and birth of the House of Avis. The **Santa Luzia Belvedere and church** of the same name are soon reached. Built on the remains of the old Visigothic walls, a small garden area and ornamental pool, used by local children to cool off in summer, provide an unexpected haven and good vantage point down over Alfama. *Azulejos* (tiles) decorate the walls of Santa Luzia with depictions of old Lisbon and the heroic Martim Moniz who, at the expense of his own life in 1147, enabled Afonso Henriques' troops to gain entry into the Moorish-held city by holding open one of the gates.

The route to the castle is to the left up Travessa de São Jorge but, by following the tram lanes a short way further, you reach a high point and site of the former eastern city gate, Largo das Portas de Sol, from where there is an extensive panorama down over Alfama and beyond. The terrace cafés provide a good excuse to linger over the views with welcome refreshment. In the Largo itself is the 17th-century palace of the counts of Azurara which houses the **Museu Escola de Artes Decorativas** (Museum of Decorative Art). The Espírito Santo Foundation was established here in 1953, by the banker Ricardo Espírito Santo Silva, to ensure the preservation of Portuguese traditional craftsmanship by setting up workshops for gilding, woodcarving and cabinet making, etc. These workshops can be visited and many fine examples of the various crafts being preserved appreciated in the natural setting of the old palace.

Castelo de São Jorge (St George's Castle)

Long recognised by a succession of tribes as a prime development spot, the city reached a new level of sophistication under the Moors who used to advantage the foundations laid by the Romans and Visigoths. A Moorish Kasba (citadel) was built within the walls on the south side of the hill, where the Phoenician settlement and later Roman acropolis once stood. The highest point was reserved for the fortress, with its ten square towers, but remnants of further walls between the Kasba and the river have become incorporated in later building works. On the Kasba site stood the Paço de Alcáçova, which was converted into a palace by Dom Dinis. It remained a royal residence down to the time of Dom Manuel but had been abandoned by the 17th century in favour of a new palace by the river.

Approaching via Travessa de São Jorge, enter the castle through the Porta de São Jorge (1846). The walls and towers have been subject to questionable renovation but the views, over the rooftops of Lisbon, from their ramparts more than compensate for any shortcomings in this respect. Tranquil shaded gardens, fountains and a small museum within the remnants of the palace, presided over by a statue of Afonso Henriques, are all that remain of the once bustling citadel. A great place to come to escape the heat of the city in summer and maybe enjoy lunch at the restaurant *Casa do Leão*, which also serves tea later in the afternoon.

Leave the castle through the old medieval quarter of Santa Cruz and its church, on the eastern side of the hill, past the church of Meninos Deus (1711–37) and left to eventually reach Largo de Rodrigues de Freitas. Calçada da Graça leads off north to Graça belvedere and church but there is an even higher viewpoint, for belvedere baggers or those with limitless energy, further on up from Largo da Graça at Monte Belvedere.

Outside the old town walls

Two imposing churches dominate the skyline further east, São Vicente de Fora and Santa Engrácia lower down the slope, and are easily reached from Largo de Rodrigues de Freitas without much uphill work. The monastery church of **São Vicente de Fora** (1582–1627) – *de fora* means 'outside' and indicates that it stood outside the medieval walls – lost its dome during the 1755 earthquake but, although the symmetry of its square, Mannerist style façade with twin towers draws the eye, it fails to excite. A charge is made to enter the **cloisters**, with some fine *azulejos* of scenes from La Fontaine's *Fables*, which hold more appeal than the gloomy, dusty interior of the church. Since 1855, the refectory has housed the tombs of members of the Braganza dynasty; their occupants, including England's Queen Catherine of Braganza, used to be displayed in their embalmed state. More *azulejos*, this time of the sieges of Lisbon and Santarém, decorate the *Portaria* to the right of the cloister entrance, but it is the ceiling (c 1710) of the Florentine Vincenzo Baccerelli which draws most acclaim.

En route between the two churches is the Campo de Santa Clara where a flea market, *Feira da Ladra* is held on Tuesday and Saturday mornings. The church of **Santa Engrácia**, begun in 1682, is the only 17th-century Baroque church in Portugal, replacing a church of the same name built on the site a century earlier. Effective use is made of marble decoration, and undulating curves are a feature of a design based on the Greek cross. Although its dome captures immediate attention from a distance, this was only completed in 1966. The length of time to its completion became a standing joke amongst the *Lisboetas*, who coined the idiom *'obras de Santa Engrácia'* as a disparaging comment for never-finished work generally. Since its completion it has been proclaimed a 'National Pantheon', with memorials to Vasco da Gama, Henry the Navigator and Luís de Camões amongst others.

From here continue down to the riverside and the location of the **Museu Militar** (Military Museum), opposite the Santa Apolónia railway station. Housed in a large building still used by the military, the museum, really for enthusiasts of military hardware and attendant paraphernalia, is entered from the Largo do Museu da Artilharia on its western side.

About 1.5km (1 mile) further east along the riverside, in the district of Xabregas, lies the Madre de Deus convent now the **National Tile Museum**. Although the museum is isolated out on a limb, in an otherwise nondescript area, it is easily located by the roadside and well worth the effort of a visit. A taxi ride from outside the railway station will save some time. Not too far away also, is the excellent **Water Museum** which details the development of Lisbon's water supply from Roman times to the present day.

Museu Nacional do Azulejo (National Tile Museum)

Founded in 1509 by Dona Leonor of Lancaster, widow of Dom João II, the Convento da Madre de Deus was built to house the relics of the Portuguese saint, Santa Auta, killed on her return from a pilgrimage to Rome, and was given to the Poor Clairs of Setúbal. Dona Leonor seemingly neglected her duties as a loving wife, preferring to lavish affection on the church, a single-minded devotion still evident in the Misericórdia charity she founded. Keep an eye open for the founder's symbol, a shrimping net, and that of her husband, a pelican, which can be located in the side portal. Little remains of the original convent foundation, which was extended by Dom João III then rebuilt after the 1755 earthquake, except for the Manueline doorway whose beauty is all but swamped by the drabness of its present surrounds.

The convent provides the perfect foil for the national collection of *azulejos* with 24 rooms around the cloisters used to depict the development of tile production. Unfortunately, they represent a lost opportunity in a failure to clearly annotate the displays and make the history of their progression down the centuries clear to visitors. Colourful or blue and white, the tiles illustrate a wide range of subjects both religious and secular. Some are Dutch, others came from Seville or the Rato factory in Lisbon, but all display the national love of *azulejos* as a form of decoration. Perhaps the most compelling tile picture is the 36m-long panoramic view of Lisbon's waterfront as it appeared c 1738.

The *pièce de résistance* is undoubtedly the magnificence of the church itself, with the richness of gilt Baroque woodwork and walls and ceilings, above tiled dados, covered with gilt-framed paintings of the life of St Francis by André Gonçalves (1687–1762). In the chancel are 16th-century paintings retrieved from the original church, and a marble basin for holy water in the sacristy is claimed to have belonged to Dona Leonor.

Fortunately, senses drained by this artistic feast can be revived in the surrounds of the bar/restaurant adjacent to a leafy garden area which, if the timing is right, makes a choice spot for a light lunch. A selection of books and information about the exhibits is on sale in the entrance hall. On leaving the museum turn right and head back parallel with the river towards the Praça do Comércio.

A foray even further along the riverside east leads to the Expo '98 site whose theme, 'The Oceans, A Heritage for the Future', explores the uses and abuses of the world's oceans in the 500 years since Vasco da Gama discovered a route to India. The Ocean Pavilion remains as one of the biggest Oceanaria in Europe.

Museu de Água *(Water Museum of EPAL)*

At times, the narrow dusty road and traffic divert attention away from route finding but, around two thirds of the way back in the direction of the Museu Militar, watch for a sign on the right to the Museu Água up Calçada dos Barbadinhos. Take the Rua do Alviela, again on the right, which appears to go nowhere in particular, and follow round left to find it opens out into a square. Enter via the gates of the *EPAL* water company on the right, then turn left up to the building at the top of the gardens which houses the museum.

The **Manuel da Maia Water Museum**, named for the engineer of the Aqueduto das Águas Livres (Aqueduct of Free Waters), started life in 1880 as the Barbadinhos Steam Pumping Station. Designed to supply the city with water from the Alviela Aqueduct, it was the first of its kind built in Portugal and was constructed in the close of the Convent of Barbadinhos, an Italian order which had established itself there in 1739.

Now redundant as a pumping station, the building has been preserved as a record of Lisbon's water supply history from Roman times which includes the story of the Aqueduto das Águas Livres and other titbits of information and objects. Still *in situ* rising majestically through three floors, are four huge steam engines one of which can be operated electrically for demonstration purposes.

The museum was awarded the Council of Europe Museum Prize for 1990 and includes the Aqueduto das Águas Livres, or Great Aqueduct, and Mãe d'Água Reservoir in Amoreiras, all of which come under the same umbrella of the *EPAL* water company.

First attempts to bring water into Lisbon via an aqueduct were mooted in 1571 but it was Dom João V, in 1731, who finally gave the go-ahead for the construction of the **Aqueduto das Águas Livres**. Only brought into service in 1748, the 11km (7 miles)-long aqueduct was built to a high specification but with an unevenly spaced arch to straddle a minor geological fault line. Fortunately, this to some aesthetic blunder saved the aqueduct from the ravages of the 1755 earthquake. Although the aqueduct was withdrawn from service in 1967, the great span of arches across the Alcântara Valley are an impressive sight and occasional group walks across this section, from Campo de Campolide to Monsanto Park, are available for those intent on closer inspection. Water from the aqueduct was collected and distributed to the city fountains at the **Mãe d'Água Reservoir** in Amoreiras, which was completed in 1834. This large covered building is now used for cultural events and guided visits can be arranged through the museum office.

Back down on Rua da Santa Apolónia, a short distance past the Museu Militar, reach the Largo do Chafariz de Dentro and location of the 13th-century city fountain, Chafariz d'El Rei. Once a busy meeting point for Alfama housewives, the square is a good jumping off point for a casual stroll around the colourful streets of this old district.

North of Rossio

Sites of interest to the north are more widespread but, with careful route planning, easily accessible. Use of the Metro comes into its own here, as the lines pass within reach of most major points of interest. The Parque de Eduardo VII, Fundação Calouste Gulbenkian (Gulbenkian Museum and Arts Centre), Jardim Zoológico and nearby Quinta do Marquês de Fronteira are along the line to the Colégio Militar, whilst the Campo Pequeno bullring and Museu da Cidade (City Museum) lie off the Campo Grande loop. Many of the major hotels are also located within reach of the Metro. To combat Lisbon's hilly terrain, for those who like to take in the sites by walking as much as possible, one option is to take transport out from the centre and, except for occasional undulations, enjoy a mainly downhill walk back.

Praça dos Restauradores, just north of Rossio, is named for the 'Restorers', who revolted against Spanish rule in 1640 and thus restored independence to Portugal. **Avenida da Liberdade** bursts forth from this square rising, in almost 1.5km (1 mile), up to Praça Marquês de Pombal (Rotunda), dominated by a soaring statue of the man himself. Initially, the Avenida was a small extension of the Praça dos Restauradores and together they formed an exclusive walled promenade area overlooked by the 18th-century Palácio Foz, which is now used for cultural events and by Turismo. This enclave was constructed to allow the upper classes some peace during their perambulations from constant harassment by the city riffraff, who thronged Rossio at that time. The walls of the enclave were eventually dismantled in 1821 and the area opened to the general public for dances and celebrations. It was not until 1879 that the Avenida became the double carriageway it is today and an elegant show-piece with palms and water gardens. Any former elegance is now masked by intrusive traffic congestion and modern rebuilding but trees still shade the way and fleeting cameos of outdoor cafés and handsome façades recapture some of the essence of its former glory days.

The Marquês de Pombal (1699–1782)

Sebastião José de Carvalho e Melo, was born into the lower aristoc-racy in 1699. Better remembered as the Marquês de Pombal, he firmly established himself in Portugal's history during his lifetime. The combination of a clear, calculating mind and powerful physical pres-ence, he stood some 2m tall, were no doubt instrumental in his mete-oric rise to fame. Dom João V, disliking the man but respecting his ability, dispatched him to London as envoy to the Court of St James's.

Pombal made a timely return to Portugal just before the death of Dom João in 1750. Untutored in the affairs of state, the new affable king, José, preferred the delights of the opera, card table and horse-riding. He made Pombal secretary of state and later chief minister, being quite happy to let him control the everyday running of the country – which included putting his signature to any document Pombal produced.

A man of vision and brilliance, Pombal nevertheless exerted a dicta-torial rule which brought him many enemies, particularly amongst the nobility and church. Matters came to a head after the 1755 earthquake when much of Portugal lay in ruins. Pombal was granted emergency powers by the king, not rescinded for 20 years, and took control. Plans were drawn up to rebuild Lisbon in neoclassical style to a geometric plan and bring piecemeal commercial activity, at home and in the colonies, under central control. Chartered companies were created for tobacco, fishing, whaling and port wine, the latter business in particular being in a state of chaos and set on a course of self destruction. The formation in 1756 of the General Company for the Cultivation of the Vineyards of the Upper Douro caused great bitterness. Demarcated areas were created for wine growing and anyone outside those areas had their vines destroyed. With despotic determination opponents were ruthlessly weeded out, some hanged others deported; only those who adapted survived and prospered. An assassination attempt on the king's life only served to provide Pombal with the excuse he needed to move against the Jesuits, although it was never really known who was respon-sible. A reign of terror followed in January 1759, when nobles known to oppose Pombal along with Jesuits were subjected to an orgy of torture, beheading and burning. Eight months later the Jesuits were expelled from Portugal and in the same year Pombal became Count of Oeiras.

All opposition quashed, Pombal now bulldozed through more, much needed change. Reforms at Coimbra University weakened religious influence, which had caused serious students to seek a broader education outside Portugal, and grammar schools were created. An observatory, botanical gardens and laboratories were established, slavery banned and distinctions between old and new (i.e. Jews) Christians abolished as was discrimination by colour in the eastern colonies.

Pombal was created Marquês in 1770 but fell from grace on the death of Dom José. In an attempt to keep his position of power, Pombal plotted to force José's daughter Maria to renounce the throne in favour of her son José, an admirer of his. The plan backfired and Pombal found himself being tried for crimes against the state. In his defence, none of his actions was shown to have been undertaken without the king's signature on the appropriate document. A new regime under an anti-Pombal queen sealed his fate: he was banished to serve out the rest of his life on his estate, but his economic and administrative reforms remained in place.

Loathed by many during his lifetime, Pombal's foresight and draconian methods of achieving his objectives only served to improve an otherwise stagnating country. His implacable will might have swept aside all that stood in his way but, despite personal ambition, he was devoted to his home and family. Today, his achievements are recognised and his memory revered rather than reviled.

Parque de Eduardo VII

This green sward slopes upwards from the nightmarish clamour of Praça Marquês de Pombal. Master of all he surveys, Pombal gazes disdainfully over the traffic which converges on and hurtles past the base of his statue – a fitting location for a man who liked to be at the heart of things. Only a step away though is the comparative peace of the park with its restful boulevards.

The park was named for the English king, Edward VII who, in 1903, made the first state visit after his coronation to Portugal, an occasion which was used to further cement the special Anglo-Portuguese alliance as laid out in the Treaty of Windsor (1386). About halfway up the park, on the right, is the unlikely neo-Baroque façade of the recently renovated Sports Pavilion and in the top left-hand corner two well camouflaged greenhouses. Entrance to the greenhouses, **Estufa Fria** (cold) and **Estufa Quente** (hot), is off Rua Castilho and there is a small entrance charge. These oases of green fronds, exotic flowers, twisting pathways, rills and mini waterfalls make an unusual diversion. In summer though, the Estufa Quente, originally built to house exotic orchids, is suffocatingly humid; the slatted roof of the Estufa Fria allows air to circulate and is much fresher. The castellated building at the top of the park belies any romantic suggestion in its use as a prison.

Fundação Calouste Gulbenkian

A short distance north of the park is the Gulbenkian Foundation complex. First-time visitors are likely to be amazed at the size of this light and airy centre of cultural excellence set in its own parkland. Besides the main collection, there is the Museum and Centre of Modern Art, and the Foundation has its own symphony orchestra, choir, ballet company, concert halls and library. The Foundation is also the most important funding body for the arts in Portugal. This remarkable collection was amassed by Calouste Gulbenkian, an oil tycoon and art patron. Born in Istanbul of Armenian parents in 1869, Gulbenkian brought together a superb eclectic collection of artistic works during his lifetime, ranging from an appealing ancient Egyptian cat to Eastern carpets and porcelain, furniture, silver, books, paintings and jewellery.

Forced to flee his Paris home at the outbreak of World War II, Gulbenkian sought refuge in Portugal, a country to which he became greatly attached. To ensure continued support of the arts he set up a foundation and, when he died in 1955, left his art collection to Portugal. The foundation financed the building of a museum to house the collection, loosely divided into Eastern and Western art for display. In the same grounds is a later building, the **Centro de Arte Moderna** (1985), which is mainly for 20th-century Portuguese art.

Books are on sale at the centres and there are self-service restaurants for a coffee or light lunch in pleasant surroundings.

Still heading north, now on Avenida da República, you come to Campo Pequena and Lisbon's pseudo-Moorish **bullring**. Bull fights in Portugal (Easter to October) are a feat of skill, not the bloodbath of their counterparts in Spain, as the bull is not killed in the ring. Close to the Monument to the Peninsular War at the end of the Avenida da República is Lisbon's permanent fairground, **Feira Popular**, open every day from March to September and limited times over winter. From here it is not far to the City Museum.

Museu da Cidade (City Museum)

The history of Lisbon is laid out from prehistory through to the revolution of 1910 in the setting of the fine 18th-century Palácio Pimenta. Built as a country residence during the reign of Dom João V (1706–50), its earlier tranquillity is now shattered by the constant roar of traffic around the Campo Grande. Even so, the museum gives a good insight into how events have fashioned the development of Lisbon, which should enhance the visitor's perception of other places visited during a stay in the city.

Even further out along the Avenida Padre Cruz, located in the gardens of the Parque do Monteiro-Mór, are the **Museu do Trajo** (Costume Museum) in the Quinta Palmela and **Museu de Teatro** (Theatre Museum) in the Quinta do Monteiro-Mór (Master of the Hounds). The **Convento de Odivelas**, further along the same Avenida, was founded by Dom Dinis between 1295 and 1305. His tomb is here, and this is where Philippa of Lancaster, wife of Dom João I, died of plague in 1415. What is surprising is that Dom Dinis, who did so much to secure the defences of Portugal, should be entombed in such a forgotten corner of the kingdom, whereas Philippa lies deservedly in stately splendour, alongside her husband, at Batalha. Some of the nuns from this convent were evidently targets for the lust of Dom João V, ensnared to assuage his known penchant for their kind. The measure of his success lies in two famous sons he had by nuns from Odivelas: Gaspar, Archbishop of Braga and José, who became a Grand Inquisitor.

Jardim Zoológico (Zoo) lies more to the north-west and is housed in very pleasant gardens covering 25 ha with roomy enclosures for the animals. Other attractions include pony rides, rowing, a train shuttle and dolphins.

Lovers of beautiful houses and gardens might be tempted to visit the **Palácio da Fronteira**, just a little west of the zoo, off Rua de São Domingos in Benfica near the Cruz de Pedra railway station. Situated on the perimeter of the Parque Florestal de Monsanto, the area around the house is distinctly seedy. Nevertheless, although hours of visiting are limited, this privately owned palace (1670) is quite a gem inside its enclosing walls. Terraces, formal gardens and a balustraded walkway are embellished with topiary, fountains, marble busts, and an ornamental lake, whilst blue and white *azulejos* provide the backcloth to a huge water tank. *Azulejos* predominate in both internal and external decoration, from the whimsical to the serious, the whole representing a large collection of captivating tiles under one roof.

Bairro Alto and points west

Rising up from the Baixo to the west, the Bairro Alto offers yet more shopping opportunities, narrow streets with flowered balconies, *tascas* for a cheap lunch and a renowned night life. The lower half, the Chiado, centred on Rua Garret, was destroyed by fire in 1988 but has since been rebuilt in the old style.

Shoppers may wish to forgo a ride on the Elevador de Santa Justa, in favour of strolling up Rua do Carmo and Rua Garret past the clothing shops and sampling another Lisbon landmark, *Café A Brasileira*. Those who opt for the lift are quickly taken up to an excellent viewpoint across the Baixo towards the Castelo de São Jorge and down to the Tagus, reached by climbing even higher to the restaurant at the very top. Although usually attributed to Gustave Eiffel, the lift was actually the work of a Portuguese, Raoul Mesnier de Ponsard, and has been in operation since 1901. Taking the level walkway from the lift exit past the poignant remains of the roofless Convento do Carmo, reach the Largo do Carmo and entrance to the monastery, which is also the Museu Arqueológico.

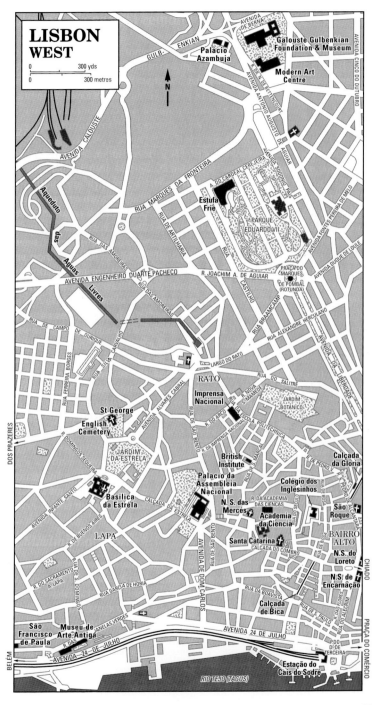

LISBON WEST

0   300 yds
0   300 metres

Palácio Azambuja

Galouste Gulbenkian Foundation & Museum

Modern Art Centre

AVENIDA DE BERNA

GULB-

ENKIAN

AVENIDA CINCO DO OUTUBRO

AVENIDA DA CINCO DO OUTUBRO

AVENIDA CALOUSTE

Aqueduto das Aguas Livres

RUA MARQUES DA FRONTEIRA

RUA DE ARTILHARIA

RUA DAS AMOREIRAS

A. DO CARDEAL CEREJEIRA

Estufa Frie

PARQUE EDUARDO VII

AVENIDA ANTONIO AUGUSTO DE AGUIAR

AVENIDA FONTES PEREIRA DE MELO

AVENIDA ENGENHEIRO DUARTE PACHECO

R. JOACHIM A. DE AGUIAR

PRAÇA DO MARQUES DE POMBAL (ROTUNDA)

AVENIDA DUQUE DE LOULE

RUA DAS AMOREIRAS

RUA DE CAMPO DE OURIQUE

RUA SILVA CARVALHO

RUA FERRERIA BORGES

RUA CASTILHO

RUA BRIAMCAMP

RUA ALEXANDRE HERCULANO

AVENIDA DA LIBERDADE

LARGO DO RATO

RATO

RUA DO SALITRE

Imprensa Nacional

RUA NOVA S. MAMEDE

JARDIM BOTÁNICO

RUA ALVARES CABRAL

RUA DE SÃO BENTO

R. DO ARCO

St George

English Cemetery

DOS PRAZERES

RUA DOMINGOS SEQUEIRA

JARDIM DA ESTRELA

R. DA IMPRENSA NACIONAL

ESCOLA POLITECHNICA

British Institute

R. DE PEDRO V.

Calçada da Gloria

R. S. PEDRO DE ALCANTARA

Basílica da Estrela

CALÇADA DA ESTRELA

Palacio da Assembleia Nacional

Colégio dos Inglesinhos

AVENIDA INFANTE SANTO

R. DE BUENOS AIRES

LAPA

R. DO SACRAMENTO A LAPA

R. S. DOMINGOS

RUA GARCIA DE HORTA

ANELAS VERDES

N. S. das Merces

Academia da Ciencia

R. DA ACADEMIA DAS CIENCAS

São Roque

BAIRRO ALTO

RUA DAS MARIAL

RUA DO SECULO

N.S. do Loreto

CHIADO

Santa Catarina

CALÇADA DO COMBRO

N.S. de Encarnação

AVENIDA DE DOM CARLOS

RUA DA BOAVISTA

Calçada de Bica

RUA DAS FLORES

RUA DE S. PAULO

PRAÇA DO COMÉRCIO

São Francisco de Paula

Museu de Arte Antiga

BELÉM

AVENIDA 24 DE JULHO

RUA DAS

AVENIDA 24 DE JULHO

P. DO DI DE TERCEIRA

Estação do Cais do Sodre

RIO TEJO (TAGUS)

Convento do Carmo and the Museu Arqueológico

Founded by Nuno Alvares Pereira who led the troops of Dom João I to victory at Aljubarrota in 1389, the monastery was a victim of the 1755 earthquake. Whilst entrance is still through the original Gothic doorway, the magnificence of the former three-aisled nave is now reduced to a peaceful oasis open to the skies, an evocative setting for occasional concerts. The **Museu Arqueológico** has found a home in the surviving section beyond, a curious miscellany of exhibits which include the tomb of Dom Fernando I who died in 1383 and a copy of that of Nuno Alvares Pereira, who spent his last eight years here as a monk from 1423. Pereira's remains have since been moved to Santa Engrácia. At least descriptions are in English.

Back in Largo do Carmo, head west along Rua da Trindade then right along Rua Nova da Trindade to emerge in Largo de Trindade Coelho or São Roque, named after the church on the opposite side of the square.

São Roque (St Rock)

Although this church is not particularly engaging externally, the original façade a victim of the 1755 earthquake, its internal decoration is something to behold. The church was begun by Afonso Álvares in 1567 but Felippo Terzi, who was responsible for Igreja São Vicente de Fora, had a hand in its construction at a later stage. A *trompe l'oeil* painted wooden ceiling, giving a vaulted effect, is a masterly foil for the eight sumptuous chapels, four either side, with their paintings, tiles and elaborate woodcarving, but the most distinctive is the chapel of St John the Baptist (Capela de São João Baptista). Commissioned in 1742 by the biggest spender of them all, Dom João V, St John's chapel was designed and built in Rome. Prior to shipment as a self assembly kit to Portugal, where it was installed in 1747, a substantial back-hander ensured it was suitably blessed by Pope Benedict XIV. The result is an extravaganza of lapis lazuli, various marbles, ivory, alabaster, jade, gold, silver, etc whose centrepiece is a painting depicting the baptism of St John. This has the appearance of an oil painting but is in fact a mosaic. A small collection of vestments and sacred art can be seen in the attached **Museum of Sacred Art**.

Solar do Vinho do Porto

Across the road from São Roque, almost opposite the Elevador da Glória, in a former 18th-century palace, is the Solar do Vinho do Porto, the Lisbon office of the Port Wine Institute. Like its counterpart in Porto (Oporto), it exudes a relaxed and discreet ambience which, combined with deep comfortable armchairs, ensures the enjoyment of port sampling. There are hundreds of port wines on offer by the glass, at reasonable cost too, except for the rare vintage variety which can only be bought by the bottle.

Turn left on leaving the Solar and pass the São Pedro de Alcântara

Belvedere on the right, with more good views down over the city, before continuing along Rua Dom Pedro V, which becomes Rua da Escola Polytécnica, to the Botanical Gardens.

Jardim Botânico (Botanical Gardens)

These gardens, just to the west of Avenida da Liberdade, are part of the Academy of Sciences and as such are not public gardens in the truest sense of the word. If open (check with Turismo), access is off Rua da Escola Polytécnica at No. 58, where steps lead down by the side of the former Jesuit Colégio dos Nobres which was later converted for use by the science faculty of the university. Founded in 1873, these shaded gardens offer a cool retreat where there are some 2,500 species of rare plants.

Mãe d'Água Reservoir and Amoreiras Shopping Centre

From the gardens heading further west, through Largo do Rato and along Rua das Amoreiras, is the Casa das Águas Livres, better known as Mãe (mother) d'Água Reservoir, a building which stands out from its surrounds by its size and simple lines. Visits here have to be prearranged through the Museu d'Água or Turismo. The Parque de Eduardo VII is quite close at this point but inveterate shoppers might be tempted to peel off further west, for the short walk towards the beckoning towers of a giant modern complex which houses the Amoreiras Shopping Centre. A popular venue with the younger set, the 300 plus shops only occupy two floors with the rest of the complex a mix of apartments, offices, banks, cinemas, a post office, supermarket and numerous small eateries amongst other services.

A short walk south from Largo do Rato, down Avenida Alvares Cabral, is the **Basilica da Estrêla**. Of interest to some might be the English Cemetery, by St George's church off to the right on reaching the end of the Avenida, which contains the grave of novelist Henry Fielding. A dominant landmark, the twin-towered and high-domed white edifice of the basilica looks especially impressive when approached through the Estrêla Gardens. Built by the fanatically religious Maria I between 1779 and 1790, in recognition of a vow made should she give birth to a living son and heir, the Baroque style marble interior has the feel of the mausoleum it has become. Maria herself died, insane, in exile in Rio de Janeiro in 1816, but her body was returned to Portugal and now lies in a black marble tomb in the church.

The **Houses of Parliament** (Palácio da Assembleia da República or Palaço de São Bento) have, since 1834, occupied the much extended former convent of São Bento da Saúde, which lies east of the basilica along Calçada da Estrêla. A written request must be submitted to inspect the post-1821 Parliamentary Archives; the Arquivo Nacional (National Archive) is also kept there.

Museu Nacional de Arte Antiga (Ancient Art Museum)

South of the basilica by the waterfront, beyond the British Embassy, is the National Museum of Ancient Art. To call it ancient stretches the imagination a little as most of the contents date from later than the 11th century, but this collection should definitely be on the museum lover's trail. The museum building itself consists of part of the 17th-century palace of the Count of Alvor, where the Marquês de Pombal lived for a time and a 20th-century addition built on the site of the former convent of Santo Alberto (St Albert), whose chapel forms part of the museum. It is also known as the Museu das Janelas Verdes (Museum of the Green Windows) from the street on which it stands. The collection is based on materials and liturgical artefacts which were amassed after the closure of the monasteries in 1834, including donations from Calouste Gulbenkian and other later benefactors. First opened to the public in 1883, the exhibits provide an excellent insight into Portuguese art, mainly from the 15th and 16th centuries. Besides paintings, silverware, glass and ceramics there are carpets, furniture and Japanese screens known as *Namban-jin* ('barbarians from the south'), with paintings depicting the arrival of the Portuguese in Japan in the 16th century.

Returning in the direction of the Bairro Alto now, the Bica Elevator rises up from Rua da Boa Vista, near the Santa Caterina Belvedere uphill from the Ribeira Market. At the top a right turn leads into Largo de Camões. Those in search of good ceramics and *azulejos* should turn left here down Rua do Alecrim to find the Sant'Anna tile shop, founded in 1741.

Go straight across from Largo de Camões into Largo do Chiado and on into Rua Garret where, just to the south on Rua Serpa Pinto, lies Lisbon's opera house and largest theatre, **Teatro São Carlos**. Built in 1792, and influenced in design by the San Carlos theatre in Naples and Milan's La Scala theatre, it has recently been renovated.

Belém

A monument in itself to the Age of Discoveries, Belém (Bethlehem) lies to the west alongside the river about 8km (5 miles) from the city centre. Historical associations are strong, with Henry the Navigator (see page 131) and Vasco da Gama key figures in its earlier development culminating in the wealth and splendidly embellished Gothic architecture of the Manueline era (see page 128). Besides the monuments, old Belém itself is worthy of exploration, whilst the local speciality, *pastéis de nata*, a particularly moreish creamy custard tart, should not be missed. This compact self-contained enclave demands a full day to do it justice and even then visitors could find themselves pushed for time. Unlike in the city centre, car drivers should find somewhere to park, especially on the river side of the main road. A novel form of transport is the tram which trundles slowly from the Praça do Comércio out to Belém, whilst there are buses, taxis and a frequent train service from the Cais do Sodré station.

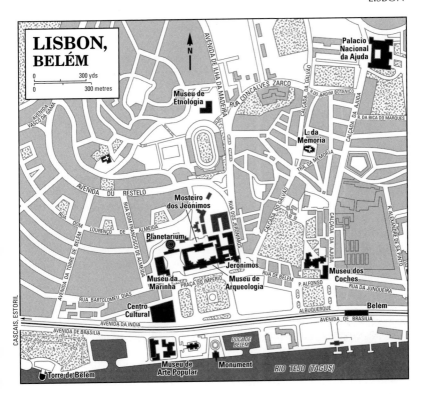

The route out to Belém passes beneath the towering suspension bridge, **Ponte 25 de Abril,** which constantly hums with traffic and connects Lisbon with the south bank of the river. Begun in 1962, it was inaugurated four years later and named the 'Salazar Bridge', only to be renamed after the 1974 revolution. It is the longest suspension bridge in Europe with a central span of 1013m. The 1959 Cristo-Rei Statue (Christ the King), its 110m overall height dominating the skyline at the southern end of the bridge, is modelled on that in Rio de Janeiro. An elevator takes visitors up to the foot of the statue.

Mosteiro dos Jerónimos (Monastery of St Jerome)

History began to unfold at Belém when Henry the Navigator founded a mariners' chapel *Ermida de Restelo* in 1460, the year of his death, which was served by the Order of Christ. Vasco da Gama prayed in this chapel before his epic voyage of 1497 but by then the site had been earmarked by Dom Manuel I for development as a modest monastery of Hieronymites. When da Gama returned two years later, having discovered a sea route to India, a euphoric Dom Manuel determined to make the projected monastery a fitting monument to the explorer's achievement. This he was able to do on profits from the spice trade, which earned it the nickname of Mosteiro da Pimenta (Pepper Monastery), and by abandoning work on Batalha Abbey. Fortunately, the monastery has suffered little earthquake damage and is probably more at risk from tourist coaches, which arrive in droves during the morning and mid-afternoon at peak times.

An impressive sight, especially when approached through the gardens of the Praça do Império, the Jerónimos Monastery, or 'Santa Maria', epitomises the Manueline style of architecture. Look particularly for Dom Manuel's symbol, the armillary sphere, which pops up everywhere. Started about 1502 with Diogo Boitac as architect, the building was to take 70 years to complete. The intricate carving of the south porch is the work of João de Castilho and easily catches the eye on approach. A cross of the Order of Christ sits atop the doorway beneath which is the figure of Nossa Senhora de Belém and below that a figure said to be that of Henry the Navigator.

The west door of Nicholas de Chanterène has been reduced in stature by bridging which connects later western extensions to the original monastery. Fortunately, statues of Dom Manuel I, his wife Maria and their patron Saints Jerome and John the Baptist remain in place round the doorway.

Just inside the west door lie the effigies of Vasco da Gama and Luís de Camões. Here, the heavily carved, low vaulted entrance contrasts dramatically with the spacious and lofty three-aisled body of the church beyond. Soaring, ornately carved polygonal columns support ribbed vaulting which is star shaped above the transept crossing. In the chancel lie the tombs of Dom Manuel I and Dom João III with those of their respective wives Dona Maria and Dona Catarina, wife number two in the case of Manuel, who had three wives in all, and mother of his ten children. Each of the plain tombs is borne by elephants, a novelty of the time, and includes those of the unfortunate Dom Sebastião, in the south transept, and Henrique, the Cardinal King, in the north transept.

An added delight are the double-storey cloisters, for which there is an entrance charge. A delicate hand crafted the beautifully carved and ornate arches which stand serenely around the central garden.

Museu Nacional de Arqueologia e Etnologia and Museu da Marinha

Next to the monastery, in its western annexe, is the Museu Nacional de Arqueologia e Etnologia (National Archaeological Museum) and at the far end the Museu da Marinha (Maritime Museum). The **Archaeological Museum** houses the national collection of early artefacts from the Copper, Bronze and Iron Ages up to Roman times. It also includes a small Egyptian collection. Portugal's nautical history is told through models, maps, charts and various other relevant items in the **Maritime Museum**. In a separate building are displayed some of the now redundant royal barges and fishing boats. Behind, is located the **Planetário Calouste Gulbenkian** which gives astronomical presentations to the general public, in a choice of languages, every Saturday

The cool cloisters of Jerónimos monastery

and Sunday afternoon. The new building on the western edge of the Praça do Império is the controversial **Centro Cultural de Belém**, opened in 1992, thought by some to impinge on the monastery setting and by others to be a bit of a white elephant.

Padrão dos Descobrimentos (Discoveries Monument)

Across the road on the waterfront is the Padrão dos Descobrimentos. Built to commemorate the 500th anniversary of the death of Henry the Navigator in 1960, it depicts Henry himself at the prow of a caravel with other leading figures of the age behind. Inside is a small museum and an elevator to the viewpoint at the top of the monument.

Museu de Arte Popular (Museum of Folk Art)

Further west is the Museu de Arte Popular. Pity about the uninspiring building, but the regional displays of local folk art are worth a diversion to see, especially the painted medieval style covered carts with solid wheels used as an early form of passenger transport.

Torre de Belém (Tower of Belém)

Beyond here is a gem, the waterfront Torre de Belém, built by Francisco Arruda between 1515 and 1521 to serve as a lookout at the mouth of the Tagus. It is an exquisite example of the Manueline style at its best, with a touch of Moorish influence in the detail. External appreciation suffices, but the five storeys can be explored and views enjoyed from the top of the tower. Those into aquariums could tramp even further west to the aptly named **Vasco da Gama Aquarium**.

Head east from Jerónimos Monastery along Rua de Belém in search of *pastéis de nata'*, delicious creamy custard tarts sprinkled with sugar and cinnamon, a speciality of the area and reputed to have been made and sold by the monks of Jerónimos, when they hit hard times at the beginning of the 18th century. The most famous place to eat the tarts is at the *pastelaria Casa dos Pastéis de Belém* (No. 86) but the café at No. 29 also sells them and has an inviting outside seated area. For a glimpse of old Belém, take a look at the 17th-century houses fronting the green along Rua Vieira Portuense between Praça do Império and Praça Afonso de Albuquerque.

Museu Nacional dos Coches

At the end of Rua de Belém, pass the pink walls of the **Palácio de Belém**. Once a royal residence, bought by João V in 1726, it is now the official residence of the President of the Republic. Except for a formal changing of the guard ceremony here on the third Sunday of the month at 10.00, the main draw is the **Museu Nacional dos Coches** (Coach Museum) just beyond the main gate. The setting for the display is in the former riding school of the palace, whose magnificence is matched by the opulent decoration of one of the best collections of coaches in the world.

Calçada da Ajuda, alongside the palace, leads steeply up to the **Palácio Nacional da Ajuda** another royal residence. Begun in 1802 to replace a wooden palace on the site, and never fully completed, it was nevertheless inhabited by the royal family whose exuberantly furnished apartments are open to the public. En route back down to Belém, divert along Rua do Jardim Botânico then left down Calçada do Galvão to the **Memória** church. The church was built in 1760 by Dom José in thanksgiving for surviving an assassination attempt on the same spot two years previously, which acted as the catalyst for Pombal to rid the country of the Jesuits. In 1923, Pombal's remains were transferred to this church. Further west, a lesser known museum, **Museu de Etnologia**, houses collections from Portugal's former colonies and can be found up the Rua dos Jerónimos, by the monastery, in Avenida de Ilha da Madeira.

Practical Information

Hotels and Restaurants

Lisbon has a selection of choice hotels either in the heart of things or on the periphery. Demand for hotels in Lisbon is high so pre-booking, especially at peak times, is recommended. Only a small selection of the hotels and restaurants available is listed. Many restaurants close on Sunday and reservations may be necessary in some of the more popular ones.

LISBON HOTELS (tel. prefix 01)
Five-star hotels
Hotel Altis, Rua Castilho, 11 (tel. 524 206). Fairly central with 307 rooms, restaurant, disabled facilities and an indoor pool.
Hotel da Lapa, Rua do Pau de Bandeira, 4 (tel. 395 00 05). Luxury based on a restored 19th-century mansion in the diplomatic district of Lapa, west of the centre. This 94-room hotel with gardens, restaurant and a pool can also accommodate the disabled.
Hotel Le Meridian, Rua Castilho, 149 (tel. 690 400). Fronts the Edward VII park, caters for the disabled, has 318 rooms and a restaurant.
Hotel Lisbon Sheraton, Rua Latino Coelho, 1 (tel. 575 757). Near Saldanha Metro station has a pool, restaurant and 386 rooms.
Hotel Tivoli, Av. da Liberdade, 185 (tel. 530 181). Halfway along the avenue with 344 rooms, restaurant, pool and garden.

Four-star hotels
Hotel Fénix, Praça Marquês de Pombal, 8 (tel. 386 2121) At the top of Av. da Liberdade with 123 rooms and disabled facilities.

Hotel Holiday Inn Lisboa, Av. António José de Almeida, 28A (tel. 793 5222). Near Campo Pequeno, 169 rooms, disabled facilities, pool and restaurant.
Hotel Lisboa Penta, Av. dos Combatentes (tel. 355 4131). North of the city near the Zoo. This enormous hotel with 588 rooms offers just about every facility including kennels.
Hotel Lisboa Plaza, Travessa do Salitre, 7 (tel. 346 3922). Convenient for centre, family owned 93-room hotel with a restaurant.
Hotel Príncipe Real (Residencial), Rua da Alegria, 53 (tel 346 0116). Cosy 24-room hotel with restaurant; fairly central.

Three-star hotels
Hotel Amazónia (Residencial), Travessa da Fábrica dos Pentes, 12–20 (tel. 387 7006). Newish hotel near Eduardo VII Park, 192 rooms and caters for disabled.
Hotel Eduardo VII, Av. Fontes Pereira de Melo, 5 (tel. 353 0141). Situated near the park of the same name with 121 rooms and restaurant.
Hotel Metropole, Rossio, 30 (tel. 346 9164). Run by same group as the excellent Palace Hotel at Buçaco. Ideal location right in the heart of things overlooking Rossio Square. It has 48 individually styled rooms, a bar but no restaurant.
Novotel, Av. José Malhoa (tel. 726 6022). North of Eduardo VII Park with 246 rooms. Good reliable standard of comfort including restaurant.
Quality Hotel, Campo Grande, 7 (tel. 795 7555). Part of the American Choice Hotels chain, handy for the Metro and Airport. 82 rooms offering a comfortable base, disabled access and restaurant.
Hotel Veneza (Residencial), Av. da Liberdade, 189 (tel. 352 2618). A pleasant and attractive converted 19th-century town house of 35 rooms near the centre of the city.
Hotel Zurique, Rua Ivone Silva (tel. 793 7111). A modern 252-room hotel near Campo Pequeno (bullring) with a restaurant.

Two-star hotels
Hotel Borges, Rua Garrett, 108-110 (tel.346 1951). A 98-room hotel in the heart of the Chiado district with restaurant.
Hotel Ibis, Av. José Malhoa (tel. 727 3181). Part of the French chain, its 211 rooms provide a reasonable standard of accommodation. Restaurant and disabled facilities.
Hotel Internacional (Residencial), Rua da Bestega, 3 (tel. 346 6401). Very centrally placed in Rossio. 53 rooms in a bright and charming building.

Four-star Albergarias
Albergaria Metro Avenida (Residencial), Av. da Liberdade, 140–142 (tel. 347 2255). Convenient for city centre with 11 rooms.
Albergaria Senhora do Monte (Residencial), Calçada do Monte, 39 (tel. 886 6002). On the heights of Graça above Alfama, near the castle. 27 rooms, rooftop terrace and bar with good views.

Built to commemorate the 500th anniversary of Henry the Navigator's death, the Discovery Monument shows Henry leading a band of Portuguese heroes including Luís de Camões

LISBON RESTAURANTS
Tascas, especially in the Bairro Alto, usually serve a delicious and cheap lunch. In more expensive establishments, the set tourist menus can be moderately priced and excellent value.

Central
Escorial, Rua das Portas de Santo Antão, 47–49 (tel. 346 4429). Shellfish restaurant with a Spanish touch. Expensive.
Gambrinus, Rua das Portas de Santo Antão, 25 (tel. 321 466). Good for seafood. Expensive.
Ritz Grill (Ritz Hotel), Rua Rodrigo da Fonseca, 88 (tel. 692 020). French cuisine a speciality. Expensive.
Sol Dourado, Rua Jardim do Regador, 19–25 (tel. 347 2570). A very popular venue for seafood. Cheap.

Alfama
Casa do Leão, inside Castelo de São Jorge (tel. 875 962). French and Portuguese cuisine. Moderate/expensive.
Malmequer Bemmequer, Largo de São Miguel, 23–25 (tel. 876 535). Serves good food. Cheap.
Michel's, Largo de Santa Cruz do Castelo (tel. 886 4338). Good reputation and selection. Moderate/expensive.
Parreirinha de Alfama, Bico do Espirito Santo, 1 (tel. 868 209). Traditional with fado. Moderate.

79

Bairro Alto
Adega Machado, Rua do Norte, 91 (tel. 346 0095). A popular place for Food, *Fado* and Folklore.
Aviz, 12B, Rua Serpa Pinto (tel. 342 8391). Good but expensive.
Bachus, Largo da Trindade, 9 (tel. 342 2828). A menu with a difference. Expensive.
Bota Alta, Trav. da Queimada, 37 (tel.327 959). Cheap and cheerful.
Faia, Rua da Barroca, 54–56 (tel. 342 6742). *Fado* and Portuguese cooking. Expensive.
O Forcado, Rua da Roas, 221 (tel. 346 8579). *Fado* and Folklore. Expensive.
Pile ou Face, Rua Barroca, 70 (tel. 342 2345). Popular and moderately priced.
Tágide, Largo Academia das Belas Artes, 18–20 (tel. 346 0570). High-class Portuguese food. Expensive.

Places of Interest

Most museums are closed Mondays and holidays with many giving free entrance on Sunday mornings. Opening times are apt to fluctuate so always check with Turismo. Ask about discounts for students and senior citizens.

ALFAMA AND EAST
Castelo de São Jorge (St George's Castle). Free daily access.
Museu de Água (Water Museum), Rua do Alviela, 12 (off Calçada dos Barbadinhos). Open 10am–4pm Tues–Sat and Sun 11am–5pm, closed Mondays.
Museu Militar (Military Museum), Largo do Museu da Artilharia. Open 10am–4pm, closed Mondays.
Museu Nacional do Azulejo (Convento da Madre de Deus), Rua da Madre de Deus, 4. Open 10am–12.30 and 2pm–5pm, closed Mondays.
Santo António and Museum, Largo de Santo António. Open 10am–1pm and 2pm–6pm, closed Mondays.
São Vicente de Fora. Cloisters Open 10am–5pm daily.
Sé (Cathedral). Open 8.30am–6pm daily, cloisters (closed Mondays) 10am–1pm and 2pm–6pm.

NORTH
Estufas Fria and Quente, Parque Eduardo VII. Open 9am–5.30pm daily.
Feira Popular, Entrecampos. Open daily March–September, otherwise 7pm–1am Fri and 1pm–1am weekends and holidays.
Fundação Calouste Gulbenkian (Gulbenkian Foundation Complex), Av. de Berna. Museum Open 10am–5pm, closed Mondays. Centre of Modern Art, Open 10am–5pm Tue, Thu, Fri and Sun; 2pm–7,30pm Wed and Sat, closed Mondays.
Jardim Zoológico (Zoo), Est. Benfica. Open 9am–7pm daily. Children under 3 free. Combination entrance ticket to include dolphin show available.

Museu da Cidade (City Museum), Campo Grande, 245. Open 10am–1pm and 2pm–6pm, closed Mondays.
Museu de Teatro (Theatre Museum), Estrada do Lumiar, Open 10am–1pm and 2.30pm–5pm, closed Mondays.
Museu do Trajo (Costume Museum), Largo Júlio de Castilho, Lumiar. Open 10am–1pm and 2.30pm–5pm, closed Mondays.
Palácio da Fronteira, Largo São Domingos de Benfica. Limited visits, arrive by 10.45am for 11am tour Mon–Fri, garden only or palace and garden. Full guided tour Sat at same time but higher entrance charge.

BAIRRO ALTO AND WEST
Convento do Carmo and Museu Arqueológico (Archaeological Museum). Open 10am–1pm and 2pm–5pm closed Sundays.
Jardim Botânico (Botanical Gardens), Rua da Escola Politécnica. Open 9am–7pm Mon–Fri,10am–7pm weekends and holidays, free entry.
Museu Nacional de Arte Antiga (Ancient Art Museum), Rua Janelas Verdes, 9. Open 10am–1pm and 2pm–5pm but open until 7pm Sun and 10pm Thu, closed Mondays.
São Roque Church, Largo Trindade Coelho. Open 10am–1pm and 2pm–5pm, closed Mondays.
Solar do Vinho do Porto, Rua de São Pedro de Alcântara, 45. 10am–10pm Mon–Sat, closed Sundays.

BELÉM
Aquario Vasco da Gama, Rua Direita Dafundo. Open 10am–6pm. Children under 10 free.
Mosteiro dos Jerónimos (St Jerome's Monastery). Open 10am–6.30pm but 5pm in winter, closed Mondays and holidays.
Museu de Arte Popular (Folk Museum), Av. de Brasilia. Open 10am–12.30pm and 2pm–5pm closed Mondays.
Museu da Marinha (Maritime Museum), Praça do Império. Open 10am–6pm but 5pm in winter, closed Mondays and holidays.
Museu Nacional de Arqueologia e Etnologia, Praça do Império. Open 10am–noon and 2pm–5pm, closed Mondays.
Museu Nacional dos Coches (Coach Museum), Praça Afonso de Albuquerque. Open 10am–1pm and 2pm–5pm, closed Mondays.
Padrão dos Descobrimentos (Discoveries Monument). Open 9.30am–6pm, closed Mondays and holidays.
Palácio Nacional da Ajuda, Calçada da Ajuda. Open 10am–5pm, closed Wednesdays.
Torre de Belém. Open 10am–6.15pm, closed Monday and holidays.

SOUTH OF RIVER TAGUS
Cristo-Rei Statue. Open 9am–6.45pm, Mon–Fri and 9am–7.15pm weekends.

Sports and Leisure

Apart from football most sporting activities centre on the Costa do Estoril, see listings in Chapter 6.

Tourist Offices (Turismo)

Pavilhão Carlos Lopes, Parque Eduardo VII, 1200 Lisbon. (tel. 01 315 1915/6/7/8, fax. 01 352 1472).

Tourism Posts

Amoreiras: Montra de Liboa Ct. Comercial das Amoreiras-Loja 2016, Piso 2 (tel. 01 657 486).

Restauradores: Palácio Foz (tel. 01 346 3314 or 346 3624).

6. SINTRA AND THE COSTA DO ESTORIL

Tucked away to the west of Lisbon is an area which has long attracted international visitors. Some of its glories are now fading, especially Estoril which once attracted royalty and aristocrats from all over Europe; not so cosmopolitan Cascais or timeless Sintra, inspiration of poets and writers throughout the ages. Add to this the sparkling Penha Longa Country Club offering quality accommodation and a wide range of sporting facilities including golf, and the whole area has taken on a new buzz.

If occasional excursions into Lisbon are planned then either Cascais, Estoril or Sintra might be considered as a base from which to explore the region. All of them are well connected to the capital by a frequent, rapid train, an inexpensive service which is faster and more convenient than using a car. It also avoids using the Marginal from Cascais into Lisbon, still regarded as one of the most dangerous roads in Europe, and avoids the considerable difficulty of finding parking space in the city.

Estoril

Estoril is a conglomerate of four different regions, all with Estoril in their title: Monte Estoril, São João de Estoril, São Pedro de Estoril and Santo António de Estoril. Collectively they are known simply as Estoril and if that is not enough to give them an identity crisis their role in modern tourism certainly will. Early in the 20th century the resort became the playground of the rich and famous who came here to relax and sunbathe, throw a cocktail party, gamble the nights away at the casino or just fish. Luxurious hotels accommodated illustrious visitors which included royalty and ex-royalty. Portugal remained neutral when World War II inflamed Europe and Estoril became a safe haven for the rich and influential. It was not long before it became a hotbed of intrigue when spies started to mingle with the guests, taking tea on the hotel terraces and gambling in the casino – a rich setting indeed for an Agatha

Christie type novel, though it seemed only to enhance the international reputation of the place. Attracted by the mild winter climate, many of the wealthy
remained and built their villas, which in turn attracted rich residents from
nearby Lisbon. These voices are now calling the tune. The town has a
declared intention of reverting to a residential area and allowing Cascais to
absorb its share of tourism.

The beach and the casino still remain big attractions. Offering a broad
stretch of fine sand, Estoril's Tamariz beach is much photographed thanks to
the castellated private house surrounded by palms at the eastern end. This
beach, like others along this coast, has been troubled by sewage pollution in
recent years but strenuous efforts have been made to tackle the problem and
the beaches are now regarded as safe for bathing once again. Tamariz, like
the other beaches nearby, becomes crowded in summer. Broad gardens, often
colourful but usually untidy, offer the opportunity to stroll in peace from the
promenade up to the casino. From the outside, the casino building is no work
of art but it has been renovated internally and offers bars, a restaurant, a floor
show, gaming machines and comfortable surroundings in which to win or
lose a fortune at roulette, baccarat and the like. Otherwise Estoril is taking on
a rather dull suburban air, offering no monuments of particular merit although
it still has quality hotels such as Hotel Palácio overlooking the gardens; built
in the 1930s, the Palacio is still offering accommodation in gracious
surroundings. In fact the town is rather well endowed with hotels of all grades
for its size. Latest for an upgrade is the Zenith Hotel, in Monte Estoril, which
has been taken over by Choice Hotels International and marketed as a
Comfort Inn. It is handily placed in a quiet area, convenient for Monte Estoril
station and nearest to Cascais where much of the action is these days.

Just inland from Estoril, along the road to Sintra, is the racing track
Autodromo do Estoril, where the formula 1 Grand Prix is held, usually at the
end of September. Be sure to pack earplugs for that particular week. Just
beyond the race track is a development which has caused enormous excitement amongst the locals, a new shopping centre with the novelty of large
department stores like C & A and Mothercare, and parking for 3000 cars.
Avoid weekends when traffic congestion in the vicinity is at its worst.

Both the railway line and the Marginal highway run along the promenade
from Estoril through to Cascais. Happily, there is a pedestrian walkway on the
seaward side at a lower level which is sheltered from traffic noise making it
a pleasure to stroll between these two adjacent resorts. Starting out from
Tamariz beach in the centre of Estoril, the next beach to the west is Praia
Monte Estoril, after which sand is replaced by rocks for a stretch until Praia
da Conceição is reached. Here pavement cafés offer a colourful atmosphere
for a light lunch or a quick snack before reaching Cascais.

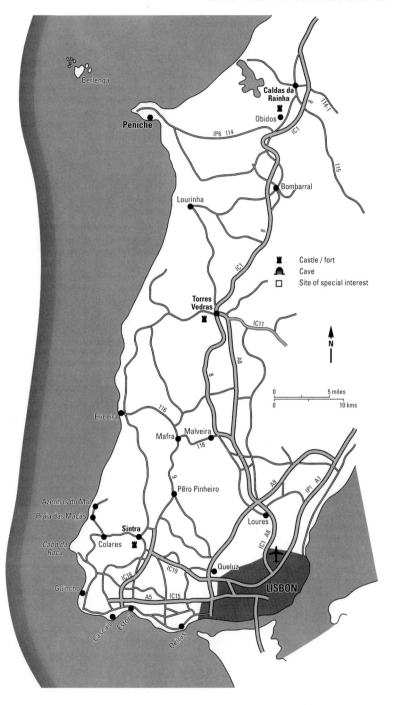

Berlenga

Caldas da Rainha

Peniche

Obidos

IP6 114

IC1

8

114-1

115

Bombarral

Lourinha

8

IC1

Castle / fort
Cave
Site of special interest

Torres
Vedras

IC11

A8

8

N

0   5 miles
0   10 kms

116

Ericeira

Mafra   Malveira

116

9

Pêro Pinheiro

A9

IP1 A1

Azenhas do Mar

Praia das Maçãs

Loures

Sintra

Cabo da
Roca

Colares

IC1 A8

Queluz

IC16   IC19

Guincho

A5   IC15

LISBON

Cascais   Estoril

Oeiras

Cascais

Once a quaint fishing village, Cascais is now a thriving resort which has warmly embraced tourism yet largely resisted spilling beyond its original boundaries. The result is an intimate and colourful resort with pedestrianised streets paved with traditional black and white *calçada* blocks re-creating a dynamic sea of waves. It might be appropriate to its heritage but it can be hard on both the eyes and the stomach, although the fishermen probably feel quite at home. Here pavement cafés and street vendors spill onto the streets endeavouring to tempt strollers away from the more fashionable boutiques and restaurants. At the heart of all this activity is Largo de Camões where a seated statue of the great poet, Luís de Camões, looks down upon a sea of green and yellow parasols shading other artistic souls busy finding inspiration in the pleasures of food and drink.

Another focal point of the resort is the fishermen's harbour, Praia da Ribeira, which many would claim as the main attraction. Mature palm trees and market stalls selling imaginative items made largely from seashells grace the promenade here which looks onto a fine sandy beach. Brightly painted fishing boats fill the bay and fishermen coexist happily with the hordes of sunbathers who crowd onto the beach in summer. It is a fascinating place to be in the evening when the fishermen's catch is auctioned off, literally as it arrives, but only the locals seem to understand the proceedings. The fishermen and the auctioneer have a day off on Sunday. Perhaps the biggest event of the week is the lively Wednesday market, repeated on a smaller scale on Saturday mornings, held near the centre of the town. This is an important market place for the local farmers who flood in to sell their home-grown fruit and vegetables and for the itinerant traders who offer everything from woolly jumpers to plastic buckets. It is a great meeting place for the locals too, but be early for the best atmosphere.

Two further beaches lie to the east, first the small and sheltered beach of Praia da Rainha, which can get very hot in summer but is particularly favoured when the sun is weaker, and beyond is the larger Praia da Conceição. There is a small beach to the west, Praia de Santa Marta, but it has barely room for a dozen bodies. A short walk beyond this beach along the main road leads to the Boca do Inferno (Mouth of Hell), a narrow inlet with arches and caverns, where the sea crashes noisily around in spectacular style, especially on those days when the Atlantic is in a restless mood.

Starting with Palaeolithic man, Cascais has attracted visitors throughout the ages but few have left significant remains. The Romans had a strong presence in the area in the 1st century AD and there was an important settlement called Casais Velhos to the west, near Guincho, where the inhabitants were believed to have extracted and exported Tyrian purple, a dye obtained from the spiny-shelled marine gastropod *Murex brandaris* and, to a lesser extent, *M. trunculus*. The Phoenicians from Tyre were the first to use the dye and they became known to the Greeks as the Phoinikes, the 'purple men'. Later the Roman emperors and senators embraced the royal purple cloth derived from

Dom Pedro I, who granted Cascais its first charter, now guards the town hall

this dye as their own and the scale of the industry boomed. The discarded shells from this process, usually left to litter the seashore, may well have given Cascais its name, which means seashells. None of the Roman sites is open to the public.

Cascais had no great mention in history until it received the privilege of self-government, granted by Dom Pedro I in 1364. Its strategic position at the mouth of the Tagus estuary became increasingly important, and when the great voyages of discovery started, Cascais was the last settlement seen by the departing adventurers and the first to greet them back home.

There is not too much to see in the way of monuments in Cascais. The citadel dominating the headland to the west of Praia da Ribeira was once the residence of Dom Luís I but is now used only by the president of the republic on official receptions. Occasional concerts provide a rare opportunity for the general public to have a look inside. Further west, near the lighthouse, is the **Museum of the Counts of Castro Guimarães** which occupies a castle-like private mansion donated to the town in 1924 after the owner died heirless. Visitors are usually escorted around the various rooms displaying period furniture, including a cupboard organ made in 1753, an assortment of Chinese porcelains, gold and silverware, oil paintings and examples of early *azulejo* tiles. Cascais' other museum, the **Museum of the Sea**, is a modern, purpose-built structure which caters fully for the disabled, including a chair lift up to the first floor. Unfortunately, the exhibits fail to match the quality of the building. Expect some stuffed fish, fishermen's costumes draped over models and no explanations in English. Save this one for a rainy day.

The opportunities for eating are good and varied in Cascais although fish often dominates the menu. Interesting restaurants to try include *Ginginha Transmontana*, which offers good Portuguese food at moderate prices in a small, cosy dining room, and *O Pescador* behind the fish market, offering an international menu in addition to fish but more expensive. There are plenty of pubs and bars for nightlife but the liveliest spot in town is the nightclub *Coconuts* on Av. Rei Humberto II da Italia, perhaps for a wet T-shirt night or similar event.

Golf in Central Portugal

The British port wine producers built the first golf course in Portugal back in 1890. It may have been slow to take off but now golf is a major growth industry and the country boasts around 40 courses. A kind winter climate makes the sport extremely popular in southern Portugal, and Costa Estoril shares the mild winter conditions. There is a choice of six courses in the Estoril area, a further four courses south of the River Tagus and one other course to the north, at Vimeiro, just north-west of Torres Vedras.

COSTA ESTORIL

1. Lisbon Sports Club. Set in spectacular woodlands at Belas, 22km (13.5 miles) north-east of Estoril and 24km (15 miles) from Lisbon, with fine views to enjoy from a number of the greens, this was built originally as a 14-hole course in 1922 by the British firm of Hawtree. It was extended to 18 holes in 1992. There are a number of testing holes but the 16th (475m, par 5) commands respect. The tee-shot is played from an elevated position to a narrow fairway with a lateral water hazard to the right and out of bounds to the left. The total distance for this 18-hole par 69 course is 5278m for men (yellow tees) and 4761m for women (red tees).

Facilities include caddies, trolleys and clubs for hire, lessons by professionals, a clubhouse with restaurant and bar, tennis, swimming pool and children's playroom.

2. Golf do Estoril. Built on rolling ground between woodlands of pine, eucalyptus and mimosa, this course lies just 2km (1.25 miles) north of Estoril. There are actually two courses, the main 18-hole course (5238m, par 69) built by E. Mackenzie Ross in 1945 and a smaller 9-hole course (2350m, par 34) added more recently. The main course offers infinite variety demanding thoughtful and accurate play. This is one of the most traditional and exclusive clubs in the country and has been host to the Portuguese Open.

There are plenty of leisure facilities including bars, restaurant and swimming pool apart from golfing aids such as a driving range and putting green. Lessons by professionals are also available.

3. Quinta da Beloura. This relatively new course, which opened late 1993, was designed by William Roquemore and lies just east of the Sintra–Estoril highway near the village of Albarraque. Six lakes incorporated into the design make sure that there is no shortage of water hazards on the 18-hole course (5878m, par 72).

Buggy, trolley and club hire is available and there is a bar and restaurant.

4. Estoril Sol. Lying some 8km (5 miles) north of Estoril in the foothills of the Serra da Sintra, this course is often described as one of the most beautiful 9-hole courses in Europe. The compact course forms part of a comprehensive golf teaching academy. John Harris and Ron Fream used the natural features and the water hazards to good effect in designing this testing course. Hole number 3 illustrates this point well, where the green perches on the far bank of a lake and is fringed in front with pampas grass. Only short – a mere 111m (par 3) – this hole is the cause of more glum faces than any other on the course. The course can be played as 18 holes by using different tee positions and this totals to a length of 3609m (par 62).

The Golf Academy covers an extensive area and offers a wide

range of situations for driving, approach shots and putting to give golfers practice under conditions encountered in real play.

There are rental facilities for clubs and trolleys as well as a restaurant and bar.

5. Penha Longa. Built with Japanese money, Penha Longa is more than just a golf course; it is a country club with a whole range of sporting facilities and includes a five-star hotel. The golf is available only to club members, hotel guests and villa residents on the estate.

Situated in a superb location between the Serra da Sintra and the Atlantic Ocean, this 18-hole championship course designed by Robert Trent Jones Jr (and inaugurated in 1992) embraces the existing woodlands and rocky outcrops to stay in harmony with the natural setting and spectacular scenery. Stretching over 6228m, the par 72 course has more than enough challenging features, including one or two testing doglegs. A second 9-hole course, par 35 measuring 2550m, has recently been added along the lines of the championship course.

Just about every imaginable facility is available, from driving ranges to golf clinics and from restaurants to jacuzzis and saunas.

6. Quinta da Marinha. The resort's full name is Quinta da Marinha Hotel Village and it is set in 100ha of privately owned land overlooking the Atlantic Ocean, just 6km (3.75 miles) west of Cascais. Open since 1984, it accommodates guests in a variety of town houses and villas amongst the pines bordering the golf course.

Designed by the famous Robert Trent Jones, this 6014m length, par 71, course has already hosted the Ladies Masters championship. Umbrella pines, Atlantic breezes, water features, wind-blown sand dunes and bunkered greens add considerable spice to this testing course which includes 5 holes at par 5 and 6 at par 3.

Clubs, trolleys and carts are all available for hire and practice facilities include a driving range and putting green. In addition there is a clubhouse, bar, restaurant, six tennis courts and two swimming pools.

COSTA AZUL (SOUTH OF THE TAGUS)

7. Aroeira. The Clube de Campo de Portugal course at Aroeira is regarded by many as one of the finest in Europe. It lies just south of the Tagus, out towards the west coast, and can be reached by car from Lisbon in about 30 minutes, assuming traffic over the suspension bridge is flowing freely.

Designed by English architect Frank Pennink, this 6040m length, par 72 course weaves through avenues of tall pine trees and by four lakes. Occupying a 365ha estate, each hole is separate from the rest creating a mood of tranquillity and peace which should help to sustain the concentration and accuracy needed to avoid the encroaching forest and narrowing doglegs.

Lessons are available on the extensive driving range and buggies, trolleys and clubs are available for hire. There is a restaurant and bar on hand too.

8. Quinta do Peru. Lying in the foothills of the Serra da Arrábida close to Vila Nogueira de Azeitão, this course is the latest addition to the circuit. This 18-hole, par 72 course which is played over 6643m was designed by Rocky Roquemore and already incorporates a club house, bar and shop. Accommodation comprising 70 apartments and 66 bungalows will shortly be available.

9. Montado. Located just to the east of Setúbal, this course designed by Duarte de Sottomeyer lies in the heart of Fonseca's muscatel vineyards. The course wends through a grove of cork oaks taking full advantage of the streams and natural lakes which are a strong feature of the countryside here. Total distance of the 18-hole, par 72 course is 6003m and, while there is plenty of challenge for top players, there is also flexibility to allow for easier options.

Locker rooms are available and there is a club house with dining room.

10. Tróia. Located just across the estuary from Setúbal and easily reached by the regular and frequent car ferry, this course is built effectively on a large sand spit and offers a spectacular location. Robert Trent Jones has indulged his penchant for deep, sandy bunkers and strategically placed greens to the full in designing this 6337m, par 72 course. Accuracy off the tee is demanded for many holes on this course which has true links character in parts. Opened only in 1979, it has already hosted the Portuguese Men's open and the European Ladies' Amateur Team Championship.

Golf carts and trolleys are available for hire and facilities include a clubhouse and restaurant. The resort Tróia offering hotels and extending the range of facilities is close by.

COSTA PRATA

11. Vimeiro. Situated on the level margins of a river estuary, Vimeiro Golf club is part of a family holiday location overlooking Praia de Porto Novo near Torres Vedras. It is a 9-hole course laid out by the English architect Frank Pennink but an alternative set of tee positions allows it to be played as a 4781m-long, par 67, 18-hole circuit.

This is an interesting rather than severe course where one hole is played across the river and where the fairways cut swathes through established trees and shrubs. The club is allied to the Hotel Golf Mar which sits astride an escarpment overlooking the sea to one side and the golf course to the other.

The golf club has caddies and trolleys for hire while the hotel offers tennis, swimming, horse riding and fishing.

Coastal excursion from Cascais

The wild and beautiful Atlantic coastline nearby is punctuated with a number of small, sometimes intimate resorts. All are worth visiting if only for their beaches but the excursion most featured by the tour operators is to Cabo da Roca, claimed to be the most westerly point in mainland Europe.

Guincho

Sandy Guincho is the first resort reached and the beach here is nothing less than spectacular with acres of soft, golden sand. All that greets the visitor is a few hotels and restaurants and virtually nothing else. The Atlantic has played a part in restricting development, crashing against this coast with great gusto and streaming an endless series of foaming white breakers onto the beach. The powerful undertow can make it dangerous for swimmers but the wind and the waves offer an irresistible challenge to windsurfers and it is a favourite venue for international competitions. A large part of this coastal region, from Cascais around to just north of Azenhas do Mar and inland as far as Sintra, shows great climatic and botanical diversity; it has been a protected area for some time and has recently been raised to the status of natural park. The dunes to the rear of the beach here are especially important as they are the habitat of the rare shrubby thrift, *Armeria pseudarmeria*, which is endemic to the western coast of Portugal but locally common here.

Peninha

Following the coast leads through Malveira da Serra to a crossroads where left leads down to Cabo da Roca and right leads to Peninha. Castle-like Peninha, actually a chapel dedicated to Our Lady of Peninha, stands etched against the skyline on the hills above. A legend relates how a mute shep-herdess had a visitation from the Virgin Mary appearing as a beautiful girl, and was given the gift of speech. News of the miracle spread and a humble chapel was built on the spot where it occurred. Later, in the 17th century, this was reconstructed by the hermit Pedro da Conceição to include outbuildings for travellers. Eventually it fell into disuse and was bequeathed to a founda-tion belonging the university of Coimbra. Currently the chapel is being restored and is expected to be open to the public very shortly. It is worth a visit if only for the sweeping views of the coastline.

Cabo da Roca

Rugged and spectacular, Cabo da Roca, is probably the most visited place of the region apart from Lisbon. A lighthouse occupies the headland at this most westerly point of mainland Europe and nearby is a cluster of shops including a restaurant. A local branch of the tourist office sells certificates to verify a visit to this supposedly unique spot. People from the west of Ireland who

Wild and windswept Guincho beach is a surfers' paradise

have travelled east to be here will not be impressed. There is little to do except wander along the footpaths through the fleshy leaves of the hottentot fig, *Carpobrotus edulis*, to get a better view of the lighthouse. This fig has proved very invasive here and has massively colonised these cliff tops, but it looks good when its large, showy yellow or pink flowers are in bloom.

Praia da Adega, next destination to the north, offers a chance to escape the hordes and enjoy a less crowded beach. It has an extensive stretch of fine sand backed by shrub-covered cliffs, a restaurant and a car park. At the moment it has no accommodation but there are indications that this could change.

Neighbouring **Praia Grande**, much favoured by the Portuguese themselves, also has a fine, spacious sandy beach but with rather more facilities. Motel da Piscina here is built into the cliffs and boasts two large swimming pools. At the south end of the resort, some 339 steps lead from the beach up to the cliff top from where there are footpaths leading down the coast to the south and it is possible to walk as far as Praia da Adega. Sand is not in short supply along this stretch of the coast and again there is a huge sandy beach at **Praia das Maçãs**, the next and rather larger resort. Praia das Maçãs is now connected by tram to nearby Colares which helps to swell the number of visitors in summer. Unlike the previously mentioned resorts, a small village here provides life away from the beach and there is a wider range of facilities from snack bars to restaurants.

The final port of call along this stretch of coast is the picturesque village of **Azenhas do Mar**, which clings and huddles on a steep headland. Surprisingly, there is no beach here but the village does have a natural swimming pool carved out of the rock at the base of the cliffs. The old part of the village is gated, with admission only for residents, so it is not possible to wander around. Grapes for the famous Colares wine are grown on the sand just inland from here.

Sintra

Magnetic Sintra, set in lush green hills and guarded by a Moorish castle, has attracted romantics through the ages. Lord Byron in particular was smitten by Sintra and, according to Rose Macaulay in her book *They Went to Portugal,* wrote to Francis Hodgson on 16 July 1809 saying, 'I must observe that the village of Cintra in Estramadura is the most beautiful, perhaps, in the world'. 'The phrase glorious Eden' was later used by Byron in *Childe Harold:* 'Lo! Cintra's glorious Eden intervenes/ In variegated maze of mount and glen', and the phrase has endured to become enshrined in almost every description of Sintra. It was not just Byron singing its praises; others before him had done so, including the native poet Gil Vicente in 1529, who described Sintra as 'a garden of earthly paradise'. If further applause is needed, then UNESCO provided it in 1995 by recognising Sintra as a World Heritage Site.

Sintra's exuberant vegetation on the hills arises from a unique microclimate created by the mountains acting as a condensation barrier in the conflict between the Mediterranean and Atlantic weather systems. Winter rains are heavier here than anywhere else in the immediate vicinity and even on a fine summer day, as the sun sets in the evening, it is not unusual for mists to form and swirl around the hilltop casting an unearthly mantle over the floodlit Pena Palace. Sintra's natural beauty drew not just the Romantics but the aristocracy and royalty, who left a legacy of palaces and mansions. No other town in Portugal can boast three palaces and a castle within such a small area. Unfortunately, such a concentration of attractions makes it a target for day trippers and the coaches pour in daily, clogging the narrow streets and main square from early morning until late afternoon. A consolation for visitors staying in the town is that the evenings are very peaceful. There are not too many tourist beds available in total. The biggest hotel is the very comfortable five-star *Tivoli,* which is so out of character many regret that it was ever built, and there is the even more expensive Setéais Palace. Otherwise, the accommodation is mainly in *quintas* or manor houses. One of the best manor houses in town is the recently restored *Casa Miradouro,* whose genial host offers bright and airy en-suite rooms in a traditional brick-red and yellow Sintra house (these colours of old Sintra have been used in the recent redecoration of Pena Palace's exterior). Some of the finest accommodation is in the *quintas* tucked away in the wooded slopes of the Serra da Sintra outside town. One of the most desirable of these is *Quinta das Sequoias* which is reached along 2km (1.25 miles) of private road, guaranteeing peace and privacy. *Quinta da Capela* is another house of character, set in extensive grounds bordering Monserrate park, which offers the opportunity of gracious living for a time.

Sintra is in three parts: Sintra Vila which is the historic centre and the main focus of interest; Estefânia which is home to the bus and train stations; and

São Pedro which has little to interest visitors except perhaps for the market held on the second and fourth Sunday in the month. This is also the best place to find some of the more traditional, and cheaper, eating places. Visitors using the very frequent train service from Rossio station in Lisbon arrive in Estefânia which leaves a 10–15 minute walk into the historic centre. This is dominated by the National Palace with its two great oast-house chimneys which seems a natural start to a tour of Sintra.

Palácio Nacional

When Dom Afonso Henriques recovered Sintra from the Moors in 1147, a small palace or castle existed on this site which passed into the possession of the crown. The builders moved in twice in little over a century, first in 1281 on the instruction of Dom Dinis, who passed control and care of the building to the enfranchised Moors of Colares, and again towards the end of the 14th century, when Dom João I set about significantly rebuilding the palace at the instigation of his wife, Philippa of Lancaster, and took up summer residence there. It was in this phase that the two great conical kitchen chimneys were built. Further modifications produced a gradual evolution over the centuries; the wings were added between 1505 and 1520 by Dom Manuel, and the result today is a fusion of Mudejar, Gothic, Manueline and Renaissance architecture and a lack of spatial continuity. The great earthquake of 1755 which virtually destroyed Lisbon also damaged parts of the palace but these were repaired on the instructions of the Marquês de Pombal.

It remained the summer residence of royalty from the time of Dom João I until the end of the monarchy in 1910. A fly on the wall throughout would have witnessed some moments of history. It was here on 21 July 1414 that Dom João I decided on his Ceuta campaign which marked the beginning of Portuguese expansion, and it was here in 1429 that he received Philip the Good, Duke of Burgundy, who came to ask for the hand of Princess Dona Isabel in marriage. Afonso V was born and died in the palace (1432–81). In 1557 Sebastião was crowned king at the age of three after his grandfather, Dom João III, died of a stroke and it was here that Dom Sebastião held a last audience before starting out, in 1578, on his ill-fated north African campaign which resulted in massive loss of life for the Portuguese, including his own. Here too the impotent Dom Afonso VI (1656–83) was incarcerated for the last years of his life after he had been persuaded to yield the reigns of power to his brother Pedro in 1668.

In 1987 an archaeological dig was started in the area of the medieval granaries and it has unearthed 7th-century remains as well as a possible tunnel entrance which may link to the front of the palace.

The present façade of the building was formerly an interior wall until it was exposed by the removal of the original porch and the buildings which formed the entrance courtyard. Now a Gothic arcade greets visitors where the ticket office lies to the left and visitors assemble for the tour which departs up the steps to the right. Guides are now not always used but information is presented in each room in various languages. Some of the highlights include the massive **kitchen** with its twin chimneys which leak so much in the rain that they are a constant maintenance problem. Only one of the great chimneys is thoroughly blackened inside which may be a clue to suggest that the kitchen only really came to life for a royal banquet or hunting party. Steps lead from the kitchen through the **Quarto do Hóspedes**, containing an early example of a bed settee from the era of Dom José (1760–70) to **Sala dos Árabes** which is half-tiled in green, blue and white Sevillian tiles with a border of Portuguese tiles (15th century). This distinctly Arabesque room, which also contains a marble fountain decorated with tritons and horses, lies in the oldest part of the palace. The **Sala dos Archeiros** (Room of the Coats of Arms) has a high domed ceiling of geometrically carved and gilded wood panels containing paintings of the coats of arms of noble Portuguese families of the period and is perhaps the most majestic room in the palace. These paintings are believed to have been completed around 1518. Hunting scenes in blue and white *azulejo* tiles surround the walls which are an 18th-century addition.

Sala das Pêgas (Room of the Magpies) has its own story to tell. It was here that the modest and pious Philippa surprised her husband Dom João I kissing a lady-in-waiting. Rather embarrassed, he explained that he meant no harm and it was only '*por bem*' – with good intentions. The queen left the room gravely and without a word but the story was instantly court gossip. João had the ceiling painted with magpies, supposedly one for each of the chattering palace ladies, their beaks silenced with his motto '*por bem*'. The magpies bear the colours of Henry the Navigator and the red rose used in the decoration represents the English House of Lancaster (Philippa's family). The main room is the **Room of the Swans**, sometimes called the Prince's Room, which is half tiled in 16th-century green and white tiles which also frame the doors and the windows. Swans decorate the ceiling, each with a gold crown around its neck.

Sintra Vila walkabout

The centre of town is effectively the large square outside the palace which is constantly crowded in the daytime. It is hard to appreciate the square is actually surrounded by shops, most serving the tourist trade with souvenirs and handicrafts. There are cafés here too with outside seating but, to sample Sintra's speciality cakes, head into Rua das Padarias, to the popular Piriquita café. Try first a delicious *travesseiro* (bolster), which is shaped as its name suggests and contains an apple and almond purée filling inside a flaky pastry case. It is hard to imagine how many are eaten in a day but the turnover of these is so rapid that they always seem to be served warm and fresh. *Queijadas*, cheese and almond tarts, are the other speciality to try but these are good to take away and are often stacked on the counter in packs of six ready to carry off. Continuing up the narrow Rua das Padarias leads into a small warren of alleyways alive with colour in the daytime from the souvenir shops and in the evening when the restaurants spread their tables outside.

Not far away, just along the road to Monserrate, is the tourist office and

Two huge oast-house-like chimneys dominate Sintra's Pálacio Nacional

following right down Rua Gil Vicente leads you to **Museu do Brinquedo**, the toy museum. This compact museum houses a collection of some 20,000 toys from the 16th century to modern times and includes some famous names like Dinky and Meccano. It is planned to rehouse the collection some time in a more suitable location.

The Moorish castle and Pena Palace lie about 4km (2.5 miles) by road above the town. Drivers should have no problem but others may have either to resort to a taxi (since the seasonal bus service is so infrequent it is best discounted), or walk. Taxis can usually be found in the road leading to the Hotel Tivoli. Most visitors walk the narrow twisting road which winds up the hillside without realising that there is a quicker and more pleasant route through the park.

From the town square head first up the cobbled Rua das Padarias, then climb the steps very shortly to join the surfaced road and turn left. Keep ahead in a moment where the road carrying traffic up to the castle swings sharply left and, for an excellent view down over the palace, simply peer over the tall wall to the left. Fork right up the cobbled road immediately beyond the fountain, also on the right, to reach the shady square by the church of Santa Maria. Just a minute later turn right up a very steep, cobbled road to pass through a large gateway into the grounds of the castle. All that remains now is to climb steadily on a good, well shaded path, but remember to turn right at the junction reached a few minutes after passing the stone seat. Mount a few steps here and head up into the castle area. At a major junction of paths, turn right to explore the castle but continue straight on to reach the exit leading to the road.

Castle of the Moors

This Moorish castle is nothing more than a long encircling wall with battlements and angle towers draped over craggy and forested hilltops known to the Romans as Mons Lunae (Hills of the Moon). Walking the ramparts provides moments of spectacular scenery, not just the walls themselves as they wind up and down the hillsides like a switchback, but also down onto the town and out over the forested Serra da Sintra mountains.

The castle is thought to have been constructed in the 8th or 9th century but there is evidence to suggest that parts were built earlier. Together with the castles at Lisbon and Santárem, it was responsible for the defence of the Muslim province of Belata and had moments of glory in resisting the advances of Dom Afonso Henriques in the 12th century. To the emerging Portuguese nation, Belata was the 'extreme' territory of the kingdom and when it was eventually liberated from the Moors it kept its name as Estremadura. Dom Fernando I (1367–83) was responsible for a large-scale restoration of the castle which left very little of the actual Moorish construction in place. With the eventual decline of military activity, the castle fell steadily into a state of disrepair until, in the 19th century, Dom Fernando II, king-consort of Maria II, was contracted by Sintra Council to repair and preserve the castle. The present state of the castle is the result of his work.

Before reaching the walls you come to the ruins of the Romanesque chapel of São Pedro which was also restored by Fernando II and nearby is the Cistern of the Moors which stores water for the palace in Sintra. Once on the walls, there is a good deal of walking to explore the ramparts and the five towers with plenty of steps to climb along the way.

Through Pena Palace gardens to the palace

There is more walking in store to reach Pena Palace but, again, it is possible to avoid dicing with the traffic along the road. Exit from the castle through the revolving gate onto the road, turn right to walk downhill to the entrance to the palace gardens on the left, reached very shortly. Enter the gardens to pass the lake on the right and go left just before reaching the Indian Fountain and now follow signs to the palace.

This 80ha park is a wonderful arboretum of trees and shrubs introduced from all over the world, full of shady paths and tracks offering hours of walking. Particularly spectacular are the tree ferns near the entrance which were brought from Australasia but there is a whole valley of tree ferns deeper into the park. Giant redwood trees thrive here, there is a Garden of Camellias, and it is possible to walk from here to the commanding viewpoint of Cruz Alta, the highest point on Serra da Sintra. It would be wise to be guided by the *Landscapes of Portugal, Sintra, Cascais and Estoril* (B. and E. Anderson) which describes this walk and others in these hills.

Chalet of the Condessa

Romantics may wish to visit the Chalet of the Condessa in Pena Palace gardens which is reached by turning right just beyond the first lake on entering the park and staying right to the far edge of the park. This is another of those love stories which punctuate Portuguese history. The Condessa was the mistress of Dom Fernando II. Fernando (Ferdinand) hailed from the German state of Saxe-Coburg-Gotha (as did his cousin Albert who married Queen Victoria of England), and he came to Portugal in 1836 to marry the 17-year-old Queen Maria II. It was Dona Maria's second marriage. A year earlier she had married the Duke of Leuchtenburg, her father's second wife's brother, but he died soon after arriving in Portugal.

Maria proved to be a loving and fruitful wife. The first child of the marriage, Pedro, was born just a year later and she continued to produce children almost annually until she finally died giving birth to her 11th child in 1853. Baby Eugénio also died.

After Maria's death, the artistic Ferdinand, who was credited with restoring a number of national treasures damaged in the anticlerical fervour following the demise of religious orders in 1834, was attracted by a lively German opera singer whom he created Condessa d'Edla. The State was not too pleased at his taking a mistress and even less pleased when Ferdinand willed everything to her rather than to his son, the king. After Ferdinand's death, the Condessa was promptly disinherited by the state, but a chalet was built for her in the grounds of the palace where she spent her time gardening.

The simulated wooden chalet with cork-lined windows still stands in an area known as the Garden of the Condessa. It is a place of pilgrimage for those with a little romance left in their souls. Nearby is another valley of tree ferns which was planted especially for the Condessa.

Pena Palace (Palácio Nacional de Pena)

A frivolous confection straight from the realms of Disneyworld, Pena Palace rarely provokes good comment but it does excite curiosity. The location, on a pinnacle of rock overlooking Sintra, has attracted developers ever since an apparition of the Virgin there. First there was a primitive chapel marking the spot but, in 1509, Manuel I replaced it with a Hieronymite monastery, Nossa Senhora da Pena (Our Lady of Sorrow) which was severely damaged in the great earthquake of 1755. When in 1838, after all religious orders had been disbanded, the government were busy selling off confiscated property, Dom Fernando II, king-consort of Maria II, was on hand to acquire the site. This sensitive and artistic man had a vision and engaged a German military

Woven around Sintra's wooded and misty hilltops, the Castle of the Moors evokes romantic images

engineer, Baron von Eschwege, to build him a Romantic baronial castle. Although work started in 1840, it took longer than the lifetime of Baron von Eschwege and was finished in 1885 by the Italian Demetrio Cinnatti and the Portuguese Possidónio da Silva. Parts of the original monastery are incorporated into the structure which turned out to be a mind-boggling concoction of Moorish, Gothic and Manueline with Renaissance and Baroque elements for good measure.

Now that it has been externally redecorated in the old Sintra colours of brick-red and yellow, the palace takes on a new fascination. Viewed from the outside there is an overwhelming jumble of crenellations, square towers, minarets, golden domes and Gothic windows presenting powerful images from any viewpoint. Entrance to the palace is through an ornamental castle gateway decorated with bartizans and over a drawbridge. It is worth a few moments to explore the outside of the edifice before starting a tour of the interior. Hard not to miss is the grotesquely carved window smothered by a grape-bearing vine which is growing from the neck of an uncomfortable-looking triton perched on a conch shell below. The small cloister of the original monastery has been preserved and the chapel with an altarpiece carved by Chanterène in 1532 for João III. The rooms visited on the guided tour are preserved in the condition they were left when the royal family took flight on 4 October 1910 on the demise of the monarchy. Although the rooms are mostly small, the intensity and richness of the furnishings and ornamentation quite overwhelm the senses and the end of the tour comes with a sense of relief.

The Sintra Music Festival

Sintra hosts a major music festival every year in June and July attracting top musicians from all over the world. All the palaces in and around Sintra, including Queluz (see page 107), are brought into action to provide magnificent settings for a feast of romantic music. A more recent addition is the ballet festival which follows the music festival and uses similar venues.

The Cork Convent

Convento dos Capuchos, with its tiny cells hewn in the rock and lined with cork, has long been known as the cork convent and may have been so christened by Byron. He was certainly fascinated by the place and used to hike over with his friend Hobbleday. The convent was built here at the request of João de Castro, Viceroy of India, and the work was carried out by his son, Álvaro de Castro, in 1560. Legend tells that the site was chosen out of respect for the Holy man Honório who lived there for 30 years surviving on nothing more than grass and water. The monastery built here reflects that poverty and hardship and the only measure of comfort in the cold, damp cells is the cork lining. Byron's view is reflected in *Childe Harold*: 'Deep in yon cave Honorius long did dwell / In hope to merit heaven by making earth a hell'.

The convent lies 8km (5 miles) to the west of Sintra. To find it, take the road out of Sintra initially towards Pena Palace but keep straight on at the final junction to ascend the ridge of Serra da Sintra. A signpost guides the way to the convent when the crossroads is reached. Hairshirts seem particularly appropriate in such a sunless gloomy spot but the fascinating tour of this uncomfortable place is mercifully short.

The Monserrate road to Colares

Both Seteais Palace and Monserrate Park are conveniently located on the scenic road between Sintra and Colares which follows along the shoulder of Serra da Sintra. The route out of Sintra Vila passes the now closed Estalagem dos Cavaleiros where Byron stayed in 1809, this is located just beyond the tourist office. From here Setéais Palace is quickly reached.

Seteais Palace, now a luxury hotel with 12 rooms, was built in neoclassical style in the 18th century for Daniel Gildemeester, the Dutch Consul in Lisbon and a diamond merchant. The two wings of the palace were joined by a triumphal arch in 1802 to commemorate the visit of Prince João (later Dom João IV) and Carlota Joaquina. Seteais means 'seven sighs' but the origins of the name are obscure; some suggest that it derives from the sound echoes in the valley here. The best way to see the palace is to take tea there or perhaps cocktails. While the hotel offers an unrivalled setting, the restaurant is expensive and has yet to earn itself a good reputation.

Monserrate

Monserrate park lies a short distance beyond the palace and there is a small parking area opposite the entrance. It is most worth visiting for its garden which is full of exotic trees and shrubs from all over the world. There is a small mansion, now belonging to the state, which at the moment lies closed and deserted. Plans are constantly being discussed for its revival but without real commitment. Monserrate, takes its name from the Chapel of Our Lady of Monserrate which was built around 1540 on the site of a previous tomb and chapel marking the spot where a prominent Arab died in a duel. In 1790 it came into the hands of a rich English merchant, Gerald de Visme, who built a house which, in 1794, was rented out to the English dilettante writer William Beckford. He described it as 'a beautiful Claude-like place, surrounded by a most enchanting country'. There is a suspicion that Beckford himself had a hand in rebuilding the place, indulging his uncertain vision, which resulted in a Gothic house of little taste, though at least the gardens and grounds benefited from his efforts at restoration.

The present neo-Moorish extravaganza was constructed in 1856 by James Knowles for the London textile merchant, Sir Francis Cook. A year or two earlier, the artist William Stockdale with the help and advice of William Nevill from Kew had laid out the 30ha of garden to produce something really fine which, although not today in the same condition, is well worth a visit.

Colares

Leafy green trees continue to crowd this narrow road twisting its way along the shoulder of the Serra da Sintra. Sharp eyes might just discern the words Quinta da Capela carved into the stone gatepost on the left. This is the entrance to an elegant old *quinta* set in spacious grounds abutting Monserrate park. It offers accommodation in the main house or in quietly located bungalows within its boundaries.

The lush greenness of the Sintra mountains is suddenly left behind as Colares is reached. This rural village is best known for its grape cultivation and for Colares wine (see page 45) and its most important monument is the **Adega Regional de Colares** where it is possible to enjoy a winetasting or even a concert in the summer months. The older and more interesting part of the village lies up the hill where the old pillory is to be seen, while the modern part is down by the riverside. Here too is a lively riverside café which is good for snacks, but the fun thing to do in Colares is to catch the **tram** to Praia das Maçãs which departs on the half hour from Banzão. Construction of this line from Sintra via Colares and Praia das Maçãs to Azenhas do Mar was started in the late 19th century and completed only in 1930. By 1954 its economic viability came into question and sections started to close, namely from Sintra Palace to Sintra railway station and from Praia das Maçãs to Azenhas do Mar. In 1975 it closed down completely, but recent restoration work has opened the Colares to Praia das Maçãs section and there are plans in hand to reopen the line to Sintra.

Practical Information

Hotels and Restaurants

ESTORIL
Hotel Apartamento Estoril Eden, Av. Sabóia, Monte Estoril (tel. 01 467 0573). Close to Monte Estoril railway station, this four-star establishment offers 160 apartments furnished in modern style. Equipped with a swimming pool, games facilities and small supermarket.

Hotel Atlântico, Estrada da Marginal (tel. 01 468 3619). Commanding good sea views, this large four-star hotel is situated rather close to the railway station. Unusually, it has a sea-water pool and offers good facilities including a restaurant.

Comfort Inn, Rua Belmonte, 1, Monte Estoril (tel. 01 468 1122). Formerly the Hotel Zenith, it has now joined the Choice Hotels International group and offers good two-star comfort in the typical style of the chain. Quietly situated and handy for both Cascais and Estoril.

Country Club Hotel Lennox, Av. Eng. Álvaro Pedro de Sousa, 5 (tel. 01 468 0424). Located in the heart of Estoril, not far from the Casino, this 32-roomed hotel offers a homely atmosphere in four-star comfort. Guests receive a discount at the Quinta da Marinha golf course.

Hotel Palácio do Estoril, Rua do Park (tel. 01468 0400). Still the place to see and be seen in Estoril. This large five-star has style, plenty of facilities and an excellent restaurant.

Restaurants are thin on the ground in Estoril since most visitors head for Cascais to eat. The major hotels offer a typically international cuisine but finding good local food is more difficult. Good eating is still to be found and places to try include:

English Bar, Av. Marginal, Monte Estoril (tel. 01 468 0413). Has built up a solid reputation for the quality of its food and offers an extensive wine list. Old-fashioned country house atmosphere; moderate to expensive, closed Sundays.

Four Seasons, next to Hotel Palácio (tel. 01 468 0400). Offers top-class food from a Portuguese and international menu. Congenial atmosphere with live music for dancing; expensive, closed Mondays.

Monte's Bistro, Av S. Pedro, Monte Estoril (tel 01 466 0106). Good food from a varied menu including some typically Portuguese dishes, cosy atmosphere. Prices are moderate to inexpensive, closed Sundays.

CASCAIS

There is no shortage of good accommodation in Cascais, from five-star hotels down to simple pensions. Only a very small selection is included here.

Hotel Albatroz, Rua Frederico Arouca, 100 (tel. 01 284 4827). A small luxury five-star hotel which was once a ducal palace. A recent extension has increased the room total to 40 but the rooms in the old palace have the best character. It has a good restaurant too but bookings are essential.

Hotel Baia, Av. Marginal (tel. 01 483 1033) A modest but adequate three-star hotel with limited facilities, recently improved with the addition of a rooftop swimming pool.

Hotel Estoril Sol, Park Palmela (tel. 01 483 2831). This large five-star hotel, lying between Estoril and Cascais, offers good facilities including an Olympic size swimming pool but succeeds most at being impersonal.

Quinta da Marinha Hotel and Village resort, Quinta da Marinha (tel. 01 486 9881). This quality resort just west of Cascais offers top facilities for golfers.

Places to eat, like the hotels, are too numerous to explore in detail. The few suggestions below are no more than a starting point.

Apeadeiro, Av. Vasco de Gama, 32 (tel. 483 2731). Good meat dishes as well as fish, inexpensive. Closed Mondays.

Ginginha Transmontana, Rua de Alvide, 366 (tel. 483 2655). Good Portuguese food at moderate prices; closed Sundays.

O Pescador, Rua da Flores, 10B (tel. 483 2054). House specialities include paella and sole; good food and service but expensive.

PRAIA DO GUINCHO

There are only three hotels in Guincho the best of which is:

Hotel de Guincho (tel. 01 285 0491). Relatively small with only 36 rooms, this five-star hotel occupies the former fortress and is particularly well situated. It has good facilities but do not expect a swimming pool.

SINTRA

Caesar Park Hotel, Penha Longa (tel. 01 924 9011). This luxury-class hotel is part of the Penha Longa Country Club which is located just outside Sintra. Guests have the exclusive use of a range of sport and leisure activities including golf, horse riding, tennis, squash, gymnasium facilities, sauna, games room and swimming pool.

Hotel Palácio dos Seteais, Rua Barbosa du Bocage, 8 (tel. 01 923 3200). Luxury hotel in idyllic surrounds with just 12 rooms. Book in advance.

Hotel Tivoli, Praça da República (tel. 01 923 3505). Centrally situated next to the Sintra Palace, this comfortable four-star hotel has only 21 rooms and is not as large as it looks. Although constantly criticised for being out of character with its surroundings, it is still one of the best places to stay.

Sintra has a number of quintas and manor houses and those listed below are part of either the TURIHAB or ANTER schemes and can be booked through them (see page 30) or directly.

Casa Miradoura, Rua Sotto Meyer, 55 (tel. 01 023 5900). Recently renovated, this quietly located traditional Sintra house set within its gardens offers six bright and cheery rooms each with a different colour theme. Has a breakfast terrace to linger over.

Quinta da Capela, Estrada de Monserrate (tel. 01 929 0170). Built originally in the 16th century by the Dukes of Cadaval, the house was rebuilt in the 17th century. Set amidst beautiful countryside, this *quinta* offers seven elegantly furnished rooms all with private facilities.

Quinta das Sequoias, Estrada de Monserrate (tel. 01 923 0342). Delightfully located 2km (1.25 miles) off the main road in the very heart of the Serra da Sintra. It is an old manor house which has been recently renovated and now includes a swimming pool. The old traditional kitchen has been retained for a dining room where guests dine around a huge wooden table. It has just five rooms for guests.

Sintra has more restaurants than first appears but they are scattered around. Those located up Rua das Padarias, out to catch the tourist trade, are not always the best choice.

Regional, Travessa do Municipio (tel. 01 923 4444). Found by the town hall, this is easily the best restaurant in town. Mostly traditional Portuguese food well presented and in more than adequate portions. The bill will delight too for the prices are very reasonable, so do not be surprised to see people queuing at the door.

Restaurant Tacho Real, Rua da Ferraria (tel. 01 923 5277). Good food from an interesting menu but expect to pay a little more; closed Wednesdays.

Restaurant Tulhas, Rua Gil Vicente (tel. 923 2378). Tucked away down by the tourist office, this small restaurant offers good traditional Portuguese food at very moderate prices; closed Wednesdays.

COLARES

Hotel Miramonte (tel. 01 929 1230). Situated along the road towards Praia das Maçãs, this two-star hotel with 72 rooms is one of the largest in the area.

Places of Interest

CASCAIS

Municipal Museum, Palace of the Counts of Castro Guimarães, open 11am–5pm, closed Monday and holidays.

Museum of the Sea, open 10am–4.45pm, closed Mondays and holidays.

SINTRA

Palácio Nacional, open 10am–1pm and 2pm–5pm, closed Wednesday and holidays.

Pena Palace (Palácio Nacional de Pena), open 10am–1pm and 2pm–5pm, closed Mondays and holidays.

Castle of the Moors, open daily 10am–6pm, free entry.

Monserrate Palace and Gardens, open 10am–6pm.

Capuchos Convent, open 10am–6pm.

Sintra Toy Museum, open 9.30am–12.30pm and 2pm–6pm, closed Mondays and holidays.

Sports and Leisure

GOLF

Course descriptions of the six high-class golf clubs in the immediate area are detailed on pages 88–91.

Lisbon Sports Club, Casal de Carregueira, Belas. (tel. 01 431 0077).

Golf do Estoril, Av. da República, Estoril. (tel. 01 468 0176).

Quinta da Beloura, Estrada de Albarraque. (tel. 01 924 0327).

Estoril Sol, Quinta do Outeiro, Lagoa Azul, Linhó, Sintra. (tel. 01 923 2461).

Penha Longa, Lagoa Azul, Linhó, Sintra. (tel. 01 924 0014).

Quinta da Marinha, Cascais. (tel. 01 486 9881).

HORSE RIDING

Lessons by experienced instructors and horses for hire from all below:

Quinta da Marinha, Cascais (tel. 01 486 9084).

Centro Hipico da Costa do Estoril, Charneca (tel. 01 487 2064).

Clube de Campo D. Carlos I, Quinta da Marinha (tel. 01 487 1403).

Escola de Equitação de Areai (tel. 01 483 9284).

WATER SPORTS

There are opportunities for water sports at most beaches and Cascais Naval Club has a weekend sailing club with yachts and motor boats for hire. Guincho beach is especially popular for windsurfing.

TENNIS

Estoril Tennis club has 18 courts with full facilities, also floodlights for evening play. (tel. 01 466 2770).

Tourist Offices

CABO DA ROCA, Azóia (tel. 01 928 0081).

CASCAIS Rua Visconde da Luz (tel. 01 486 8204).

COLARES Várzea de Colares (tel. 01 929 2638).

ESTORIL Arcadas do Parque (tel. 01 468 0113).

SINTRA Praça da República (tel. 01 923 1157).

7. EXCURSIONS NORTH OF COSTA LISBOA

A number of worthwhile excursions, like the walled town of Óbidos, the coastal resorts of Peniche and Ericeira and the palaces of Mafra and Queluz, all lie within easy reach for visitors staying anywhere in the general area of Costa Lisboa. Queluz, is particularly convenient to reach by public transport since it lies on the rail line between Lisbon and Sintra. A car is essential for travelling to the other destinations which are a little further afield. Set aside half a day for Mafra Palace since the guided tour is quite lengthy, but Ericeira is not too far away and can be easily included to make it a full day out. Óbidos and Peniche can also be contemplated as another day tour but be sure to visit historic Óbidos first and give it as much time as it deserves.

Queluz Palace (Palácio Nacional de Queluz)

Located 9km (5.5 miles) west of Lisbon, the palace is easily reached by road or rail. Visitors using the Sintra–Lisbon train need to alight at Queluz-Belas station and head downhill south to reach the palace.

This pink Rococo palace started life as a country mansion which was confiscated by the royal family in 1654. It remained virtually untouched until Infante Dom Pedro, son of Dom João V, decided to rebuild the place for himself. With the aid of the Portuguese architect Mateus Vicente de Oliveira, who had also been involved with the building of the palace at Mafra, Queluz Palace was substantially rebuilt as a two-storey edifice in 1747–52. Shortly afterwards, around 1758, further single-storey additions in a more neoclassical style were made with the assistance of Jean-Baptiste Robillon.

Forming the main entrance are the **courtyard gardens**, also designed by Robillon who took inspiration from Versailles. These are largely geometrical with lots of straight lines and circles formed by neatly trimmed box hedges, and feature topiary, ponds, urns and statues. The gardens were particularly favoured by Carlota Joaquina, wife of Dom João VI, after they came to live there

LISBON & CENTRAL PORTUGAL

in 1794 during João's regency, following a fire at Adjuda Palace in Lisbon.

The Rococo character is reflected throughout the interior with light-coloured walls decorated in fine gilded relief. Spatial effects too are introduced with oval and round rooms. A guided tour of the palace visits some of the finest rooms, including the oval **Hall of Mirrors** and the circular **King's Room** in which Dom Pedro IV was born and died.

Even if the palace is closed, it is possible to visit the old **kitchens** since these have been converted into a quality restaurant known as Cosinha Velha. Queluz is often used as one of the romantic locations in the Sintra music festival.

Mafra

Mafra lies about 24km (15 miles) by road north of Sintra and it can be reached with equal facility from Lisbon, although the journey is a little longer (40km/25 miles). Ericeira is only 12km (7.5 miles) to the west so the two destinations can easily be accommodated in a single tour.

Once north of Sintra, marble factories dominate the roadside for a time in the region of Pero Pinheiro which is famed for the quality of its pink marble. Beyond here the rolling farmland was once graced by windmills and there are one or two still around, but the best place to see the style of them is in the handicraft shops. Nearer to Mafra, on dipping down into Cheleiros, there is a restored bridge of Roman origin which can be seen on the right. The huge **monastery** which so dominates the town announces your arrival in Mafra.

An old town has been in existence here from Roman times and survived through the Moorish occupation to be liberated in 1147 by Dom Afonso Henriques. It was granted its first charter in 1189 by Sancho I and donated to the Bishop of Silves. A new charter was granted by Dom Manuel I in 1513 and the town developed around the castle (now no more) and the church of Santo André built around 1400. The construction of the new convent started early in the 18th century when Brazilian gold was flowing freely into the royal coffers and Portugal was becoming a wealthy and powerful state.

One-fifth of all the gold discovered went to the crown but this was not enough for Dom João V. He set in motion a series of ambitious projects of which the most extravagant was Mafra, built to commemorate the birth of an heir to the throne. Up to 45,000 workmen at peak times, including many skilled stonemasons, laboured the best part of 18 years to construct the monument and the statistics are staggering: it contains 5200 doorways and 2500 windows. Under Dom João, the revenues flowed out of the royal coffers faster than they entered. Many of the men working on Mafra convent were paid little or late and may not have been paid at all. The king even had trouble paying his soldiers and Lisbon was bankrupt. Seemingly against all the odds, the convent was finally completed in 1735.

The design of the monastery-palace was entrusted to the German-born Johann Friedrich Ludwig who had studied architecture in Rome while in the service of the Jesuits. In 1700, at the age of just 30 and still in the service of the Jesuits, he moved to Lisbon. In building the convent he was assisted by an Italian builder Carlo Baptiste Garbo and his own son. The original plan and scale were not followed too strictly and the monastery ended up with accommodation for 280 friars and some 150 novices against the original plan for only 13 friars. Today parts of the convent are used by the Portuguese military.

Mafra Palace and Convent

It has the distinction of being quite different from any other piece of architecture in Portugal, and the façade in particular, flanked as it is by bulbous-domed square towers, is more reminiscent of German monastic architecture. Taking an overview of the front – all of 220m long – is not easy and the monumental façade of the centrally placed **church** tends to demand all the attention. It achieves pleasing symmetry, with two multi-stage belltowers guarding the colonnaded two-storey entrance which is crowned by a triangular pediment. Four statues are incorporated: from left to right, St Dominic and St Francis above and St Clara and Elizabeth, Queen of Hungary below. The belltowers boast a huge assembly of bells, around 57 in each, 48 of which form the carillons, made in Liège and Antwerp and reputed to have cost a whole shipload of gold. Ringing the bells is now easier since their electrification and carillon concerts are held in the church from time to time. Entrance to the church is free and is not part of the monastery tour.

Pink, white, blue, yellow, red, grey and black marbles are all richly used in the elegant interior. The single tunnel-vaulted nave is flanked by side chapels containing sculptures by artists of a local school directed by an Italian, Alessandro Giusti, and takes the form of a Latin cross. The church was consecrated in 1730, five years before the monastery complex was actually completed.

If the tour of the **palace** takes in the military wing and museum, as it usually does, then set aside about one and a half hours and do not expect the guide to have much English. It is unlikely that the charming young Portuguese girl encountered by the authors will be around with every party to liven things up with her excellent English and good knowledge of history. She turned out to be a true romantic when she declared envy for Inês de Castro, her favourite character in history, and was completely unshaken when it was pointed out that she was murdered.

The military wing and museum usually starts the tour and includes the old kitchens which have now been refurbished with stainless steel fittings and pressed into use to serve the hungry young soldiers. One exhibit here is a contoured model of the hills in this region showing the lines of defence used in the Peninsular War (see pages 113–114). Endless galleries, all with polished wooden floors, lead to countless rooms including the hospital with its small cubicles and royal bedrooms, bathrooms, the dining room with hunting trophies, and the music room. A highlight of the visit is the magnificent Rococo **library** which preserves some 40,000 gilt volumes, many yet waiting to be researched.

Azulejos

The Portuguese fascination with surface decoration extends to *azulejos*, coloured ceramic tiles, which are inescapable throughout the country. They are not unique to Portugal – it is just that the Portuguese have a passion for them and use them imaginatively in a whole variety of ways, from simple patterns to large scenes or even documentaries, to decorate churches, water fountains, railway stations, palaces, public buildings and house fronts.

This love affair started around the 15th century, inspired by tiles with a geometric pattern imported from Seville. Home production of essentially blue tiles started and the patterns were established in firing by separating the colour with rivulets of linseed oil or by ridges of clay. In the 16th century, the Italian majolica technique was introduced by which the clay tile was covered with a white enamel which could be painted onto directly. This greater freedom allowed the Portuguese to introduce a design element to create patterns and by the 17th century coloured tiles, chiefly dark blue, yellow, green and white were used to make up either geometric, carpet or tapestry designs, often based on a module of four tiles. Exotic designs with animals, fish and flower motifs made an appearance too, but the polychrome fashion waned with the appearance of Delft blue. Europe had been captivated by the imported blue and white Chinese porcelain and the Dutch responded by developing a delicate blue and white tile which quickly found favour in Portugal.

Towards the end of the 17th century, narrative tiles made their appearance, telling a story of events in life like harvesting grapes, fishing or hunting, and these increased in size and realism to become very popular. Tile painting rapidly became recognised as an art form, both in its creation and use as a complement to architecture to enliven interiors. One of the recognised masters, António de Oliveira Bernardes, together with his son Policarpo set up a school in Lisbon which rapidly became influential in the development of this art. A number of beautiful works in the first half of the 18th century are often assigned with authority to the Bernardes family; works by António can certainly be seen in the chapel of Nossa Senhora da Cabeça in Évora and by Policarpo in the chapel of São Filipe fort at Setúbal. Quite a number of artists became well known but one outstanding craftsman remains unknown to this day apart from the initials P.M.P. which adorn his works.

Blue and white tiles were dominant throughout this period, but the mid-18th century saw the return to favour of polychromy at more or less the same time as an earthquake shattered much of Lisbon. During the rebuilding phase, when the demand for tiles was high, a large number of factories opened, not all maintaining the previous high standards. The use of azulejos for the exterior decoration of church façades and house walls was imported in the 19th century, when the royal family and other emigrants returned from Brazil where they had moved to escape the French invasion. One of the best places to trace the history and development of azulejos is in the Museu Nacional do Azulejo in Lisbon.

Mafra town itself has little to offer apart from a snack bar or two useful for catching up on refreshments after the long tour of the monastery, although the church of Santo André with its simple Gothic lines is worth a moment.

Ericeira

Electric blue and white adobe houses crowd the streets of this small fishing village which has more recently become a tourist destination for packaged holidays. Apart from the bustle of fishermen there is a pleasing ambience to enjoy and some narrow streets to wander. Life centres mostly around Praça da República where shops and cafés benefit from the leafy shade of giant plane trees. Diners might be tempted to try a local speciality, *açorda de mariscos* or shellfish soup, made from bread soaked in shellfish stock then cooked in olive oil with garlic and coriander followed by the addition of eggs and shellfish; it is almost a meal on its own. Down on the waterfront, the main beach is reserved for the fishermen and not available for swimmers although the cliff-backed Praia do Sul to the south offers fine sand and bathing opportunities. To the north is Praia de São Sebastião which is named after the young king who led an unwilling army to slaughter in the battle of Alcácer Quibir in 1578. A stunned Portugal refused to believe that the king and some 8000 soldiers died in battle. Since nobody actually saw the king killed, a belief grew that he was not dead and that he would reappear to lead them back to glory. These dreams were bolstered by fears that the ageing Dom Henrique would not be able to avert Spanish claims to the throne. Sebastianism, as it became known, inspired poets to verse and produced its share of impostors like the hermit in Ericeira who proclaimed himself to be Dom Sebastião, crowned a queen and gathered behind him a small army of local farmers. The state dished out terminal punishment to him in 1584.

The town's second mark on history had a slightly happier ending. It was from here that Dom Manuel II 'the Unfortunate' and his family escaped in 1910, after the monarchy was overthrown. They went first to Gibraltar and then on to England to settle at Twickenham where the exiled king devoted himself to building a library of early Portuguese books. A plaque on the side of the tiny Santo António chapel above the harbour records this event and there are related documents, including British newspaper reports, in the small municipal museum.

The old fishing quarter at Ericeira

The Peninsular War (1807–10)

In 1807 Napoleon delivered an ultimatum to Portugal, to close its ports to British ships and declare war on Britain. Unwilling to turn against such a long-term ally and valued trading partner, Portugal defied Napoleon, whereupon General Junot marched French troops on Lisbon and met with little resistance. The royal family fled to Brazil for safety and the country turned to Britain for help. Sir Arthur Wellesley, later the Duke of Wellington, arrived in August 1808 with an initial force of some 9000 troops, landing near the Mondego river at Coimbra. These were soon joined by a further 13,000 British forces and, together with 8000 Portuguese, they defeated the French at Roliça and Vimeiro, just north of Torres Vedras. This led to negotiations and to the remarkable Treaty of Sintra by which the French withdrew, using British ships to be safely transported home complete with their booty. It was a treaty which mystified and angered both the Portuguese and the British.

The French were not finished and there were to be two further invasions before this war reached a conclusion in 1810. Wellington, now familiar with the countryside around Torres Vedras, recognised its potential should defensive action prove necessary in the face of superior French forces. In anticipation, Wellington secretly started work on a double line of defence in the autumn of 1809. The **Lines of Torres Vedras** which he organised comprised two lines of hilltop fortifications extending across much of the country. Some 126 strong masonry forts with 247 guns fortified the defences, earthworks were raised, ravines walled with stone and homes destroyed. All of this was constructed within a year with conscripted and underpaid Portuguese labour. In the north, the line ran from the Atlantic west of Torres Vedras to just below Vila Franca de Xira on the River Tagus, and in the south from the Atlantic passing just north of Mafra, through Bucelas to meet the Tagus just north of Pávoa de Santa Iria. A scorched earth policy was operated north of the lines and when the French did attack, the local population complete with their livestock were moved to the south. There is a contoured model showing these defences on display in Mafra Palace.

Napoleon himself planned the second attack in 1809, led by Marshal Nicholas Soult. Chaves in the north quickly fell and Soult marched on Porto which was unable to resist. Wellington, with a force of some 17,000 English troops and 7000 Portuguese, again came to the rescue and pushed Soult north into Galicia. The French threat switched to the west from Spain as an army captured Abrantes and set up headquarters there before Wellington's defeat of the French at Talavera. For this victory he earned himself the title of Viscount.

In May 1810, the third and final attack was ordered by Napoleon. This was intended to be decisive and a massive force of 65,000 men under the command of Marshal Masséna marched on Portugal, heading first for Viseu. Wellington established a strong position in the hills of Buçaco and waited. Undeterred, the French on 27 September mounted an attack, a scene vividly recalled in the *azulejo* panels in Buçaco Palace Hotel; they lost 5000 troops. By this time the final pieces of Wellington's plan were in place and the trap was ready to spring. He judiciously pulled back his army, allowing the French to advance. Filled with a new confidence, Masséna marched towards his ultimate goal, Lisbon. To his unimaginable shock, he found the way blocked by a defensive line which had totally transformed the landscape. Wellington's well-provisioned troops lay in wait and Masséna realised that their position was impregnable. On 15 November the dispirited French troops finally left Portuguese soil bringing the Peninsular War to a conclusion.

Just as the Portuguese built the defences, they also pulled them down, but there are still earthworks and masonry identified with the northern line of defence to be seen to this day. A handy booklet published by the British Historical Society of Portugal will assist avid historians wishing to track down the remains, such as they are.

Óbidos and Peniche

A round trip taking in both Óbidos and Peniche involves about 200km (125 miles) of driving from Sintra and only a little more from Lisbon. Some new stretches of road, mostly bypassing towns, quickens the journey and the road between Óbidos and Peniche is particularly good.

Torres Vedras, passed en route, is the centre of a wine-producing area and a market town of some size. For a time before the 16th century it was a royal residence but it is better known now for its role in the Peninsular War and as the headquarters of the Duke of Wellington.

Óbidos

A first breathtaking view of the incredibly picturesque walled town of Óbidos is in store along the approach road, just before the car parking area beneath the walls is reached. Visitors' cars are excluded from entering through the town walls. Perched on a limestone ridge, Óbidos has been settled at least since Roman times and possibly before. The Moors occupied it for 400 years or so before Dom Afonso Henriques came along to recover it on the morning of 10 January 1148. Dom Sancho I carried out some restoration work on the walls but it was Dom Dinis (1279–1325) who was responsible for most of the significant rebuilding. He was quite fond of giving his saintly wife Isabel extravagant presents, like the town of Trancoso which he gave her as a wedding present. So, in another of his magnanimous gestures, having tidied up Óbidos and restored the castle, he presented the town to his wife and it remained the property of the Queens' Household until its abolition in 1834. The castle and the walls were considerably damaged by the 1755 earthquake but have since been restored.

Still huddled within crenellated walls and guarded by a castle, blue and white houses decked with bougainvillaea crowd narrow cobbled streets. Souvenir shops and cafés find space to spill out into the alleyways and there is some eye-catching colourful pottery on view. The **castle** has been converted into a *pousada* known as Castelo but, with only nine rooms which include three suites, it gets booked up for months ahead. It does have a restaurant so why not call in to try the asparagus with smoked ham or the kid Obidense style and perhaps view some of the *pousada*? One of the simple pleasures to enjoy in Óbidos is walking the **walls** which completely encircle the town. This provides some fascinating viewpoints down onto the houses and streets, although the walls are not guarded and are high in parts, which may not suit those with an inclination to vertigo.

Monuments to see include the **Igreja de Santa Maria** which dominates the market square. The present church dates from the 17th century, the later Renaissance period, but it sits on the location of an earlier church which predated the Reconquest, and contains paintings by Josefa of Óbidos depicting the mystic marriage of St Catherine. Born Josefa d'Ayala in Seville around 1630, the artist spent most of her life in a convent at Óbidos. Her early art work was with etchings and miniatures but later she turned to full-scale religious works and quickly gained respect as one of the country's finest painters. She died in 1684 and was buried in São Pedro. More of her work can be seen in the municipal museum in the old town hall.

Standing just to the west of Óbidos, on the same ridge, is a working **windmill** which is most clearly seen from the walls of the town. A closer inspection requires a short uphill walk but, if the miller is around, the reward is an opportunity to inspect the workings.

Peniche

The onward route to Peniche crosses flat land which makes it easier to appreciate that this was once sea, with Óbidos a coastal town and Peniche an island. Silting dramatically changed the landscape, much to the benefit of the farmers.

An important fishing port, Peniche occupies a large promontory. Dom Manuel I raised the question of defending the port, or Ribeira d'Atougia as it was known then, for a number of reasons. It was already steadily silting up, making Peniche a convenient landing point with easy access to the mainland, and armed piracy was a serious problem. The Count of Atougia was charged with the task of drawing up plans and costing the project but it was under Manuel's successor, Dom João III, that work actually started on the defences,

Óbidos, one of the most picturesque walled towns in Portugal

Colourful souvenirs on sale in Óbidos

with the **fort** in 1557. The first stage ended in 1570 in the reign of Dom Sebastião but much yet remained to be done to finish the planned walls and bastions which would complement the natural rock defences. Under Spanish rule (1581–1640), the fortification of Peniche was all but forgotten but shortly afterwards, in the reign of João IV, Count Jerónimo de Ataide was able to bring the plan to a conclusion and finish the work necessary to make Peniche an important military stronghold. Once its military purpose was served, the Fortaleza, as it is known, became a prison in the repressive Salazar regime.

The whole peninsula is walled and the road enters through the one and only gate. The fort and fishing harbour lie to the left but can also be reached by keeping straight ahead and following around the coastline of the promontory. Steep cliffs along the northern shore provide many precarious footholds for the intrepid Portuguese for whom fishing is a national obsession. The Santuário de Nossa Senhora dos Remédios enjoys magnificent coastal views; Cabo Carvoeiro offers nothing more than an unattractive lighthouse. From here the road heads back along the southern coast to the fort (now containing a museum) and the large fishing **harbour**. It is a busy harbour, shared by fishing boats and yachts, and equally busy onshore in the surrounding cafés and restaurants, especially along Avenida do Mar where sardine-grilling on the outside barbecues seems to start as early as breakfast and continues through to supper. Just a couple of blocks inland from Avenida do Mar is the fishermen's church of **São Pedro** which has a model of a sardine trawler complete with nets. Another pleasant café area is the leafy main square which is also the location of **Igreja Misericordia** worth visiting to study the paintings by Josefa of Óbidos. At the other end of the square is the tourist office.

Berlenga

Throughout the main summer months, ferries from Peniche take trippers to Ilha Berlenga, the largest island of a small archipelago just 12km (7.5 miles) offshore. It is now a nature reserve overflowing with gulls, puffins and cormorants, and to meet concerns over the growing number of visitors, ticket sales are limited to 300 per day. It does not take too many bodies to make the landing stage and small sandy beach look crowded, but those prepared to walk a little can cross the narrow causeway to visit the Forte de São João Baptista, now a very basic hostel. A fish lunch can be enjoyed at the *Mar e Sol* restaurant.

Practical Information

Hotels and Restaurants

ERICEIRA
Albergaria D. Fernando, Quinta da Calada E.N. 247 (tel. 061 55 204). Recently upgraded from a five-star pension, it lies out of town on the northern side.
Hotel de Tourismo de Ericeira (tel. 061 64 045). With 154 rooms, this three-star hotel is the largest in town. Good facilities including a swimming pool and games room.
Hotel Pedro Pescador, Rua Eduardo Burnay, 22 (tel. 061 64 200). A modest two-star hotel with limited facilities, located on the main street.
     There is no shortage of eating places and, for its size, Ericeira offers a remarkable choice although seafood restaurants predominate.
Marisqueira Ribadouro, Largo das Ribas (tel. 061 62 631). A good seafood restaurant with moderate prices.
O Barco, Rua Capitão João Lopes (tel. 061 62 759). Excellent seafood but expensive.

MAFRA
Pensião Castelão, Av. 25 de Abril (tel. 061 812 050). This two-star pension is the only accommodation in town; it has 19 rooms all with private facilities.

ÓBIDOS
Albergaria Rainha Santa Isabel, Rua Direita (tel. 062 959 323). This four-star establishment has a good location inside the town walls looking onto a cobbled street. Some 20 rooms all with private facilities.
Estalagem do Convento, Rua Dr João de Ornelas (tel. 062 959 214). Situated just outside the town walls, this former nunnery is now an interesting four-star hotel with 29 rooms. It has a small restaurant serving good food at moderate prices.

Pousada Castelo (tel. 062 959 105). Converted from part of the 16th-century castle, the *pousada* offers six comfortable rooms and three suites; one of the most popular pousadas so book well in advance.

Residencial Mansão de Torre, Casal do Zambujeiro (tel. 062 959 247). A couple of kilometres out of town, this four-star *residencial* is built around an old tower. Simple and clean, it is one of the few places with a swimming pool and tennis courts.

The **Pousada Castelo** has an excellent restaurant but it is expensive and the **Estalagem do Convento** restaurant is worth a visit, otherwise:

Restaurant Alcaide, Rua Direita (tel. 062 95 220). Serves good food with some Azorean specialities on the menu; moderate. Closed Tuesdays.

PENICHE

Hotel da Praia Norte, Av. Monsenhor Bastos (tel. 062 781 166). This three-star hotel with 92 rooms is the only hotel in town. Facilities include a swimming pool and restaurant.

Nau dos Corvos, Cabo Carvoeira (tel. 062 72 410). One of the most respected restaurants in town but on the expensive side of moderate.

Residencial Félita, Largo de Prof. Francisco Freire, 12 (tel. 062 782 190). Modern and fairly comfortable, this two-star *residencial* has just eight rooms, five with private facilities.

Places of Interest

Queluz Palace, open 9am–1pm and 2pm–5pm; closed Tuesdays.
Mafra Palace, 10am–1pm and 2pm–5pm, closed Tuesdays.

Tourist Offices

ERICEIRA Rua Dr Eduardo Burnay, 33 (tel. 061 63 122).
MAFRA Av.25 de Abril (tel. 061 812 023).
ÓBIDOS Rua Direita (tel. 062 959 231).
PENICHE Rua Alexandre Herculano (tel. 062 789 571).
TORRES VEDRAS Rua 9 Abril (tel. 061 314 094).

8. ROTA DO SOL

The southern half of Costa de Prata is now promoted for tourism as Rota do Sol, a region which centres on Leiria. It covers the broad coastal area from Alcobaça in the south to an imaginary line just north of Pombal. Many parts of the area are well known and well visited, such as the monasteries at Alcobaça, Batalha and Tomar, the religious sanctuary of Fátima and the seaside resort of Nazaré, and the region is rich in other interests. Limestone mountains, such as the Serra de Aire and Serra dos Candeeiros, are a Mecca for flowers lovers but these mountains, now

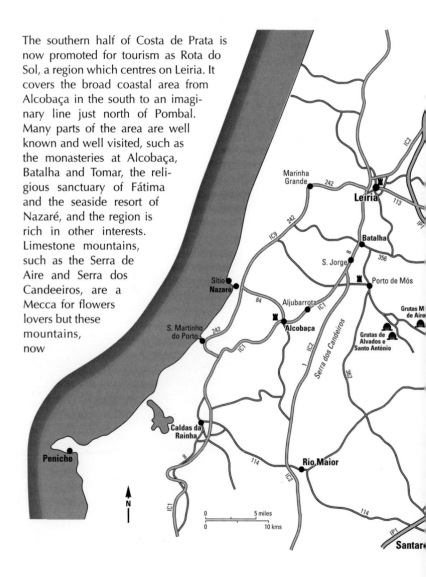

protected as a natural park, also contain some spectacular deep caves (*grutas*). Perhaps the most famous of these is Mira de Aire where the descent is on foot and the return by elevator; others would press the claims of Grutas de Alvados or Grutas de Santo António for spectacular beauty. Since they lie fairly close together, any argument can be resolved by visiting them all. No area of Portugal is without its castles and Rota do Sol has its share, including those at Porto de Mós, Leiria and Pombal, but none is so romantic as Almourol defending a tiny island in the river. The only charge here is for the boatman who rows visitors across the water.

Much of the interest in this region lies south of Leiria, but choosing a base may be dictated by securing accommodation. In spite of the vast influx of tourists who arrive by coach to visit the major sites, there is very little hotel accommodation available. Nazaré offers some as does the busy town of Leiria, but both Batalha and Alcobaça have surprisingly few hotels. Some of the country manor houses and *quintas* offer a quieter alternative and there are a number around, like the spacious and comfortable *Casa da Padeira* at Aljubarrota. Outside the towns driving is rarely hindered by traffic, so exploring the whole region from a single base is perfectly feasible.

Santarém

Heading north from Lisbon into the Rota do Sol area, it is quite possible to consider a side trip to Santarém, the capital of the Ribatejo region and one of Portugal's most historic cities. It was of strategic importance to the Romans, the Visigoths and the Moors, but little remains in evidence of its early history. The Moors made sure it was well fortified and, after losing it briefly to Alfonso VI of León in 1093, managed to hold on to it until displaced by Dom Afonso Henriques in 1147. The king's men scaled the wall under the cover of darkness and overcame the unsuspecting guards: to commemorate this victory, Dom Afonso Henriques founded the Abbey of Alcobaça. Santarém slowly established a reputation for its good hunting and it became a regular haunt of royalty between the 13th and 16th centuries. Dom Dinis died here in 1325 and here also the murderers of Inês de Castro were executed in 1357. The tomb of the unfortunate Inês lies in Alcobaça, visited shortly.

Santarém sits on high overlooking the River Tagus and commands extensive views over rich agricultural plains to the south and east. There is not too much to see in town and everything is nicely grouped within walking distance. High on the list are a couple of fine churches, two out of a number, and outstanding views from the *miradouro* (viewpoint), Portas do Sol. Largo Sá da Bandeira, at the heart of the old town, is a good starting point. Here the 17th-century many-windowed façade of the Jesuit seminary, which now serves as the town's cathedral, is prominent. Heading out along Rua Serpa Pinto and following signs to Portas do Sol, the route conveniently passes the two churches of particular interest. First of these is **Igreja de Marvila**, interesting for its unusual stone pulpit incorporating eleven miniature Corinthian columns and some outstanding 17th-century diamond-patterned *azulejos*. The next right turn leads to **Igreja de Graça**, famous for its outstanding rose window carved from a single piece of stone. Here lie the tombs of two of Portugal's famous sons. The more elaborate is of Pedro de Menezes, the first governor of Ceuta, who died in 1437, and his wife, while a rather austere tombstone belongs to Pedro Alvares Cabral, the discoverer of Brazil. This discovery is not recorded on his tombstone since the importance of Brazil was not fully appreciated at the time.

Returning to the main street, signs can be followed to the gardens of **Portas do Sol** within the walls of the Moorish citadel. From here there are sweeping views of the Tagus and the plains of Alentejo.

Early June is a good time to visit Santarém when the **Feira Nacional de Agricultura** is in full swing. Starting the first Friday in the month, it includes horse shows and bull fights as well as all the usual festivities like feasting and dancing. Another highlight of the festival calendar is the **Feira Nacional de Gastronómia** which takes place from the end of October into November. Here there is plenty of regional cuisine to sample as well as folk art and handicrafts from all over the country to tempt the visitor into spending a little money.

From Santarém the EN114 cuts across country via Rio Major to reach the spa town of Caldas da Rainha and from there Alcobaça, the next destination, is reached by travelling north on the IC1.

Alcobaça

In the midst of a rich fruit growing area, Alcobaça sits at the confluence of two rivers, the Alcoa and the Baça. It is totally dominated by the abbey which was founded for the Cistercians in 1153 by Dom Afonso Henriques to commemorate victory over the Moors at Santarém six years earlier. Work on the present structure started in 1178 and was finished by around 1223.

The Royal Abbey of Santa Maria de Alcobaça is a magnificent piece of medieval architecture, a delight of Cistercian Gothic simplicity – a simplicity not immediately obvious, for the Baroque façade, remodelled around 1725, is quite out of character with the interior. Only the doorway retains simple Gothic lines, otherwise there is plenty of ornamentation including a figure of the Virgin set high up between the two square bell towers. The niches which flank the portal contain statues of Sts Benedict and Bernard, whilst the narrow ledge above the doorway and below the rose window carries personifications of the Four Cardinal Virtues.

Inspired by the famous French Cistercian abbey of Cîteaux, the elegance of the proportions and austerity of the church combine to breathtaking effect. Three-aisled and cruciform, the church is very long (109m) with narrow side aisles to accentuate the towering loftiness of the interior (20m). Nine chapels radiate from the ambulatory in the apse and one of these now leads through to a sacristy and chapel added later. To the left of the entrance is the King's Room (Sala dos Reis) which is well decorated with *azulejos* and contains statues of the kings of Portugal up to Dom José I.

Two of the abbey's greatest treasures, drawing romantics by the thousands, are the 14th-century tombs of Portugal's most famous lovers, **Inês de Castro and Dom Pedro I**, lying feet to feet on opposite sides of the transepts. Their story is featured on page 124.

The tombs are skilfully sculptured and delightfully ornate. Each figure resting on top is attended by six angels while the sides are intricately carved with scenes from the scriptures. The dog lying at Pedro's feet could yet prove his undoing when he rises on the day of judgement to rush into his lover's arms.

The tombs of Afonso II and Afonso III and their respective wives, Urraca and Brites, lie in a small chapel off the south transept.

A door in the left aisle leads into the lower storey of the **Cloister of Dom Dinis** also known as the Cloister of Silence. This was constructed between 1308 and 1311 and the upper storey added in the 16th century. Ribbed vaulting decorates the galleries which surround the gardens, the ribs springing from corbels on the walls. A number of rooms lead off the galleries but the two not to be missed are the refectory and the kitchen. The **kitchen**, with its huge chimney rising over equally large ovens, has a tributary of the River Alcoa flowing through which was used to provide flowing water for the fish tank to keep fish fresh for the table. Simple austerity might have been the rule for architecture but was not necessarily the code by which the monks lived. Beckford, who visited Alcobaça in June 1794, kept notes which were published 40 years later as *Recollections of an Excursion to the Monasteries of Alcobaça and Batalha*. Here in Alcobaça he found 300 monks, including servants, 'living in a splendid manner'. In the kitchen he admired the vast wooden table and observed: '… pastry in vast abundance which a numerous tribe of lay brothers and their attendants were rolling out and puffing up into

Infante Dom Pedro and Inês de Castro

The epic love story of Pedro and Inês has become inextricably bound up in the folklore of Portugal. Ideal subject matter for minstrels and poets, it is a classic tale of uncontrollable passion, jealousy, intrigue and gory revenge. The die was cast as soon as Inês arrived from Spain to attend her cousin Constanza, with whom she had been brought up and who had married Pedro, son of Afonso IV, in 1340. As soon as Pedro laid eyes on Inês he fell madly in love, which led to her banishment from court. When Constanza died in 1345, Inês returned and went to live with Pedro as his mistress, bearing him several children.

Inês de Castro's only crime appears to have been her Spanish connections – she had a Galician nobleman for a father and ambitious brothers. Jealousy and suspicion over Inês' foreign connections gained momentum. Afonso IV forbade their marriage on the grounds that she was a potential Spanish influence over the heir to the throne, but ignoring his father's wishes, Pedro whisked Inês off to Bragança where it is claimed they married secretly in 1354. Prime movers in the political intrigue at court were three nobles, Pedro Coelho, Diogo Pacheco and Álvaro Gonçalves, who persuaded Afonso that Inês would have to be disposed of permanently. At first the king gave his agreement but, when it came to the crunch, backed down. Fired with zeal for their mission, the three nobles took matters into their own hands and sought out Inês in the grounds of what is now the Quinta das Lágrimas in Coimbra, where they murdered her in cold blood on 7 January 1355.

Pedro was inconsolable and threatened revolt. Intervention by the archbishop of Braga seemed to cool the situation and an uneasy truce was negotiated between Pedro and his father. Two years later, when Pedro succeeded to the throne, he gave full rein to his vengeance and hunted down the perpetrators of the crime. Pacheco managed to elude capture but Coelho and Gonçalves were tracked down and executed at Santarém. In the meantime, Pedro swore before the Cortes (national assembly) that he had indeed married Inês at Bragança. He had her body removed from its tomb in the church of Santa Clara (now Santa Clara-a-Velha) and setting her on a throne at his side, he crowned her as his queen and forced his courtiers to kiss her decomposing hand before she was finally entombed in the church at Alcobaça.

Each of the lovers' tombs is inscribed with the motto 'Até ao Fim do Mundo' ('Until the End of the World'), and Pedro expressly left instructions that the tombs be placed foot to foot, so that on Judgement Day the first thing to meet their eyes will be each other.

During the ten years of his reign, Pedro I diverted his all-consuming passion into the administration of justice and became known as the Justeiro (Justicer).

a hundred different shapes, singing all the while as blithely as larks in a corn field. "There," said the Abbot, "we shall not starve. God's bounties are great, it is fit that we should enjoy them".'

Next to the kitchen is the huge **refectory** with a vaulted roof supported by columns with foliate capitals. A colonnaded staircase within the wall here leads to a pulpit. On the other side of the kitchen, reached by climbing stairs, is the **dormitory,** again with a ribbed vaulted roof, here sustained by two rows of columns. From the south end there is a view down across the transepts of the church.

The rest of the monastery, which includes four other cloisters, is closed to the public. Exploring Alcobaça is a rich experience to be savoured and enjoyed while allowing ample time to digest its pleasures. It seems a little unfortunate that there is another even richer feast in store only a relatively short distance away at Batalha. If the order can be dictated, visit Alcobaça first and allow ample time, preferably a day or two, before heading for Batalha.

It is worth stopping for the **Wine Museum** which lies to the right of the main road on leaving Alcobaça for Aljubarrota.

Batalha

Batalha (Battle Abbey) was built to commemorate the Battle of Aljubarrota. The small village of Aljubarrota passed soon after leaving Alcobaça en route to Batalha, is not the scene of the battle, despite the name. The battleground, visited shortly, is much nearer to the abbey. The main road slides past most of the village of **Aljubarrota** and it is easily missed today. There has been a settlement here for more than two millennia; the Romans called it Arruncia which became Aljamarrota under the Moors. At the end of the 12th century it was one of the 13 farming regions under the control of the monks of Alcobaça, and in 1312 it received special privileges, among them the rights to press oil, to make wine and to bake bread. Dom Manuel I declared Aljubarrota a city in 1514 and it became the administrative centre for the area until this role passed to Alcobaça in 1833. Brites de Almeida, a baker's wife, became locally famous when she reputedly killed seven Spaniards single handedly with her oven-peel (Baker's shovel) in 1385 during skirmishes in the battle of Aljubarrota. She is commemorated by a statue, shown holding a long-handled baker's peel, whilst the name of the guesthouse here, *Casa da Padeira* (the House of the Baker), takes advantage of this locally popular story.

For the Aljubarrota battleground, turn right following signs to São Jorge just south of Batalha; the greenfield site, marked by a chapel and symbolic lines of soldiers, lies immediately on the left.

Worth visiting on the site is the **military museum** which attempts to re-create life at the time and illustrate the military hardware available to the soldiers. Drawings show how the weapons were used and models are used to great effect to depict the battle formations.

The Battle of Aljubarrota

The Battle of Aljubarrota was one of the defining moments in the history of the country. In 1383, when the first dynasty – the House of Burgundy – came to an end, Portugal was suddenly caught up in rivalries with Spain. The past decades had been troubled by frequent battles with the Castilians, and marriages and alliances between the royal families of Portugal and Spain had been used partly to build bridges but mostly to keep the old enemy at bay. This almost proved the country's undoing on the demise of the last Burgundian king, Dom Fernando. His 12-year-old daughter Beatriz had married the recently widowed Juan I, King of Castile, on the understanding that she would eventually succeed to the Portuguese throne and Juan would bear the title of King Consort. However, on the death of Dom Fernando, his unpopular wife Leonor Teles assumed the throne as Queen Mother together with her lover, Galician count João Fernandez Andeiro.

Juan instantly ordered that Beatriz should be declared queen and prepared to enter Portugal, but João, Master of Avis (a military-religious order) and illegitimate son of Dom Pedro I, also laid claim to the throne. His first action was to assassinate Andeiro, Leonor's lover. The country was divided: the support of the nobility and clergy fell behind Leonor while João won support amongst the middle classes. After the death of Andeiro, Leonor fled to Juan of Castile and both sides made preparation for war. On 6 April 1385, with popular support, João was crowned Dom João I and a new dynasty, the House of Avis, was born.

On 14 August of the same year the new king was forced to defend his title against the Castilian enemy in a battle on these fields near Batalha. The Portuguese army, captained by Nuno Álvares Pereira, heard mass at Porto de Mós before marching to take up position here on the battlefield at dawn. Juan, approaching from Leiria with vastly superior numbers, made a flanking move to approach from the west. The Portuguese troops, reinforced with a small contingent of English archers, took up carefully prepared positions and waited to engage the enemy. Before battle commenced Dom João I prayed to the Virgin Mary for support and promised to build her a great church should his forces win.

The Spanish forces, supported by some Portuguese aristocracy opposed to Dom João I, were undisciplined and too eager to engage. Unplanned preliminary skirmishes led to a full battle which had lasted barely an hour when the Spanish royal standard went down, throwing the Castilians into panic. Juan himself escaped towards Santarém, his troops were overrun by the Portuguese and as many as 2500 were slaughtered. A great victory was recorded which secured the monarchy for almost two centuries and with it the country's independence.

The impressive façade of Batalha Abbey

The town of Batalha owes its existence to the **Monastery of Saint Mary of Victory** (Mosteiro de Santa Maria da Vitória). Dom João offered the abbey to the Dominicans and the plan is in general accord with their principles but otherwise incorporates the best elements of architectural styles prevalent at the time. Some details recall the English Perpendicular style, especially the façade, others show French influences as in the tracery of the windows; German elements too can be observed, particularly the spire. The result is a masterpiece of Portuguese architecture which rivals anything in Europe from this period.

Work started on the abbey in 1388, three years after the battle and continued in phases to reach completion around 1515. Dom João I built the church, the founder's chapel, the first cloister and the chapter house using Afonso Domingues, a Portuguese architect, and then one Huguet, a foreigner thought to be English since it was he who was responsible for the façade which contains vertical elements associated with the English style. Dom Duarte, the eldest son of Dom João, carried on the work and built the octagonal chapel behind the apse (1437) while Dom Afonso V commissioned the construction of the second cloister (1438–77). Two masters from Évora, Martins Vasques and his nephew Fernão de Évora, were used for this latter work and it reflects the austere Gothic style of Alentejo. The final major phase of building was between 1485 and 1515, in the Manueline period, when the Unfinished Chapels were largely built and some carving to fill the arches in the Royal Cloisters was added.

The main road to Leiria once gave the abbey a respectfully wide berth but the route was recently rerouted and, in spite of many protests, constructed close to the monument. Passing motorists can now enjoy an excellent view

Architecture in Portugal

Influenced perhaps by the country's early history or simply reflecting the nature of the people, Portuguese buildings often have the solidity of Roman construction. Stable rectangular forms have their clean lines emphasised by a neat facing of white plaster which leaves the bare stone of the aperture frames and structural members free. Portuguese architects have always favoured horizontal structures, so that most buildings are of no great height, and have not shown any inclination towards curves and domes. Even in the Romanesque churches of the north, the curved apse is often ignored in favour of a square wall. The oval plan favoured by church architects of Germany, Austria and Italy in the 17th and 18th centuries was almost completely ignored, although Nasoni built the 18th-century Clérigos church in Porto in this style. Domes too are rare in Portugal and barrel-vaulted roofs are by no means common.

In total contrast to this simplicity of line and style, the Portuguese found great delight and demonstrated extraordinary creative talent in surface decoration. This is evident in the decorative sculptures on the Romanesque churches, where doorways are often adorned with carvings. The Manueline, Baroque and Rococo periods provided opportunities for expanding this art which was fully embraced by the sculptors, stonemasons and woodcarvers of the time.

This same genius for surface decoration spread inside the church, especially to the retable behind the altar which evolved into a highly carved and usually gilded piece of woodwork, often embellished with cherubs and vine leaves. Uniquely Portuguese, this style developed until sometimes the whole church interior was entirely covered in carved and gilded wood.

Gothic architecture, which brings together a number of elements like the pointed arch, the principle of the flying buttress as half arches or half tunnel vaults, and generally more slender elements, was introduced by the Cistercians; the most outstanding early example is the abbey of Santa Maria de Alcobaça (1178–1252). The style only really found support towards the end of the 16th century and reached full expression in the Monastery of Batalha.

The Manueline style, which developed out of late Gothic, sprang from the great riches pouring into the country and it represents Portugal's unique contribution to the world's architecture. Its peak coincided roughly with the reign of Dom Manuel (1495–1521), after whom the style was named (but not until much later). Apart from lavish surface decoration, the style also involved transformation of structural members, with a particular passion for twisted columns and ribs. There was no great uniformity within Manueline architecture, which used borrowed ideas like sea motifs, and incorporated other effects such as *mudéjar* elements – a style which evolved in Spain when Christian architects absorbed Muslim influences. Most of the finest examples of Manueline occur south of Coimbra, with Jerónimos monastery at Belém and the Convent of Christ at Tomar, the latter famous for its carved stone window frames with twisted tree trunks, coral, knots and ropes.

Preoccupation with Manueline meant that Italian Renaissance was late in reaching Portugal – its influence creeps in around 1530 at the earliest. French architects were the first practitioners in this return to the harmony, stability and poise of the Greco-Roman style which extended to statues, portals, retables, tombs and whole chapels. Amongst the most elegant and harmonious of the early works is the chapel of São Pedro in the Old Cathedral at Coimbra (1537). From the middle of the 16th century, Portuguese architecture responded to changes arising in Italy and evolved the Mannerist style. This involved a shift away from the basic classical proportions to characteristic distortion and exaggeration to present an ideal of beauty opposed to a simple representation.

Baroque architecture emerged in Europe in the 17th century and was initially resisted in Portugal. This style is characterised by exuberant decoration, curvaceous form, a delight in large-scale and sweeping vistas with a preference for depth over plane as in the Baroque staircase leading to the sanctuary of Bom Jesus near Braga, for example. It was gold and diamonds from Brazil and the munificence of João V which attracted foreign craftsmen to Portugal and stimulated architectural advances. Complex surface ornamentation was not neglected and the Portuguese took to woodcarving with particular enthusiasm, retables emerging with twisted chestnut columns decorated with theatrically gilded grapevines and birds.

The first truly Baroque church is Santa Engrácia in Lisbon, begun in 1682 but not actually completed until 1966, whilst the most extravagant project launched by João V was the huge complex of Mafra Palace near Sintra. A movement away from the dark and ponderous Baroque to the lightness and colour of Rococo represented the dying phase of this style of architecture, which eventually faded away around the middle of the 18th century.

of the front of the monastery without leaving their cars. The **façade** is worth a much closer look than that, however. Built in honey-coloured limestone, the vertical elements are immediately striking but there is a delicacy in the detail that needs more than a moment to absorb. Pinnacles adorn every semblance of a column and fine tracery balustrades decorate the whole of the front. Anxious to see the inside, many visitors enter the portal without stopping, yet there is so much to admire in the craftsmanship and carvings. In the tympanum, above the door, is Christ enthroned with Evangelists, while the archivolts are filled with tiny figures of angels, kings and saints. The larger figures, representing Christ's twelve disciples are copies – the originals can be seen in the museum room inside. A wander around the outside of the building to explore its proportions and wealth of architectural detail is suggested at some time; in any case, if the Unfinished Chapels are to be visited there is no alternative but to walk around the outside since they have only an external entrance. A fine statue of Nuno Álvares Pereira mounted on his horse, fresh from leading his forces in the Battle of Aljubarrota, guards the side of the monastery.

Inside, the three-aisled lofty church has the same startling proportions and purity of form as Alcobaça. It is long (80m), narrow (22m) and tall (32m). Two rows of eight relatively plain piers separate the nave from the side aisles and help to accentuate the height. Immediately to the right on entry is the **Founder's Chapel** (Capela do Fundador), which was designed as the burial chamber of Dom João I and his family, including his English wife, Philippa of Lancaster and their son, Henry the Navigator. Cruciform piers support an octagonal lantern with some of the oldest stained-glass windows in Portugal which illuminate a star-shaped vault. In the centre lie the tombs of Dom João I and Philippa of Lancaster. Unfortunately, the tombs are raised just above eye-level which makes it difficult to appreciate the details of the craftsmanship, but the figures lie side by side and can be seen to be holding hands. Along the south wall are the tombs of their children, the princes Pedro, Henry the Navigator, João and Fernando. Dom Duarte, who succeeded João, lies in one of the Unfinished Chapels, visited shortly. All the children distinguished themselves but none achieved the fame of Henry the Navigator whose story is featured on page 131.

The tombs on the west wall of the Founder's Chapel are modern imitations and contain the remains of Afonso V (died 1481), João II (died 1495) and his only son Afonso (died 1491).

Entrance to the **Royal Cloister** is from the north aisle. This was built by the first master builder, Afonso Domingues, but the Manueline embellishments like the tracery and slender columns which fill the Gothic arches came later (1485–1515). Note the armillary sphere of Dom Manuel embodied within the tracery. The roof line of this single-storey cloister is decorated with tracery balustrades to match the exterior. Access to the **Chapter House**, the monks' meeting room, is through a graceful arch in the east walk. Designed and executed by Huguet, this large room (19m square) is remarkable for its ribbed vaulted ceiling which has no intermediate supports and is claimed to be one of the boldest vaults of Gothic architecture in the Iberian Peninsula. It is said to have collapsed at least twice during its construction. The **Adega dos Frades**, the monks' cellar, on the north side, now contains some museum pieces including original carvings removed from the front portal and replaced with copies. The adjacent **Cloister of Afonso V**, smaller and simpler than the Royal Cloister, is the work of Fernão de Évora.

Infante Dom Henrique – Henry the Navigator 1394–1460

The foundations of the British connection with Portugal were cemented in 1385 when, with the aid of English archers, João I defeated the Castilians at the battle of Aljubarrota. In gratitude for English assistance in securing Portugal's independence, the Treaty of Windsor was signed in 1386 as a declaration of lasting peace between the two countries. More than anything, it served as formal confirmation of an earlier Anglo-Portuguese Alliance of 1373. As a further seal of good intent, John of Gaunt, Duke of Lancaster, a signatory to the Treaty, gave his daughter Philippa of Lancaster in marriage to João I. They were married in Porto cathedral on 14 February 1387, and their third son Henry, later known as Henry the Navigator, was born in 1394.

A serious son of an equally studious and serious mother, Henry's curiosity regarding seafaring matters was most likely developed during childhood whilst growing up close to the Douro riverside in Porto. What motivated Henry is a matter of conjecture but expeditions were still very much bound up with the Crusades. Interest in voyages of discovery was fuelled by talk of the legendary Christian Kingdom of Prester John and its untold riches, said to lie somewhere in Africa. Conquering Moorish lands in North Africa was a prerequisite to gaining access to the hinterland of that continent; the seeds had been sown for thoughts of wider possibilities.

With a fleet of 200 ships, the building of which Henry himself supervised, he set sail from Porto with his father and brother on a Crusade against Ceuta in North Africa where they won a resounding victory. A lasting impression on Henry was not so much the victory itself as the oriental riches they looted. What of these lands where such a wealth of gold, silver, silks and spices originated? Henry returned to Portugal a thoughtful man but his energies were still channelled into taming the north coast of Africa. Only later, on hearing tales from other sailors, was Henry drawn into the search further afield although he himself remained a landlubber after his foray to north Africa.

Taking himself off down to the untamed wilderness of Sagres in Algarve, Henry established an observatory and school of navigation, where he devoted time, effort and money to improving navigational aids and boat design. Using revenue from his position as Duke of Viseu, Governor of the Algarve and also Governor of the Order of Christ, he gathered together experts in astronomy and astrology, cartography and geography as well as knowledgeable mariners. His shipyard at Lagos built the boats, and from here they set sail, the red Cross of Christ, emblem of the Order of Christ, prominently displayed on their white sails. Trading gradually took precedence over crusading as Henry developed a tidy business from financing and equipping excursions down the west coast of Africa.

A huge leap forward came in the form of a new boat, the caravel, which Henry and his team designed and perfected. The caravel's light weight gave it manoeuvrability and speed, whilst a shallow draught enabled it to sail close inshore. Another advantage was the need for a smaller crew, giving more storage space for goods.

Under Henry's patronage Gil Eanes finally passed Cape Bojador on Africa's west coast in 1434, a barrier beyond which 15 earlier expeditions had been too afraid to penetrate. Explorers were encouraged to set up trading posts at each new landing place, where they erected stone pillars (*padrões*) topped by a cross and engraved with the Portuguese coat of arms. They also brought back samples of plant life, fruit and nuts. It was to be a further decade before Gil Eanes returned with the first cargo of African slaves, which prompted an escalation of trade along the west coast of Africa.

An austere man who shunned worldly pleasures in favour of a monkish existence, Henry remains something of an enigma, his striving after wealth inconsistent with a frugal personal image. Desire for wealth to fuel his life's interest at Sagres seems a more probable motive than personal gain. By the time he died at Sagres in 1460, his expeditions had reached as far as Sierra Leone.

Extending from the rear of the church are the **Unfinished Chapels** (Capelas Imperfeitas) which can be accessed only from the outside. Although they were started in 1435 by Huguet, much of the Manueline decoration was completed in the last phase of work between 1485 and 1515. Open to the skies, the chapel complex houses the tomb of Dom Duarte (1433–38), son of João I. Built around an octagonal centre are seven radiating chapels with the eighth side occupied by a remarkable doorway considered a masterpiece of Manueline art. An inscription repeated frequently in the arch is the motto of Dom Duarte, '*leauté faray tam yaserey*' ('loyal I shall ever be'). The tombs of Dom Duarte and his queen, Leonor of Aragón, lie in the chapel opposite the door; the Duke of Aveiro and an infant son of Dom Afonso V are also entombed in this chapel.

The surrounding town is full of the usual tourist shops out to trap their share of custom from the great tide of visitors who sweep through daily. While the cafés are good for coffee and cakes, the restaurants do not need to try too hard with so much custom. Batalha cannot therefore be recommended as a place to eat.

Exploring the coastal region

There are two resorts on the west coast worth visiting which can easily be incorporated in one trip. The first of these, Nazaré, is a popular resort living on a past reputation, while the other, São Martinho do Porto, is a small but expanding summer resort.

Nazaré

Lying just 11km (7 miles) west of Alcobaça, Nazaré is quickly reached by road. Don't expect the traditional fishing village of old with teams of oxen busy pulling brightly painted sardine fishing boats up onto the sand. All that changed some years ago although attempts are still made to sustain the image. The oxen were replaced with tractors long ago but even these are redundant since there is now a new port to the south for the fishing boats. However, the huge sweep of fine golden sand ending abruptly under the cliffs to the north is still there and still as popular as ever. High summer sees the town under strain from the weight of visitors and the sands crowded with tents, awnings and sun umbrellas shading an even greater number of bodies. Ladies in coloured headscarves arrive on the beach with buckets of fish on their heads and still go about their business of drying fish on racks using the free heat of the sun – and all this amidst the ebb and flow of curious tourists.

Bars, cafés and the inevitable souvenir shops are scattered plentifully around, but there is not too much to see in the way of buildings, except perhaps for the narrow streets lined with fishermen's cottages in the lower town at the end beneath the cliffs. The other part of Nazaré, **Sitio**, sits on top of the 110m cliff top which can be reached by funicular or by road. It offers a dramatic view down over the Praia area of Nazaré but little else except – as always – a church. This one, Nossa Senhora de Nazaré, was built originally at the behest of a 12th-century knight, Fuas Roupinho, who was in danger of riding over the cliff one foggy day while out hunting a deer. Fortunately, he was saved at the last moment by a timely vision of Our Lady of Nazaré after whom the church is named. The present 17th-century chapel replaces the hermitage built by Fuas Roupinho in 1182.

São Martinho do Porto

The road leading south out of Nazaré runs first past the new fishing port then onward down the coast to the emerging resort of São Martinho do Porto. An almost complete circle of fine sand dominates the landlocked bay which has the smallest of openings to the sea. With such good shelter, the sea is shallow, calm and warm and offers some of the best swimming on the west coast although there is a downside; pollution can sometimes be a problem. The town's resources have not been able to keep up with its sudden rise in popularity so finding accommodation here can be difficult throughout the main season.

The traditional method of drying fish in the sun is still practised in Nazaré

The Natural Park of Serras de Aire and Candeeiros

For a refreshing change from an over-rich diet of monasteries and monuments, head for the Natural Park of Serras de Aire and Candeeiros, just to the east of Alcobaça, to explore limestone countryside, deep caves and the castle of Porto de Mós. The town of Porto de Mós is an entry point to the park and a good place to start a tour.

Porto de Mós

It is the **castle** capped with green cones and standing on a hill above the village, which is the main attraction. There was clearly a settlement here in Roman times – some of the stonework in the present castle is Roman and bears votive inscriptions. The Visigoths were here to remodel the fort and later it was taken over by the Moors. Dom Afonso Henriques conquered the castle in 1148 and appointed the legendary Fuas Roupinho as its alcaïde; this was the same Fuas Roupinho who featured later in the miracle of Nazaré and proved the scourge of the Moors on both land and sea. With the Moors still troublesome, Dom Sancho I (1185–1211) carried out large-scale reinforcements and Dom Dinis (1279–1325) ordered further strengthening. The army of Dom João I rested here on the way to the Battle of Aljubarrota (see feature on page 126), and the king later gave the castle to Nuno Álvares Pereira in gratitude for his role in leading the troops. The castle passed with his title, Count of Ourém, down to his grandson, Afonso, who was a cultured and much travelled man. Afonso endeavoured to convert the castle into a palace by hiding its strong military lines. Ourém castle received similar modifications under his ownership and there are some strong similarities between the two castles.

Built on an irregular pentagonal plan with five towers, one at each corner, the castle was severely damaged in the great earthquake of 1755 and further damaged in 1919, again by an earthquake. The National Monument Service carried out work to restore it to its present state. Now only four towers project above the walls and two of these are capped by green pinnacles. The castellations are no longer evident but the distinctive and decorative elongated corbels on the walls and towers are preserved.

Although the town itself is pleasant, there is little to detain visitors from heading straight away into the natural park. The route due south on the EN 362 to Mendiga is perhaps the most picturesque in the park and offers an overview of the park's typical limestone scenery, with dry valleys, walled fields and dolines (the funnel-shaped depressions formed by solution). An alternative route, and the one followed here, goes through the Vale de Alvados to Mira de Aire and has the advantage of good park scenery, three magnificent caves and the option to extend the tour to Torres Novas.

Limestone grottoes

All three caves lie relatively close together and all are sufficiently different to be worth visiting. The temperature inside the caves is relatively constant at 16–18°C so, if the weather is hot, it is a good escape from the heat. Grutas de Alvados and Grutas de Santo António lie on a spur off the main road and are conveniently visited together, but there is no especially recommended order. If only one is visited then Mira de Aire is the best choice.

Grutas de Mira de Aire is the largest of the caves and was first discovered on 27 July 1947. Although some 4km (2.5 miles) have been explored, only around 700m is open to the public. There are over 600 steps leading steadily down through well illuminated caverns, with imaginative names like Hell's Mouth and Spaghetti Cavern attached to particular caverns or recognisable shapes amongst the stalactites and other rock formations. Visitors are taken down in groups in the company of a guide who may, with luck, speak English, but written information in English, is posted in various halls. The climax of the visit is the underground river with bright and colourful illuminated fountains, one resembling a green Christmas tree. Having descended through some 110m over 45 minutes, the return by elevator is more than welcome. There is a small seasonal aquatic park outside this cave with a water slide, swimming pools, a sunbathing area and a café. All-day tickets are available (10.30am–8pm) or half-day tickets (3pm–8pm).

Grutas de Santo António was discovered in June 1955 by two men who observed a bird disappear into a crack in a rock. The sound of silence is masked by piped music while exploring this cave, essentially one huge cavern offering superb stalagmite displays and some striking vistas. Taken gently, the tour around the cave lasts about 20 minutes and it is necessary to cope with some ups and downs. There is a huge car park and café facilities on site.

Grutas de Alvados came to light in 1964 when a group of men working in nearby marble quarries noticed that stones falling into a particular hole took a long time to drop. It took workmen two years to provide access to the cave for the public but the result is an attractive walk through a succession of caverns. While it may not have the dramatic vistas of the other two caves, Grutas de Alvados does offer some very beautiful cameos featuring stalactites and stalagmites, with some joined as columns. It takes around 20 minutes to walk through from the bottom entrance up ramps and steps to emerge at the pay area, although the gain in height is not great.

If time allows, the road through the mill town of Mira de Aire leads beyond the IP1 motorway to the industrial town of Torres Novas dominated by its 14th-century castle, although only the outer walls and towers now remain. Just north of the town is the Vila Cardilo (1st to 4th century) with little standing above ground but with some remarkable geometric mosaics. Normally protected by sand, these are uncovered for visitors if the caretaker is around. In the Lapas area, to the north-west, are some cave-like cellars which have puzzled historians over the years.

Exploring east of the region

Tomar is not strictly in the Rota do Sol area but it can be conveniently reached from the region with Fátima and Ourém to visit along the way and, if time permits, one of Portugal's most romantic castles, Almourol.

The EN 356 out of Batalha leads eastwards towards Fátima which while holding no special interest for general sightseers, is a magnet for the religious.

Fátima

Often described as the Lourdes of Portugal, Fátima attracts pilgrims by the thousand on the 12th–13th of each month, with massive crowds, topping 100,000, on those days in May and October. Those who don't attend can usually watch the event on television.

It was an unknown village in the middle of wild unaccommodating country until 1917 when, on 13 May, a vision of the Virgin Mary appeared to three children. The vision appeared again to the same three children, Lúcia, Francisco and Jacinta, on the 13th of every month until October, when 70,000 pilgrims witnessed strange movements of the sun, since known as the Miracle of the Sun. Two of the children died before the age of 12 but Lúcia, the only one who could actually converse with the apparition, eventually joined the Carmelite Convent at Pontevedra in Coimbra.

A vast white **basilica** was consecrated in 1953, built in recognition of the importance of this site to pilgrims, and in front is a huge esplanade large enough to hold hundreds of thousands of visitors. The church contains the tombs of the two visionary children who died, Jacinta and Francisco, in chapels on either side of the entrance. The original oak tree in which the Virgin first appeared has long since disappeared; in its place stands the small Chapel of Apparitions.

Large notices advise that Fátima is not for the curious but for the pilgrims, who should be respected at prayer. They also say that what matters here is the heart. Non-believers will be struck by the grotesque commercialisation, some in very questionable taste, which thrives on the sick, the poor and those who come with hope. Other notices advise you to lock your car.

The EN356 north from Fátima joins the IC9 which leads first to Ourém and then to Tomar.

Ourém

Forget the market town of Vila Nova de Ourém and climb straight up to **Ourém Velha** poised on top of an easily defended hill overlooking rolling countryside and valleys below. Park outside the entrance of this old walled enclosure and prepare to explore on foot. The castle, which existed in Moorish times, and the restored tomb of Afonso, Count of Ourém, in the crypt beneath the church, are what attract most attention, but there is also a 15th-century Gothic fountain and a 17th-century pillory to find.

The history of the castle is known only from the time it was recaptured from the Moors by Dom Afonso Henriques in 1148. Little further was done in the way of reconstruction until Dom Dinis (1279–1325) arrived on the scene, although it must have already been defensibly strong since it was used to imprison Dom Sancho II's queen in 1246. Dom Pedro I (1357–67) created the title of Count of Ourém which was held for a short period by João Fernandes Andeiro, lover of Dona Leonor Teles, who was assassinated by João in events leading up to the Battle of Aljubarrota (see feature page 126). After the battle, Dom João I awarded the title to Nuno Álvares Pereira who later, on entering the Convento do Carmo at the age of 62, passed it to his grandson Afonso. It was this wealthy and much travelled man who attempted to convert the castle into a fit place to live and was responsible for the Italian-influenced additional decoration seen also on his other castle, Porto de Mós. Still to be seen is the base of a round tower and the secret passage which connected it to the castle.

Afonso, the Count of Ourém who would have become the Duke of Bragança had he not died before his father, lies in the crypt below the church, entered by a side door. It was desecrated by Napoleon's retreating troops early in the 19th century when they were searching for loot.

From here, the ride through attractive countryside to Tomar (20km/12.5 miles) is quickly accomplished.

Tomar

The small town of Tomar with its cobbled streets and flowery window boxes nestles on the banks of the River Nabão. Overlooking this peaceful scene are the crenellated walls of a 12th-century castle enclosing the **Convento de Cristo**, headquarters of the Knights Templar and enduring symbol of the power and importance which once resided in this now quiet part of the country.

Founded by the French in Jerusalem during the first Crusade, around 1118, the **Knights Templar** were a religious military order pledged to defend the Holy Sepulchre, protect Christians and fight the Moors. In 1157, in recognition of their services in helping to expel the Moors from Portugal, they were rewarded with a gift of land, the site of the old Roman Nabantia on the banks of the river. Work was started on a church and a castle but was abandoned in 1160 in favour of the present, more secure hill site. After a second false start, the Grand Master, Gualdim Pais, finally selected a satisfactory site and, in 1162, the church, the Charola, was built within fortified walls. By 1190 it was sufficiently reinforced to withstand an attack by the Almohad forces.

Answerable only to the Pope, the Templars became rich and powerful through the land and castles they demanded for their services. Feeling his authority threatened by their growing power, Pope Clement V ordered them to be disbanded around 1307. Spain took vigorous action against the knights, many of whom took refuge in Portugal, but a reluctant Dom Dinis only nominally enforced this papal decree, dissolving the order in 1314. Recognising

Manueline architecture seen at its most exuberant and ornate in the Santa Barbara window at Tomar

their utility to the crown, he allowed the order to reform in 1319 under the banner of the Order of Christ and to inherit the wealth and extensive property of the Templars. Its first headquarters was at Castro Marim in Algarve, then moved to Tomar in 1356. Henry the Navigator was Grand Master of the order from 1417 to 1460. Under his leadership, the red Cross of Christ was emblazoned on the white sails of the discoverers' caravels. In 1492, the Mastership passed to Dom Manuel and subsequently remained with the crown.

Built over a period from the 12th to the 17th centuries, the monastery complex has at its heart the **Charola**, the original church modelled on the Rotunda of the Holy Sepulchre in Jerusalem. It is a 16-sided church with the high altar enclosed in a central octagon. On the east side, a passage leads to two cloisters built on the instruction of Henry the Navigator: the Claustro do Cemitério decorated with *azulejos* and the Claustro da Lavagem. When Dom Manuel succeeded to the Grand Mastership in 1492, he invested some of the country's seemingly endless flow of wealth into building a rectangular nave to the west of the Charola. This was built on two storeys with the lower serving as a chapter house and the upper as the Coro Alto (choir). The highly decorative Flamboyant Gothic south portal leading directly into the nave was designed and built in 1515 by the architect João de Castilho. He later carried out considerable modifications to the monastery when Dom João III ascended to the throne in 1521 and converted the Order into a monastic brotherhood. This resulted in the addition of dormitories, kitchens and four new cloisters. Ascending from the nave, you come to the upper storey of the Renaissance-style Great Cloister which abuts the chapter house, partially obscuring one of its fine windows. From a gallery here there is a view of the famous, highly ornate **Santa Bárbara window** located on the west wall of the chapter house. The frame is a contorted mass of ropes, seaweed and coral-stems in an extravagant expression of the Manueline style. It is crowned by the Cross of the Order of Christ surmounting the royal arms and flanked by the armillary spheres of Dom Manuel, and all is supported by the figure of an old sailor with the roots and stump of a tree on his shoulders. Steps here lead down into the Claustro de Santa Bárbara from where there is an even closer view of the window.

Leaving the south portal and keeping to the right leads down to an access point to the castle walls and also gives a view of the aqueduct which once brought water to the monastery. From there, the rampart of the castle walls can be walked all the way back to the main entrance.

The Town

Wandering the old quarters of the town will bring you eventually to the Praça da República which is bounded on one side by the elegant 17th-century town hall and on the other by **Igreja São João Baptista**. The church is remarkable for its octagonal belfry standing on a square tower and for its elaborate Flamboyant Gothic doorway. Inside there are 14th-century paintings by Gregório Lopes, one of Portugal's most famous painters. To the south of the church, in Rua Dr Joaquim Jacinto, stands a 14th-century **synagogue** which houses a small museum of ancient inscriptions in Hebrew. Water pitchers, embedded high in the corners of the room, act as sound amplifiers. The Jews suffered extensively under the Inquisition (see the feature on page 15, and this is one of the few remaining synagogues in Portugal. It was vacated in 1496 when the Jews were under pressure and all signs of worship were removed. Bought by a private individual, it was resold around 1516 for use as the town prison, which had been in the castle until then. On 29 July 1921, the building was recognised as a National Monument.

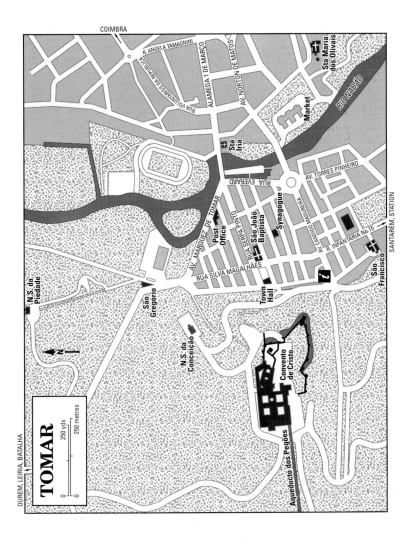

Almourol Castle

The onward route from Tomar follows south down the IC3 then out eastwards along the IP6. Once through Vila Nova da Barquinha, it is only a short distance to Tancos and the first glimpse of the castle out on the River Tagus. Follow the sign to the right which leads down to the river bank where a rowing boat waits to ferry visitors across.

Almourol castle enriches a location which inspires painters to paint and photographers to take more pictures than they will ever need. All it lacks is a fairy-tale princess with long, flowing hair looking over the battlements.

The Romans loved the location and built a castle there, although they were probably not the first builders on the site. It was an especially important fortification in those early years, since the river was a key route for communication and, with a plentiful supply of fish, attracted many settlements. After the Romans, the castle had a succession of new tenants: the Visigoths, the Moors and, finally, the Christians. After its recapture from the Moors by Afonso Henriques in 1147, it was entrusted to the Knights Templar since it fell within the lands awarded to them for their assistance in overcoming the Moors. The Grand Master Gualdim Pais rebuilt the castle and left an inscription over the door. After the demise of the Knights Templar, the castle passed to the Order of Avis but gradually, with the Moors effectively extinguished, the defensive role of the castle was no longer required and its military garrison was withdrawn. Although time and the elements weathered the castle, its isolated river location protected it from being despoiled by those seeking to reuse its stone. In the second half of the 19th century it was taken over by the National Monuments department.

Anything but regular in shape, Almourol castle crowns its rocky, granite island, towering to a height of 18m. Round towers of varying diameters, ten in all, strengthen the outer walls and there is a stout square keep with two wooden floors. Battlements, ramparts and arrow slits are reminders of its original purpose. There is no entrance fee to explore the castle which takes only a few minutes, but the ferryman extracts a small charge on return.

Northern Rota do Sol

Except for two major towns, Leiria and Pombal, which can both be explored while moving northwards out of the region towards Coimbra, the northern section has little to detain the visitor.

Leiria

Reached by following the main road north from Batalha, Leiria is a busy town usually humming with traffic, and parking is not easy. It is best to head straight up to the imposing castle on the hill where there is parking space, and use that as a base for exploring both the town and castle. On entering the

Romantic Almoural castle crowns a rocky island in the River Tagus

town follow signs first to Turismo and from there the castle is signposted.

The palace-castle of Leiria changed hands a few times in the battles against the Moors. In 1135, Afonso Henriques had control of the castle, virtually rebuilt it and left it well garrisoned, but it was retaken by the Moors two years later. It remained in the battle line for some time and constantly changed hands until, by 1144, it was firmly back with the Christians. Such was the importance invested in this castle that a settlement was encouraged and this grew fairly rapidly. The very first Cortes was held at the castle in 1254 indicating its importance and, following that, Dom Dinis (1279–1325) carried out considerable reconstruction work and lived there for long periods with his wife, Dona Isabel. Leiria was lost to the French under General Junot in the Peninsular War early in the 19th century and they sacked and looted the town on their retreat.

Enclosed within the **castle** walls are the keep and the ruins of a 15th-century church, Nossa Senhora da Penha, and forming part of the walls is the royal palace itself. The keep is intact but not usually open to the public. A delightful Gothic doorway of five archivolts leads into the ruins of the simple, unadorned apsidal church erected by João I, now open to the sky. The palace has received more recent renovations and is still used for certain functions. Perhaps its most outstanding feature is the elegant loggia with a view down to the town through eight Gothic arches supported on a double row of columns. Each of the arches is provided with window seats.

Below the castle lies the old part of town which is easily reached on foot. The place to head for first is the tall 16th-century cathedral in Largo de Sé, but the heart of the old town lies around Praça Rodrigues Lobo where there are some fine arcaded buildings. The narrow side streets hide plenty of cafés where you can try some of the local specialities which include *bolo de pinhão*, a cake made with pine nuts, and *brisas do Lis*, an egg and almond fantasy.

Pombal

There is no reason for stopping at Pombal other than to see the **castle**. The Romans might have defended the hill where it stands, but there is no evidence apart from a find of Roman coins, so it was essentially deserted when Dom Afonso Henriques handed the territory to the Knights Templar. In 1160, under the direction of the Grand Master Gualdim Pais, a castle quickly rose providing safe conditions for settling the immediate area. How it came to be named 'Pombal', which means dovecote, is not really known but the best guess is that it attracted more pigeons than people in its early life. Typical of the Templars' constructions, this is another towering castle with the walls strengthened by angle-towers, ten in this case. There is no public access to the sturdy keep but the extensive walls remain in excellent condition. It is possible to walk around the ramparts but these are without guard rails and not for the nervous or young children.

The town's main claim to fame is that it gave its name to Sebastião José de Carvalho e Melo (1699–1782) when he was elevated to Marquês. Marquês de Pombal, a brilliant but dictatorial minister (featured on page 63), retired here in disgrace in 1777 and died at his residence in the main square.

Practical Information

Hotels and Restaurants

ALCOBAÇA
Hotel Santa Maria, Rua Dr Francisco Zagalo (tel. 062 597 395). The only hotel in town, two star but good and reasonably priced, 34 rooms.
Pensão Carações Unidos, Rua Frei António Brandão, 39 (tel. 062 42 142). A cheap and cheerful three-star pension with 16 rooms. The restaurant downstairs offers even better value.
Restaurant Celeiro dos Frades, Arco de Cister, 2. Fairly basic but popular restaurant; inexpensive.

ALJUBARROTA
Casa da Padeira, (tel. 062 508 272). Attractive country house, part of Turismo Rural, in quiet location offering eight rooms in the main house with apartments in the grounds, swimming pool.
Restaurant Casa da Sofia. Located in the old village, near the shopping centre, this restaurant offers traditional Portuguese food at a reasonable price.

BATALHA
Motel São Jorge, Casal da Amieira (tel. 044 96 210). This three-star motel offers 34 rooms and reasonable facilities which include swimming and tennis.
Pousada do Mestre Afonso Domingues (tel. 044 96 260). A new building within sight of Batalha Abbey, this *pousada* offers 21 rooms, which include two suites, and a restaurant.
Quinta do Figaldo, (tel. 044 96 114). Close to Batalha Abbey yet in a quiet location surrounded by gardens, this 17th-century house full of period furniture offers four rooms.

FÁTIMA
Fátima has more accommodation that any other town in the region but, even so, many of these are booked up by the endless Portuguese and international pilgrimage groups which visit the town throughout the year. Avoid particularly the 12th–13th of every month from May through to October. Two possibilities are:
Hotel de Fátima, Rua João Paulo II, Cova da Iria (tel. 049 532 351). A large four-star hotel with 126 bedrooms. Facilities include covered parking and restaurant.
Hotel Pax, Rua Francisco Marto, 52, (tel. 049 533 330). With 76 rooms this three-star hotel is not especially large for this town but it does offer good facilities, including a restaurant.

LEIRIA
Hotel Dom João III, Av. D. João III (tel. 044 812 500). This comfortable three-star hotel with 64 rooms is about the best in town, facilities include a restaurant.
Hotel Eurosol, Rua D. José Alves Correia de Silva (tel. 044 812 201). Located on the southern side of town, this large three star hotel also has an adjacent sister hotel, **Hotel Eurosol Jardim**, of similar standard. They share the swimming pool.
Hotel Lis, Largo Alexandre Herculano, 10 (tel. 044 814 017). Two-star hotel by the river bridge, fairly basic but inexpensive.
Monte Carlo, Rua Dr Correia Mateus, 32/4. A good restaurant serving generous portions; inexpensive.
Restaurant O Manuel, Rua Dr Correia Mateus, 50. Good Portuguese food in robust portions at a moderate price.
Tromba Rija, Rua Professores Portelas, Marrazes (tel. 044 32 072). Just out of town to the north, this is the best restaurant in the area. Good home cooking of typical Portuguese dishes and at moderate prices.

NAZARÉ
For an important seaside resort, there are surprisingly few hotels, just four, but a larger number of pensions, although many quite small. Expect to find it booked up in high season.

Hotel de Nazaré, Av. Largo Afonso Zuquete (tel. 062 561 311). Just off the esplanade, this three star 52 roomed hotel is the largest in town.

Hotel Praia, Av. Vieira Guimarães, 39 (tel. 062 561 423). The limited facilities at this three-star hotel do include covered parking.

Residencial Beira Mar, Rua dos Lavradores (tel. 062 561 358). One of the brighter two-star pensions with 15 rooms, reasonably priced.

Most of the numerous eating places are concentrated along the seafront, Av. da República, and the roads leading off it. As expected in a fishing village, fish dominates the menus and fish in Portuguese restaurants is usually expensive.

Aquário, Largo das Caldeiros, 13. Good seafood and inexpensive.

Mar Bravo, Praça Sousa Oliveira. A very popular seafood restaurant and moderately priced.

São Miguel, Av. da República. More fish but this time with a good view, moderately priced.

TOMAR

Estalagem de Santa Iria, Parque do Mouchão (tel. 049 313 326). Located in a quiet corner of Tomar, this elegant four-star Estalagem, which offers 14 rooms, had a facelift recently. Not too many facilities but comfortable.

Hotel dos Templarios, Largo dos Reis, 1 (tel. 049 321 730). A fairly large four-star hotel with 84 rooms, it offers a good view of the Convento and plenty of facilities including restaurant and swimming pool.

Pensão Nuno Álvares, Av. D. Nuno Álvares Pereira, 3 (tel. 049312 8730). This two-star pension with 11 rooms is particularly good value, with the added benefit of a good restaurant.

Pousada São Pedro, 2300 Tomar (tel. 049 382 274). This *pousada* lies 16km (10 miles) south-east of Tomar alongside the Rio Zêzere, more particularly near the Baragem de Castelo de Bode. It offers 24 rooms including one suite.

Quinta da Anunciada Velha, Cem Soldos (tel. 049 345 218). This rustic house built on the remains of a former convent and part of the Turismo Rural scheme, offers four rooms and one apartment.

Places of Interest

ALCOBAÇA

Abbey. open daily: Apr–Sep 9am–7pm and Oct–Mar 10am–1pm and 3pm–6pm.

BATALHA

Abbey, open 9pm–6pm.

Military Museum, open 10am–12noon and 2pm–5pm, closed Mondays.

Grutas de Alvados, open Mar–Oct 9.30am–6pm early and late season and until 8pm or 9pm in high season.

Grutas de Mira de Aire, open 9am–9pm from 1 Apr to 30 Sept and 9am–7pm for the rest of the year.

SERRAS DE AIRE AND CANDEEIROS PARK
Grutas de Santo António, open Mar–Oct 9.30am–6pm early and late season and until 8pm or 9pm in high season.
TOMAR
Convento de Cristo, open: May–June 9pm–12.30pm and 2pm–5.30pm; Jul–Sep 9.15am–12.30pm and 2pm–6pm; Oct–Apr 9.15am–12.30pm and 2pm–5pm.
Synagogue, open 9.30am–12.30pm and 2pm–6pm (5pm in winter), closed Wednesdays.

Tourist Offices

Regional Office:
Jardim Luís de Camões, 2400 Leiria (tel. 044 23 773).
Tourism Posts
ALCOBAÇA Praça 25 Abril (tel. 044 42377).
BATALHA Rua N. Sr do Caminho (tel. 044 96 180).
FÁTIMA, Av. José Alves Correia da Siva (tel. 049 531 139).
NAZARÉ Av. da República (tel. 062 561 194).
OURÉM, Praça do Municipio (tel. 049 42 194).
POMBAL, Largo do Cardal (tel. 036 23 230).
PORTO DE MÓS Jardim Publico (tel. 044 491 323).
S. MARTINHO DO PORTO Praça Eng. José Frederico Ulrich (tel. 062 989 110).
TOMAR, Rua Serpa Pinto, 1 (tel. 049 323 113).

9. COIMBRA AND NORTHERN COSTA DE PRATA

Firmly woven into Portugal's historical tapestry, Coimbra holds court in this northern section of Costa de Prata. Easily accessible though, as escapes from pulsating city life, are the bucolic havens of the Serras do Buçaco and da Lousã, Bairrada wine country or bracing Atlantic coast from Figueira da Foz to the canal town of Aveiro, capital of the Rota da Luz.

Coimbra

Lying on the banks of the Mondego river, Coimbra is crowned by the university buildings perched atop Aláçova hill. The city's foundations go back into misty prehistory, but it became Roman Aeminium before taking the name Coimbra from the Roman settlement of Conimbriga close by. During more than 300 years of Moorish rule, it became an important centre of Mozarabic culture before succumbing to the Christians in 1064. Dom Afonso Henriques moved the capital of the emerging Portugal from Guimãres to Coimbra, where he was crowned in 1154. Its spell as capital was relatively short lived, that honour being transferred to Lisbon in about 1250.

After reconquest by the Christians, Coimbra became an important river port but there were problems with flood water and silt along the south bank of the river. Financed by the church as a means to produce more priests, the first university in Portugal was established in Lisbon (1290) by Dom Dinis, then transferred to Coimbra in 1308, where students were tutored by the monks of Santa Cruz Monastery. However, political wrangling between the monarchy and the Church caused the seat of the university to be moved back and forth between the two cities a number of times. The **University** was finally settled in Coimbra in 1537 and remained the only university in the country for nearly 400 years. Despite efforts by a succession of Portugal's kings to raise standards and put the University firmly on the map, the

148

Church's stranglehold stifled development and caused serious students to pursue academic success outside Portugal. The country had to wait for the Marquês de Pombal finally to prise away the stagnant grip of the Church, in the 18th century, and lay the foundation for the university's reputation as a recognised seat of learning. Coimbra has developed and grown around its university which is the heartbeat of the city. Its reputation as a major learning centre remains intact, even though the more recently founded university in Lisbon now exceeds Coimbra in numbers of students. The buzz of city life is highly charged whilst the students are in residence, with something going on somewhere almost all the time. Outside term time a much quieter ambience prevails.

Medieval traditions are an integral part of the fabric of everyday student life, and in themselves inject additional colour and interest. The usual form of lodging, which has survived down the centuries, is in *repúblicas*, where a group of students share furnished accommodation. Many students now opt to wear casual dress but the sense of being transported to another time accompanies those who wear the traditional long, black capes. Faculty ribbons (*fitas*) pinned to the capes denote the wearer's area of study, with blue for Arts, red for Law and yellow for Medicine. Perhaps more intriguing is to check a student's tally of amorous conquests by counting the number of tears around the bottom of his cloak. A carnival atmosphere accompanies the end of final exams in May, the highlight of which is a ceremony called *Queima das Fitas* (Burning the Ribbons), when faculty ribbons are ritually burnt.

Coimbra's greatest contribution to traditional folk music is the soulful and expressive musical art form, **fado**. This style of singing is an instinctive expression, which springs from the soul in the form of a lament about love, longing, life, etc., and a lone voice can often be heard winging through the night. These plaintive sounds make sense if, as one story goes, *fado* in Coimbra developed around homesick students of yore, but its origins are thought to stem from the songs of African slaves, laments which found an echo in the hearts of homesick Portuguese sailors on voyages of discovery. It is not really intended for organised public performance, which probably accounts for the tradition of not applauding a rendition, although some restaurants employ a *fado* singer at weekends. Unlike the *fado* in Lisbon, which is more commercial and sung by men and women, Coimbra *fado* is performed only by men and has a more serious and intellectual content. Singers are accompanied by a 12 string guitar, although spontaneous snatches of a few bars of unaccompanied *fado* are not uncommon.

Approaching Coimbra from the Santa Clara side of the Mondego river, across the bridge of the same name, affords the best overall view of the old city. This south-facing elevation, encompassing the main area of interest, is dominated by the hilltop University. What remains of the city's medieval past clings tenaciously to the steep gradients below. Fortunately, much of Salazar's more recent characterless, angular faculty blocks are somewhat masked from this angle. Even the Mondego river is a celebrity for, unlike the Douro and Tagus rivers, it springs from and flows its entire length through Portuguese soil. As such, it has fired the passions of writers and musicians over the centuries to the extent of becoming known as O Rio dos Poetas (The River of Poets). The spread of the city degenerates into a jumble of old and new, the new not always in harmony with its heritage, but this soon ceases to intrude. Walking is the only way to absorb the sights and sounds of this fascinating city. Evening, especially, can be very atmospheric and a different experience again from a daytime jaunt over the same ground. Distance is not a problem, as the centre is fairly compact, but the steep inclines may be a deterrent to some. Pedestrianised shopping streets in the Baixa (lower town), which although outside the old city is almost as old, keep heavy traffic at bay. This effectively creates an island within which the original city streets are concentrated, although cars wend tortuously through some of the streets around the University. Cars are not an option really as parking is limited. Best to park along Avenida Emidio Navarro, to the right on crossing the Ponte de Santa Clara, or in the metered car park to the left. If these options fail, there is parking on the Santa Clara side before crossing the bridge.

The Largo de Portagem, immediately opposite on crossing Ponte de Santa Clara, is a good place to start a tour. Those who stay at Hotel Astoria, to the left of Largo de Portagem, are well placed for touring on foot. This friendly and recently refurbished hotel retains much of its 1920s ambience with modern-day comforts. The restaurant is one of the best in town and the wine list includes the excellent but elusive Buçaco wines, only available in this hotel chain. The *Almedina Coimbra Hotel* offers a good level of comfort and is also fairly central.

To the upper town

To the right of Largo de Portagem is the helpful Turismo, who supply a good map and can advise on other hotels and *residencials* close by. Starting out along pedestrianised Ferreira Borges causes problems from the start. Cafés displaying trays of the delicious local speciality *arrufadas*, wrapped in layers of filo-type pastry, act like a magnet. These are not actually baked on the premises but transported daily by the trayful from the small village of Tentúgal, near Figueira da Foz. The *Café Briosa* does a particularly brisk business and offers other mouth-watering specialities such as *queijades* (cheese cakes), *manjares brancos* (blancmange cake) and *pastéis de nata* (custard tarts). Temptation doesn't stop there, for Coimbra's large student population ensures a generous sprinkling of inviting cafés along the route. Rua de Ferreira Borges becomes Rua de Visconde da Luz, leading to Praça 8 de Maio, and is lined with fashionable shops. For now, head only as far as the **Arco de Almedina** (Almedina Gate), a few hundred metres along Rua de Ferreira Borges on the right. Its name suggests a Moorish connection as `medina' is the Arabic word for city. Once a gate in the medieval city walls, it leads into Rua do Quebra Costas (Street of the Broken Backs) which was then, as now, the main pedestrian route between the Sé Velha (Old Cathedral) and the Baixa. The tower above was the Town Hall until 1878 and is where the Sino de Correr (Warning Bell) is still housed along with the city's archives.

Coimbra is a city shared by students and tourists

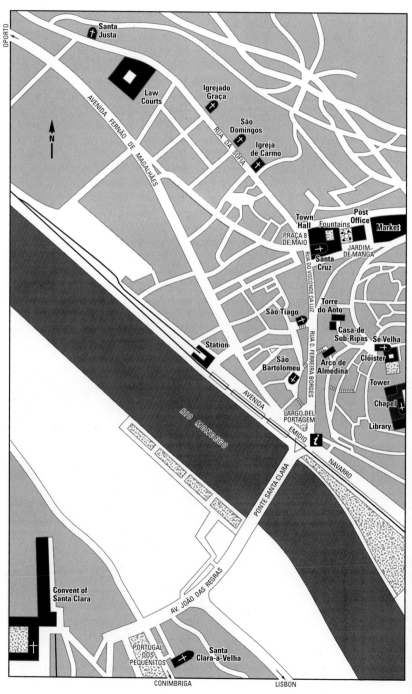

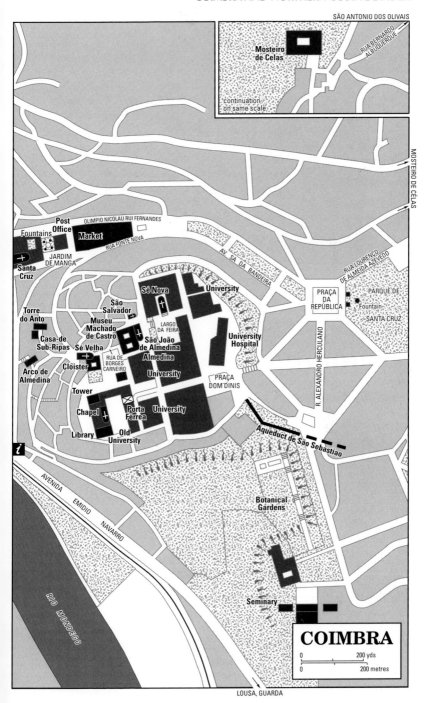

SÃO ANTONIO DOS OLIVAIS

Mosteiro
de Celas

continuation
on same scale

MOSTEIRO DE CELAS

Post
Office

Fountains

OLIMPIO NICOLAU RUI FERNANDES

Market

RUA FONTE NOVA

JARDIM
DE MANGA

Santa
Cruz

AV SA DA BANDEIRA

Sé Nova

University

PRAÇA
DA
REPÚBLICA

RUA LOURENÇO
DE ALMEIDA AZEVEDO

PARQUE DE

Fountain

SANTA CRUZ

Torre
do Anto

São
Salvador

Museu
Machado
de Castro

LARGO
DA FEIRA

University
Hospital

Casa-de
Sub-Ripas

Sé Velha

São João
de Almedina
Almedina

Arco de
Almedina

Cloister

RUA DE
BORGES
CARNEIRO

University

PRAÇA
DOM DINIS

R. ALEXANDRO HERCULANO

Tower

Chapel

Porta
Férrea

University

Library

Old
University

Aqueduct de São Sebastiao

Botanical
Gardens

AVENIDA EMIDIO NAVARRO

RIO MONDEGO

Seminary

COIMBRA

| 0 | 200 yds |
| 0 | 200 metres |

LOUSA, GUARDA

Artesanato (craft) shops lining the way provide plenty of excuse for stops on the upward haul. Divert left into Rua Sub Ripas to the **Casa de Sub-Ripas** on the left, just before the archway. A Manueline doorway and windows (attributed to João de Ruão) grace the external walls of this 16th-century mansion but a glimpse of the plain interior suggests an earlier foundation. This is believed to be the site of the murder of Maria Teles, who had secretly married João, the eldest son of Inês de Castro. It is a tale of jealousy and intrigue, which revolved around Maria's own sister, Queen Leonor of Portugal. With the promise of her own daughter in marriage, Leonor successfully persuaded João that Maria was being unfaithful. He dutifully disposed of his wife, only for Leonor to renege on her promise and have him banished from the country. The mansion is now the Archaeological Faculty of the University. Continue beneath the archway, whose façade is studded with sculpted cameos by João de Ruão, a prolific sculptor of the 16th century, to the **Torre do Anto**. The 12th-century tower was once part of the city walls but now serves as the Casa de Artesanato da Região de Coimbra (Regional Craft Centre). It was the home of the 19th-century poet António Nobre for a short while when he attended the University. The multilingual curator offers expert guidance around the four floors of the tower. Two floors are dedicated as permanent salesrooms for local handicrafts, whilst the other two are used for rotating craft displays from different areas. This is an ideal place to purchase local souvenirs of pottery, delicately carved white poplar, weaving and lace from local villages – all good quality and at a reasonable price. Return to the main route and continue climbing the steps to Largo da Sé Velha.

The Old Cathedral

The sloping square is dominated by the Sé Velha (Old Cathedral) one of the finest Romanesque cathedrals in Portugal. Built between 1162 and 1184, its fortress-like appearance is testament to the need for continuing protection from Moorish incursions into the area at the time. Within its walls, the unfurling of history has included the coronations of Sancho I and João I and the ordination of the Lisbon-born Saint Anthony of Padua. The main entrance was the work of João de Ruão who had a workshop close to the Casa de Sub-Ripas. Later embellishments attempted to soften the austere lines of the exterior, especially the Renaissance Porta Especiosa (North Portal), which is unfortunately crumbling, and the door of the north transept, which was altered at the same time. The 1837 domed belfry is out of character, as domes are not a feature in Portuguese architecture, but only really noticeable from above. A stark interior comes as no surprise, yet maybe the warmth in the colour of the stone compensates for a lack of elaborate decoration and makes this church seems more welcoming than most. All that is left of the *azulejos*, bought from the Seville workshop of Quijarro in 1508, are unobtrusive panels along the side walls. Tiles once also decorated the pillars of the nave, where it is difficult to imagine them having done much in the way of interior enhancement. The intricate and delicately carved Gothic main altarpiece, executed by the

Flemish masters Olivier of Ghent and Jean d'Ypres, is aesthetically pleasing and enjoys a more natural relationship with the surrounding simplicity than the chunkier, more commonly encountered later Baroque style might. It was presented by Bishop Jorge de Almeida (1483–1543) whose tomb lies in the **chapel of São Pedro** (1537), in the north transept. This chapel is exemplified as one of the most elegant and harmonious examples of Renaissance architecture. Amongst a collection of mainly bishops' tombs, lies that of Dona Vetaça, who was governess to Queen Santa Isabel. Steps lead from the south aisle to the Gothic cloister which once housed the University press. Giant conch shells, used to hold holy water, are an unusual reminder of the Age of Discoveries and Portugal's exotic colonies. In 1772 the episcopal see was moved to the Sé Nova but the impression is that today the Old Cathedral acts more as a focal point of city life than its later replacement.

Sculpting and Sculptors

A type of limestone known as *pedra de Ança*, from the village of Ança to the north-west of Coimbra, was responsible for the town's development as a centre for sculpture. Being softer than limestone from other areas, Ança stone lent itself particularly well to the art of the carver. It was used in abundance for decoration, during a 200 year period from the 1300s onwards, until its popularity declined in favour of woodcarving.

An early exponent of the art of stone carving was Pêro, who is said to have introduced the Gothic style to Coimbra. Frenchmen particularly, attracted to Coimbra as much by the wealth being poured into new building as the quality of local stone, were prolific exponents of the art during the 16th century. Of these, Nicolas Chanterène produced some of the finest Renaissance work, whilst the carving of João de Ruão (Jean de Rouen), although extensive, never achieved the same acclaim.

A kaleidoscope of life swirls round the Largo da Sé Velha, an ideal place for people-watching from one of the surrounding cafés. Music students from the nearby faculty practice their scales or perform in the cathedral; for a Saturday-night fado treat with tasty food, the Trovador restaurant is a good choice.

The University

Move on and up behind the Sé Velha along Rua do Norte, passing the 16th-century Casa dos Melos, now the Faculty of Pharmacy, to the **Velha Universidade** (Old University). Enter the courtyard known as Patio das Escolas (Courtyard of the Schools) through the 17th-century Porta Férrea (Iron Gate). Niches on the top hold statues of Dom Dinis and Dom João III. Tickets are available for the Sala dos Capelos and Biblioteca from the administration offices to the right. Buildings fill three sides of the courtyard and have evolved from the original royal palace donated by Dom João III in 1573. They still form the nucleus of the University. The south side is open, with elevated views over the River Mondego across to the convent of Santa Clara, and a portly statue of Dom João III (reminiscent of Henry VIII of England) takes centre stage in the courtyard. The double stairway, to the right on entering, leads to the Via Latina (Latin Way) gallery where students process to their graduation. Pass through the door marked 'reitoria' onto the balcony of the **Sala dos Capelos** (Ceremonial Hall), one-time throne room but now the setting for degree ceremonies, where portraits of Portugal's kings hang beneath a 17th-century painted wooden ceiling. In the corner of the courtyard stands the 18th-century Baroque clocktower which has become a national symbol. Christened *cabra* (goat) by the students, it was once used to summon them to lectures as well as signalling a dawn-to-dusk curfew. Further round is the 16th-century university chapel, **Capela de São Miguel**, entered via a Manueline portal. The elaborate interior decoration is a mix of styles added over the next 200 years. 'Carpet'-style *azulejos* are placed alongside the painted and gilded altarpiece, which is highly regarded as a fine example of Mannerism, but the *pièce de résistance*, not to everyone's taste, is a heavily gilded Baroque organ which is apparently as 'loud' as it looks. Finally, the 18th-century library **Biblioteca Joanina,** is regarded as one of the world's most magnificent Baroque libraries. Ring the bell at the side for admittance. Constructed by Dom João V, whose coat of arms hangs above the entrance, the interior consists of three connecting gilded and painted rooms lined with double-storey shelves of rare books. The elaborately framed connecting doors create a telescopic effect through all three rooms to the large framed portrait of Dom João V on the far wall.

The New Cathedral

Move through Largo da Porta Férrea between the nondescript modern university faculties to Praça Dom Dinis. A huge statue of Dom Dinis dominates the large open square where Coimbra Castle stood until its demolition in 1772. There is a small Turismo office located here. Steps lead down then along Oliveira Matos to the Praça da República, its bars and cafés a popular haunt of students, and beyond to the Parque de Santa Cruz. To the right, the 16th-century São Sebastião Aqueduto, built on the site of an earlier aqueduct, stretches across the edge of the **Jardim Botânico** (Botanical Gardens). The gardens were laid out to a circular design at the instigation of the Marquês de Pombal, and although started in 1774 they took over a hundred years to complete. Possibly of more immediate interest, is the huge building dominating the landscape at the end of the aqueduct. This 18th-century building, with 19th-century additions, was once a seminary and is noted for its octagonal domed church; it now does service as the local prison.

From Praça Dom Dinis, the **Sé Nova** (New Cathedral) is only a short walk down Rua dos Estudos. Originally founded in 1598 by the Jesuits, and taken from them when they were suppressed in 1759, it took a hundred years to build. The bleak expanse of the Largo da Sé Nova matches the equally lacklustre Renaissance frontage of the Cathedral, whose interior does nothing to dispel the ominous portent of its exterior. Inside, an eerie bluish tinge strikes a chill through the lofty emptiness. Paintings of the Life of the Virgin, mostly Italian copies and framed by carvings, line the walls behind the 17th-century redwood choir stalls which were originally in the Sé Velha along with the Manueline font. Even the Jerónimo Luís gilded main altarpiece, two ornate Baroque organs and an abundance of gilded vine leaves, cherubs and further paintwork fail to have much impact on the pervading gloom.

Machado de Castro Museum

By contrast to the Sé Nova, a visit to the Machado de Castro Museum is like a breath of fresh air. Not surprisingly considering Coimbra's reputation as a centre for sculpture, the museum – founded in 1912 – was named after an 18th-century Portuguese sculptor. Housed in what served as the old Episcopal Palace and church of São João de Almedina, whose foundation stems from the 12th century, it stands on the site of the Roman Forum. A two-storey Roman Cryptoporticus (crypt), built into the side of the hill to support and give height to the Forum that once stood there, was left to do similar service for the later building. This provides one of the most fascinating aspects of a visit here as it is possible to explore the passages of the upper storey (the lower storey is closed to the public). A torch is useful as the low, but atmospheric lighting makes close inspection of the stonework difficult. The tower by the main entrance along with the church, probably built on the site of a mosque, provide a Moorish connection, although much of the building seen today is the result of 16th-century additions and rebuilding. Besides sculpture, which includes an appealing 14th-century knight on horseback attributed to Pêro, the museum contains paintings from as early as the 14th century, furniture, ceramics and the bishop's coach. The same ticket covers access to the gold, silver and jewellery treasures, reached via a separate entrance at the foot of the steps from the Sé Nova. Along the edge of the pleasant quadrangle runs a loggia, providing an elevated view of the city and connecting the museum café with the entrance to the Cryptoporticus in the other part of the museum. There is no concession to foreign visitors and information on exhibits is presented in the Portuguese language only, a problem all too frequently encountered.

The lower town

Soak up the atmosphere on the way down to Praça 8 de Maio by making for the 18th-century **Igreja de São Salvador** (Saviour) with its earlier Romanesque doorway, and wandering in the area of Rua de São Salvador and Rua da Matemática where many of the student *repúblicas* are located.

Down in Praça 8 de Maio at the end of Rua do Visconde da Luz lies the **Igreja de Santa Cruz**, one-time monastery and one of Coimbra's most important churches. Dom Afonso Henriques is reputed to have sanctioned its foundation as a monastery for Augustinian monks in 1131, his confessor São Teotónio being installed as its first prior. Dom Manuel started enlarging the monastery in 1502 and exempted the priors from the jurisdiction of the bishop. This eventually led to Dom João III giving the priors automatic succession to the chancellorship of the new University, when it was moved from Lisbon in 1539, a privilege which lasted until monasteries were disbanded in 1834. The Portal da Majestade (west front) is somewhat over the top, with the original 16th-century doorway masked by an early 19th-century arch. Floor level is now below street level, so steps lead down into the church which is lined with 18th-century *azulejos*. Here it is not the ornate altarpiece which excites attention but Nicolas Chanterène's intricately carved pulpit of 1522 and, in the chancel, the tombs of Portugal's first two kings Dom Afonso Henriques and his son Dom Sancho I, disinterred and placed here after lying for 400 years in nearby graves. A door from the sacristy, which contains furniture and notable paintings, opens into the lovely Manueline Casa do Capitulo (Silent Cloister).

A favourite of the Portuguese is the Café Santa Cruz next door. Formerly a chapel attached to the church (as the Manueline ceiling and stained-glass windows testify), it has served as a café for about 70 years.

Behind the church is the **Jardim de Manga** (Garden of the Sleeve), so named because Dom João III is reputed to have drawn the design for this oddity on his sleeve; its design is also attributed to João de Ruão. Curiously modernistic, the unwieldy construction was completed in 1535 as a representation of the fountain of life, and was originally a cloister of the Santa Cruz monastery.

Rua da Sofia (Street of Wisdom), so called because it was once lined with theological colleges, could be of interest to church collectors. The churches of Carmo, Graça, São Pedro and Santa Justa were connected with the colleges when the University of Coimbra was established and, in an effort to preserve the 16th-century architecture, this street has been declared a national monument.

A plunge into the bustling rabbit warren of streets leading off Praça 8 de Maio is a wonderful diversion from monuments and a journey of discovery in itself. When refreshment calls, the outdoor cafés in the irregularly shaped Praça do Comércio, former Roman circus but now lined with shops in 17th- and 18th-century houses, seem an attractive proposition. Two more churches can be found here, the 12th-century Romanesque church of São Tiago (St James) and the nearby São Bartolomeu, its 18th-century rebuilding in Baroque style masking a 10th-century foundation. The wiggle of narrow streets encompassed within a triangle marked by the squares of Comércio, Meias and Portagem, contains a concentration of good and very reasonably priced eating places, including the very Portuguese Zé Manuel.

The Santa Clara Convents

On a hill across the Mondego lies the brooding bulk of the 17th-century Convento de Santa Clara-a-Nova (New Santa Clara Convent), a shorter walk than might at first appear, especially as there are diversions along the way. Here lies the body of Rainha Santa Isabel (Queen Saint Isabel), wife of Dom Dinis, who freely spent her husband's money on helping the poor and needy. Her canonisation was the result of a life spent founding hospitals and orphanages and because of the Miracle of the Roses (see page 183).

After crossing the bridge over the Mondego, keep heading up past Avenida Inês de Castro but take the next narrow road left to come up behind the sunken Gothic **Convento de Santa Clara-a-Velha** (Old Santa Clara Convent). Dona Mór Dias founded the convent in 1286. It was refounded in 1330 by Santa Isabel and is where she and the ill-fated Inês de Castro were originally interred. Annual flooding of the Mondego river and consequent silting caused the convent to be finally abandoned in 1677, the tomb of Santa Isabel being transferred up the hill to the new convent, whilst that of Inês now rests alongside that of Pedro I at Alcobaça. The absurdity of a sinking church, with the tops of arched vaulting wallowing in green weed-covered water, is compounded by a recently renovated roof and cleaned stonework. To view the convent and its rose window from the front, approach from off Rua António Augusto Gonçalves down the side of the Portugal dos Pequeninos park. Further along the same road on the right is the 19th-century **Quinta das Lágrimas** (House of Tears), now a four-star hotel, the traditional site of the home Inês de Castro shared with her lover Pedro I. Legend states that the Fonte dos Amores (Fountain of the Lovers) in the grounds of the *quinta* gushed from the spot where Inês was murdered, a tale compounded no doubt by the poetic licence of Camões in *The Lusiads*.

The **Portugal dos Pequeninos** is a fanciful Lilliputian-style outdoor museum for, as the name implies, children. Individual displays of indigenous artefacts from Portugal's former colonies and small-scale models of Portuguese buildings, in which children are free to clamber around, make a worthwhile side trip for all ages.

Keep heading up Rossio Santa Clara towards the new convent, passing the dilapidated and forlorn façade of the former monastery of São Francisco (1602), a chimney denoting its demotion to a factory. Cobbled Calçada de Santa Isabel, climbs steeply to the gate of the convent. One of the best overall views of Coimbra is from the terrace in front of the church. Except for a small military museum, the main body of the convent is now a barracks and barred to the public. The **Convento de Santa Clara-a-Nova**, constructed between 1649 and 1677, has become a shrine to Santa Isabel (1271–1336) since the relocation of her remains in 1696 from the waterlogged old convent below. These remains now lie in a silver casket, purchased with donations from the people of Coimbra, above the main altar, whilst her original stone tomb lies empty in the lower choir. Gilded carvings and paintings, especially six panels depicting the removal of Santa Isabel's body from the old convent, adorn the interior. Dom João V is reputed to have been fascinated by nuns and it was he who provided the convent with its large cloister.

Luís de Camões

Portugal's greatest epic poet started life in the bosom of an impoverished aristocratic family. It is probable that he was born in Lisbon in 1524 (the year Vasco da Gama died) and studied at Coimbra University, where he would have received a thorough grounding in the classics, but accounts of the early part of his life tend to be based more on supposition than fact.

The passionate nature of Camões can be gleaned from biographical elements in his early writing, and indiscreet amours eventually led to his being banished from the Portuguese court at Lisbon, where he had gone in 1544 to write poetry and plays.

An adventurous life now beckoned and Camões went off to Ceuta in Morocco around 1547, where he lost his right eye. Five years later he was imprisoned for being involved in a street brawl in Lisbon and injuring a royal official. His life over the next 17 years appears to have been fraught with danger and deprivation. After gaining an early release from prison by agreeing to serve in Goa for an obligatory three-year stretch, a stroke of good fortune saw his safe arrival in India on the *São Bento*, the only ship of the fleet to survive the journey. From there he travelled on to Macau in the Far East and, on the journey either to or from Macau, was shipwrecked in the Mekong estuary and lost everything except the half-completed manuscript of his epic poem. Eventually returning to Goa, he was again thrown into prison for some unknown transgression. Intent on returning home to have his poem published, Camões reached Mozambique where he lived for two years from 1567. Sympathetic compatriots funded the by now penniless poet's journey back to Portugal in 1570.

Os Lusíades ('The Lusiads') was finally published in 1572. Named for the sons of Lusus, the mythical founder of Portugal, *Os Lusíades* was inspired by Camões' hero Vasco da Gama, whom he used in a similar manner to Homer's hero in the *Odyssey*. Unlike the *Odyssey*, where fact becomes immersed in ancient folklore, Camões' genius lay in his ability to blend historical accuracy with mythical elements of classical Graeco-Roman culture. The poem reflects the Portuguese spirit of the time when it grew rich and powerful from the Voyages of Discovery.

Camões received scant acclaim when the poem was published, although he managed to win a small royal pension. Now one of Portugal's most famous sons, he died in poverty and with no heirs in 1579.

Traditional farming methods still abound in rural Portugal

Excursions from Coimbra

Coimbra makes a good base from which to explore the surrounding area and a visit to Conimbriga is a must.

Conimbriga

A 20-minute drive, south along the IC2 then off left through Condeixa onto the IC3 will take you to **Conimbriga**, the largest and most important Roman archaeological site on the Iberian Peninsula. Its natural defences, with gorges to two sides, would suggest its use as a settlement even before the Celts arrived.

When the Romans first came along at the end of the 2nd century BC, Conimbriga's strategic position on the road between Lisbon (Olisipo) and Braga (Bracara Augusta) made it an obvious target for expansion. Over the following centuries the site grew to cover around 13ha, much of which still lies waiting to be excavated. Conimbriga developed in importance to such an extent that Vespasian granted it *municipium* status around AD 70. Prosperity lasted until the Roman Empire began to crumble, towards the end of the 3rd century. Incursions by the Suevi (Swabians) increased in frequency and persistence and it became necessary to strengthen defences. The inhabited part of Conimbriga was drastically reduced and a large wall hurriedly constructed to protect a smaller area of the town. This wall, much of it still in evidence today, cut a swathe through existing housing. It is evident from the materials used to build the wall that it was constructed in haste, with rubble

from destroyed buildings incorporated as building material. Heavier fortification failed to repel the Suevi who, after repeated attacks in the 5th century, eventually forced the inhabitants to succumb. Many of the townspeople were taken as slaves, including the wife and children of a nobleman who lived in **Casa do Cantaber** (House of Cantaber), the foundations of which now provide an insight into the lifestyle of the Roman nobility of the time.

After such a decimation of the population, many that were left removed to Aeminium (Coimbra) which was better defended, although a pocket of the inhabitants remained. It appears that the final abandonment of Conimbriga occurred around the time the episcopal see was transferred to Aeminium, along with its name, sometime during the 6th century. Those who did remain, formed a community on the site where the amphitheatre once stood, which eventually developed into modern-day Condeixa-a-Velha.

Pleasantly situated in countryside on the outskirts of Condeixa, Conimbriga is high on the list of places to visit. Most visitors are unaware on the approach to the car park that the accompanying wall to the right is actually a stretch of the original Roman wall. A modern **museum** building houses an imaginative display of finds in two parts. To one side, a series of windows open onto collections of artefacts depicting different aspects of Roman life: Health and Hygiene, Personal Adornment and Military Equipment to name but some. The other room contains mosaics, one of which is a picture of the Minotaur's head in a maze, fragments of friezes, statuary and a scale model of the Forum and Temple. A good café/bar/restaurant is also part of the complex, where lunch is available, but those who prefer to eat *al fresco* will find a specially designated picnic area in the grounds.

The excellent plan of the site, on sale at the ticket office, is invaluable to have to hand. Access to the site is along the remains of the Lisbon to Braga Roman road, which passes through the previously mentioned heavy defensive wall at the main gate. On the right, just before reaching the wall, is the **Casa das Fontes** (House of Fountains). Excavations have revealed the function of the various rooms which surround the large ornamental pool, and have uncovered mosaics and wall paintings. A 50-escudos coin is all it takes to set the fountains playing again. Once through the gate, the largest and possibly the most luxurious villa on the site lies to the left – the House of Cantaber, with its own private baths. To the right is an aqueduct which ran underground from Alcabideque 3km (1.8 miles) away and was then raised on arches to cross the town to a distribution tower. At some time, possibly when Suevi attacks became more frequent, an underground cistern was brought into operation as insurance against deliberate sabotage of the aqueduct. Further along on the same side was the Roman Forum and other monumental buildings. It is quite easy to while away an hour or two enjoying this elevated country location.

Serra do Buçaco

From Coimbra a short trip north-east up the IC2 to Mealhada, famous for *leito assado* (suckling pig), then east via the EN234 leads to the spa town of **Luso**. This small town is dedicated to spa tourism with thermal baths, swimming pool and, for when the serious business of the day is over, a casino. Commercially bottled Luso water can be bought throughout Portugal, but the town's functional Fonte São João (St John's Fountain) draws the crowds, complete with a motley collection of plastic water containers, for free spa water which is claimed to be especially beneficial for the liver and kidneys. A visit to the 19th-century Salão do Chá is a must for those in search of a nostalgic leap back in time.

Exit Luso south down the EN235 to the countryside location of the **Buçaco Forest**. Enter through Portas das Ameias, signposted to the Palace Hotel. There is a pay box on entry for those just visiting the grounds, as they are overseen by the national parks department; guests at the hotel are refunded this charge and entrance is free on 27 September.

Benedictine monks were the first to found a hermitage here in the 6th century, although this arboreal enclave was created by the monks of the Order of the Barefoot Carmelites. The Carmelites bought the site from the Bishop of Coimbra in 1628, built the boundary wall and planted both native and foreign trees amongst whose leafy fronds they constructed hermit cells as retreats. Only one door, facing Coimbra, penetrated the monks seclusion in those early days, and a rule of their order also forbade entrance to women. Cutting down trees in the forest was banned on pain of excommunication by a Papal Bull of 1643, unless two-thirds of the community consented, so by the time religious orders were suppressed in 1834 the forest was thriving. Even evidence of its brief appearance centre stage in the Peninsular War, when Wellington based himself in the monastery, is kept outside the walls in the **Museu Militar** (Military Museum), near the Porta da Rainha (Queen's Gate). **The Battle of Buçaco**, on 27 September 1810 marked the first serious setback for Napoleon, and Wellington's victory is still marked every year on that date. Reveille sounds at 7.30am, signalling the start of morning celebrations, the highlight of which is a re-enactment of the engagement in period costume.

For years the forest lay untouched, until the monastery was all but destroyed to make way for the present building. Ferdinand of Saxe-Coburg-Gotha, the widower of Dona Maria II, had earlier converted a monastery at Pena, above Sintra, into a whimsical palace and took the notion to do the same with the monastery in the Buçaco Forest. His son Dom Luís proved intractable when pressed to turn the dream into reality, but his grandson Dom Carlos agreed to the building of a hunting lodge. Between the years 1888 and 1907 Luigi Manini, an Italian architect, somehow managed to incorporate his penchant for Romantic Revivalism into the grand neo-Manueline edifice of today, leaving only the church, small cloister and a few cells of the former monastery intact. Originally intended as a modest hunting lodge for the royal family, the opulent palace it became was used only once by Dom Manuel II before his exile in 1910. In 1920 the property, by then government owned, was put under the management of a local man, Alexandre d'Almeida, whose family still run this and other high-quality hotels.

A leaflet from the tourist office in either Luso or Coimbra, shows the layout of paths in the forest. The fanciful turreted confection which is now the five-star luxury *Palace Hotel do Buçaco* is rated as one of the finest in Europe, with a service to match. A delectable menu is matched by an impressive wine list, which includes the excellent quality Buçaco own label. Non-residents are welcome to call in for lunch or dinner.

Colourful moliceira *boats are fast disappearing from the lagoons of Aveiro*

Figueira da Foz and Aveiro

If a whiff of tangy sea air is the order of the day, head out of Coimbra along the south bank of the Mondego and across the river into Montemor-o-Velho, before moving on to Figueira da Foz at the mouth of the River Mondego (*foz* means 'mouth'). Continue from there up the coast to the lagoon town of Aveiro before returning through the heart of Bairrada wine country via another spa at Curia.

To enjoy a rural atmosphere, take the south bank road of the Mondego (EN341) through the village of Pereira to **Montemor-o-Velho.** A slower pace of rural life, presenting a series of interesting cameos, is likely to be encountered along this slow but scenic route, especially in spring and late summer. The **castle** at Montemor dominates the skyline as the road skims slightly above the flat areas by the river, used for cultivation of rice and cereals, before swinging right to cross a pontoon bridge over the river. Access to the castle for vehicles is to the north of the town.

The castle site, on the most prominent mound around, was probably occupied even before its fortification by the Romans and then the Moors. By the time the Moors were ousted in the 11th century, the castle was derelict. Its strategic importance, as part of the defence system of the Mondego river and Coimbra, was such that Dom Sancho I ordered its rebuilding. Early kings of Portugal seem to have been quite attached to this castle, and it was here that Dom Afonso IV sealed the fate of the tragic Inês de Castro (see page 124).

It is worth a diversion up to the castle for the views and the well

165

manicured gardens within the walls. Also inside are the ruins of a 16th-century Manueline palace and the restored **Igreja de Santa Maria da Alcáçova**. Although the church dates from the time of the castle's restoration, subsequent rebuilding has resulted in an interesting amalgam of decorative fashions with twisted Manueline columns, raised Moorish style *azulejos*, a small Baroque retable, frescos and a wooden painted and gilded pulpit.

Figueira da Foz is quickly reached along the IP3 and at first sight is not encouraging, with off-putting views of the industrialised river mouth. Although not to everyone's taste, Figueira da Foz, besides being a deep-sea fishing port, is a major Portuguese resort with a casino and is also popular with the Spanish. Ignoring the high-rise apartment blocks lining the seafront, Figueiro's big asset is a huge expanse of fine sandy beach where the Atlantic rollers make for good surfing. Beach huts in candy-stripes of yellow and blue add a freshness to the scene, and piped music accompanies strollers along the *calçada*-patterned promenade above.

Fishing boats and tile-fronted houses add a touch of character at the northern end of the promenade, where Figueira merges with the village of Buarcos, before the road wends up onto the cliffs to pass the *farol* (lighthouse) and eventually reach a viewpoint. The view stretches endlessly northwards over the pine-studded plain which backs an unbroken silver strand of sand, and inland over the Bairrada vineyards. Leave the cliff top and make for the village of Quiaios and the IC1 for a quick run north to Mira.

Turn left in the centre of Mira for **Praia de Mira**. The road heads seawards past the Hotel Quinta da Lagoa and in 6km (4 miles) comes to the inland lagoon behind the fishing village, the most southerly point of the lagoon and canal system of the Ria da Aveiro – a spot sheltered from the unpredictable wildness of this exposed coast. Activity on the lagoon centres on boating and picnicking in the pine woods which fringe the edges. Candy-striped beach huts again lend a jaunty holiday air to the superb sandy beach, but pride of place goes to the immaculate blue-and-white-striped wooden church of the fishermen. Those in search of a local fishing village atmosphere may be disappointed, as much of the old way of life is fast being stifled by development. There are still some houses on stilts but brightly painted boats pulled ashore by oxen have all but disappeared. Fishing remains a focus of village life though and fishermen gather to barbecue fish on the shore and share a drink.

Back on the main road at Mira, turn left for Aveiro. A possible diversion to the left, before reaching Aveiro, is **Vista Alegre** and its famous porcelain factory. Founded in 1824, it is still owned by the same family and a museum and shop is open to the public on weekdays (closed 12.30pm–2pm). On reaching **Aveiro** follow signs to the centre and Turismo. Entering from the south, cross the bridge over the canal in the centre and turn left. Turismo is now on the right – painted boats moored on the canal opposite usually mark the spot – and there are car parks or parking opportunities a little further along near the fish market.

Aveiro sits on the edge of the Ria da Aveiro, a shallow estuary stretching some 45km (28 miles) between Ovar and Mira and 10km (6 miles) wide, into which the River Vouga flows. During the Middle Ages the town thrived on trade from metals, salted fish and tiles, but in the 1570s, storms created a sand barrier which effectively cut off shipping access to the sea. Over the next 200 years the town declined until a canal was cut through the sand barrier at Barra in 1808. This and a further network of canals effectively drained the silted estuary of the River Vouga encouraging some return to prosperity. Traditional industries connected with fishing, salt, seaweed (for fertilisers) and tiles still exist but are rapidly being replaced with modern ones.

Dubbed the Venice of Portugal (though comparisons other than a few canals are thin on the ground), Aveiro is pleasant enough for a short visit. Other than the Museu de Aveiro, housed in the former Convent of Jesus, there is a cathedral and a few churches. To search out local character head for the fish market and the streets of the old town beyond. The Cais dos Mercanteis leads from the market to the Cais de São Roque where old fishermen's cottages gaze seawards beyond the graceful Venetian-style bridge over the canal. Turismo organise trips by boat on the lagoon, where you may catch sight of the rapidly disappearing *moliceiro* boats, specially designed to dredge for seaweed, and to other places of interest in the vicinity.

Magnificent sandy beaches protect the lagoon from the ravages of the Atlantic, similar to the Ilhas of Algarve. Unfortunately, those easily accessible from Aveiro have become fairly built up and are crammed with sunseekers at holiday times. Candy-striped decoration of summer houses is commonplace along this coast and there are some fine examples at Costa Nova, reached by heading first for Barra then down the coast. Birdwatchers might be interested in Reserva Natural das Dunas de São Jacinto. Check with Turismo about access and the ferry from Barra to São Jacinto.

The route back to Coimbra penetrates the heart of **Bairrada wine country**. Leave Aveiro in the direction of Oliveira do Bairro along the EN235 which crosses the IP1. On the right, between Oliveira and the IC2, are three wineries which offer free tasting without prior booking: *Caves Borlido, Caves Aliança* (Aliança Velha *aguardente* will tempt brandy lovers) and *Caves Império*. For details of other wine producers in the area ask for the special Bairrada map at Turismo in Curia. Turn right towards Coimbra on reaching the IC2, and in a short distance take a right turn to the spa at **Curia**. The *Palace Hotel da Curia* belongs to the same chain as the Hotel Palace do Buçaco and offers an excellent standard of service, along with the exclusive Buçaco wines. Curia with its wide range of recreational facilities makes a pleasant country base for a day or two.

Villages of the Serra da Lousã

For a more traditional country experience head out south-east from Coimbra to the cluster of villages south of the Mondego, with **Lousã** the main objective. The views from Penela castle, situated south of Conimbriga off the IC3, are worth a stop, before heading north then east via Miranda do Corvo. A map of the Serra can be obtained from Turismo in Lousã which shows the

Tucked away in the hills of Serra da Lousã is the Hermitage of Our Lady of Compassion

location of six old stone villages – Casal Novo and Talasnal are two – abandoned nearly half a century ago, but now being renovated for tourist accommodation. To find **Castelo de Arouce**, take the road out of Lousã towards Castanheira and look for the sign to 'Castelo' on the right. Wind along the narrow road for around 2km (1 mile) to find the castle sitting on a mound in a gorge, with the white chapels of the hermitage of Our Lady of Compassion rising on a sister mound opposite. Park at the castle and walk down the narrow road to the river where there is a natural swimming pool and a café.

Other main villages of the Serra are Góis, Arganil, Vila Nova de Poiares and Penacova. Black clay pottery is made at Olho Marinho, between Góis and Poiares, and willow baskets are a speciality of Arrifana, just north of Poiares. Time, and plenty of it, is what is really required to search out and savour the hidden delights of this area.

Onwards to Serra da Estrela

Make initially for Viseu from Coimbra, north on the IC2 to join the IP3, then turn off right on the IC7 or IC6 towards the Serra da Estrela. The IC7 to Covilhã skirts the southern edge of the Serra where, just south of Vide, lies another pocket of hidden Portugal in the ancient slate and schist village of Piódão.

Practical Information

Hotels and Restaurants

There is much more accommodation than the listings below, even in out of the way places, including Turismo Rural properties.

AVEIRO AND ENVIRONS
Estalagem Riabela, Torreira, 3870 Murtosa (tel. 034 48 137) Four stars. Modern, near the beach with restaurant.
Hotel Imperial, Rua Dr Nascimento Leitão, 3800 Aveiro (tel. 034 22 141). A comfortable and convenient 108-roomed three-star hotel and restaurant.
Hotel Quinta da Lagoa (Residencial), Mira (tel. 031 451 688) Two-star with 49 rooms on the road between Mira and Praia de Mira. Restaurant and range of other facilities.
Pousada da Ria, Bico do Muranzel, Murtosa (tel. 034 48 332/3/4) Only ten rooms but pool and restaurant.

COIMBRA
Almedina Coimbra Hotel, Av. Fernão de Magalhães, 199 (tel. 039 29 161/2). Friendly three-star hotel, fairly central, good bed and breakfast base.
Casa da Azenha Velha, Caçeira de Cima, 3080 Figueira da Foz (tel. 033 25 041). On a farm estate just south of Montemor-o-Velho. Six rooms, bar, pool and nearby restaurant.

Casa dos Quintais, Carvalhais de Cima, Assafarge (tel. 039 438 305). 6km (4 miles) outside Coimbra in quiet surroundings, part of the Turismo Rural scheme. Three rooms and swimming pool.

Hotel Astoria, Av Emídio Navarro (tel. 039 220 55/6). Comfortable three-star hotel, very central with excellent restaurant.

Hotel Dom Luís, Quinta da Várzea, Santa Clara (tel. 039 813 196). Three-star in the country, facing city across river, about 3km (2 miles) out; restaurant.

Hotel Ibis, Av Emídio Navarro (tel. 039 491 559). Part of French chain, this two-star comfortable hotel is fairly central; restaurant.

Hotel Tivoli, Rua João Machado (tel. 039 269 34). Four-star and fairly central, swimming pool, restaurant and disabled facilities.

Restaurant Trovador (tel. 039 254 75), next to Sé Velha. Atmospheric, good food and *fado* if a trifle pretentious. Moderate.

Zé Manuel (tel. 039 237 90), behind Hotel Astoria in Beco do Forno, very Portuguese. Good and cheap.

CURIA
Palace Hotel da Curia, Curia, 3780 Anadia (tel. 031 512 131/2). Three-star hotel with excellent restaurant and other facilities which include a pool.

LUSO
Hotel Palace de Buçaco, 3050 Mealhada (tel. 031 930 101/2/3). Incomparable luxury five-star hotel in exquisite location and with service to match.

Places of Interest

COIMBRA
Convento de Santa Clara-a-Nova, open daily 9am–12.30pm and 2pm–5.30pm.
Igreja de Santa Cruz, open daily 9am–12.30pm and 2pm–6pm.
Museu Machado de Castro, open Tue–Sun 10am–1pm and 2.30pm–5pm, free Sunday mornings. Closed Mondays.
Museu Militar (Military Museum next to Santa Clara-a-Nova), open daily 10am–12noon and 2pm–5pm.
Portugal dos Pequeninos, open summer daily 9am–7pm and winter daily 9am–5.30pm.
Sé Velha, open daily 9.30am–12.30pm and 2pm–5.30pm.
Velha Universidade, daily 9.30am–12.30pm and 2pm–5pm.
COIMBRA ENVIRONS
Conimbriga, open summer daily 10am–12.30pm and 2pm–5pm, closes one hour earlier in winter.
Montemor-o-Velho, castle open 10am–12.30pm and 2pm–5pm, closed Mondays and holidays; free entry.
LUSO
Peninsular War Museum, open 9am–5.30pm summer, 10am–5.30pm winter, closed Mondays.

Tourist Offices

Regio de Turismo do Centro
Largo da Portagem, 3000 Coimbra (tel. 039 330 19).
Região de Turismo da Rota da Luz, Rua João Mendonça, 8, 3800 Aveiro (tel. 034 23 680)
Tourism Posts
ARGANIL: Câmera Municipal (tel. 035 22 859).
COIMBRA: Largo Dom Dinis (tel. 039 325 91).
CONIMBRIGA: Condeixa-a-Nova Câmera Municipal (tel. 039 941 114).
FIGUEIRA DA FOZ: Av. 25 de Abril (tel. 033 22 126).
LOUSÃ: Câmera Municipal (tel. 039 993 502).
Junta de Turismo da Curia, Praça Dr Luís Navega, 3780 Anadia (tel. 031 512 248).
Junta de Turismo do Luso-Buçaco, Rua Ermídio Navarro, Luso, 3050 Mealgada (tel. 031 939 133).

10. SERRA DA ESTRELA

Located to the east and slightly north of Coimbra, Serra da Estrela is Portugal's highest and most admired range of mountains. It is a treasure house of wonders for lovers of the countryside. It acts as a barrier across the country, a point where Mediterranean, Atlantic and Continental influences dramatically converge to shape the character of the vegetation, the land use and the customs of the people. Descend from any corner of the mountain and it is a different country to that on the others. The wetter north-west to the drier south-east shows the greatest contrast when driving across the mountains. Lush small farms worked with hand tools and the grazing sheep of the north and the west are replaced by drier, goat-grazed hills and large, mechanised farms in the south and the east. Most of the villages surviving on the slopes of the mountain are found around the northern tip and down the western side.

The central mountains form a plateau with a high point of 1993m at Torre and a considerable area above 1200m. Granite dominates the geology of these old-fold mountains and much of it is exposed on the heights with extensive flat polished surfaces and great tors strewn about. With a little imagination, some of these massive granite boulders can be likened to particular shapes – to a man or an animal – and many are individually named (some rather fancifully). Even so far south, these mountains suffered glaciation in the last ice age and many of its effects are still very evident in glacial lakes and extensive moraines, especially the classic U-shaped glacial Zêzere valley in the heart of the mountains. A road penetrates the full length of this valley and it is one of the highlights of a drive in the mountains. In the higher regions, the environment is hostile to human activities but the shepherds make intensive use of the natural grasslands for summer pasturing. At slightly lower

Castle / fort
Cave
Site of special interest

N

Marialva

Figueira do
Castelo Rodrigo

Castelo
Rodrigo

Trancoso

Pinhel

Almeida

Malta

226

226

340

Freixadas

Leomil

102

226

221

332

340

332

Celorico
da Beira

IP5

IP5

IC6

IP5

IP5

16

Vilar
Formoso

Carrapichana

Castelo
Mendo

221

324

232

Linhares

GUARDA

Gouveia

232

IP2

Seia

Manteigas

Valhelhas

232

324

233-3

232

Sabugueiro

Penhas
Douradas

Poço do
Inferno

Caldas de
Manteigas

IP2

Belmonte

Sortelha

Sabugal

IC12

Serra da Estrela

Penhas
da Saúde

233

Torre
1993m

Covilhã

Caria

Unhais
da Serra

IC7

Tortozendo

Capinha

233

Fundão

Penamacor

SPAIN

18

233

Aranhas

332

Salvador

Monsanto

332

Idanha-a-Velha

233

Alcafozes

IP2

Idanha-
a-Nova

0   5 miles
0   10 kms

**CASTELO
BRANCO**

173

levels, but still above 1200m, rye is grown extensively. Stone-built houses with straw roofs known as *casais*, seen dotted about the higher regions and usually by water courses, are for the protection of shepherds and summer farmers. One of the most important products of the area, Serra da Estrela cheese, is famous throughout the country.

Choosing a time to visit is critical. Snow lies on heights above 750m usually from late November to early April, which has allowed the development of the country's only ski resort at Penhas da Saúde. The ski season is short since the snow is only reliably present from January to March. For hotels on or near the mountain this is high season for prices, the low season being the non-skiing summer months. Rainfall is very high and can reach 3000mm in a year with most of this falling between October and May, usually in torrents. Recorded hours of sunshine are equally generous over the year, totalling on average 2650 hours with July as the sunniest month. Summer, mostly dry and sunny, is a good time to visit but flower lovers may well wish to risk the spring, when May is the optimum month.

In July 1976 the whole upland area was declared a Natural Park to protect and preserve not just the land itself, but the cultural activities which take place there and to control rural development. An excellent, contoured 1:50,000 scale map of the park area was published by the Instituto Geográfico e Cadastral in 1992 and is available for purchase at any of the park information offices around, principally at Manteigas, Gouveia and Seia (see page 190, for addresses). Walkers too are well catered for and a major network of walking routes criss-crossing the whole of the mountains has been established, waymarked and detailed in a book entitled *Discovering the Serra da Estrela*, available in English, also from the park information offices.

Apart from exploring the mountains of the Serra da Estrela for its landscapes and villages, there are a number of interesting excursions into the surrounding district, which is riddled with old invasion routes of the Moors and the Spanish. The legacy of this turbulent period is a rich heritage of hilltop walled towns and castles all within easy driving distance for a day excursion. In choosing a base to explore the region, the *Hotel Quality Inn* at Penhas da Saúde, situated at an elevation of 1500m, is there essentially for the ski trade but open throughout the year. If many excursions off the mountain are planned then a hotel at the foot of the mountain, like the modern *Hotel Turismo da Covilhã*, might be considered. This is located on the western fringe of Covilhã with easy access to the IP2 for escaping on excursions.

Touring Serra da Estrela

There is no convenient circular tour to encompass all the spectacular scenery and cultural diversions which the park has to offer, but this suggested tour covers many of the attractions of this beautiful area. Starting for convenience at Penhas da Saúde above Covilhã, the route follows the fascinating, glacial

Flowers of the Serra da Estrela

The activities of man over the centuries in cutting and burning timber has destroyed the natural forest that covered the high mountain slopes in earlier times. Heathlands and grasslands have developed in their place and only a few remaining patches of trees are thought to be relic woodlands providing clues to the vegetation of the past. Pine plantations, mainly *Pinus pinaster*, now give a more forested look to the lower slopes while the montane zone, at 800–1600m, contains chestnut, *Castanea sativa*, and oak, *Quercus rotundifolia* (thought to be one of the relic species), although there are many more trees now introduced by the Forestry Department.

In spite of this deforestation, there is a rich flora which makes its appearance the moment the snow melts. Amongst the most delightful of the flowers are the spring bulbs, which include *Crocus carpetanus*; the delightful dwarf daffodil, *Narcissus bulbocodium* which is particularly common in some areas; two other narcissus species, *N. asturiensis* and *N. triandrus*, the deep blue *Scilla monophyllos* mostly found in a touch of woodland; the elegant *Fritillaria lusitanica*; and bluebells, *Endymion nonscriptus* – all ably supported by that other harbinger of spring (although not bulbous, the primrose, *Primula vulgaris*. Only the early visitors will catch a sight of the dog's-tooth violet, *Erythronium dens-canis*, although its lovely marbled leaves are around for some time after the flowers finish. Orchid buffs will be disappointed that the orchid flora is represented only by the early purple *Orchis mascula*, and the broad-leaved helleborine.

Typical of heath areas, the heather family is well represented in *Calluna vulgaris*, *Erica arborea*, *E. australis* and the compact *E. umbellatum*. Growing in similar areas is the strawberry tree, *Arbutus unedo*, prized down in Algarve for its fruit which is used to make *medronho*, a fiery spirit. At the shrub level, the blaze of yellow in spring is provided by the broom family of which the tall, endemic *Cytisus grandiflorus* is outstanding; there is also a white broom in *C. multiflorus*.

Even on the apparently barren summits dominated by the tough *Nadus stricta* grass there are always flowers to be found, usually in crevices and sheltered habitats. The small yellow-flowered *Gagea nevadensis* or the pink-flowered endemic *Silene foetida*, easily identified by its unpleasant smell, take their place with the expected saxifrages like *Saxifraga granulata* and *S. spathularis* as well as sedums, *Sedum anglicum* and *S. brevifolium*.

This is only a very brief summary of the flora. There is a book available – although not very comprehensive and in Portuguese – from the park offices (for addresses, see page 190).

Cut by an ancient glacier, Zêzere valley is used by farmers throughout summer

Zêzere valley to Manteigas before climbing west and leaving the park through Gouveia only to re-enter further north to visit the historic town of Linhares, the focal point of the tour. The return heads south down the IC6 to Seia and recrosses the park via its highest point, Torre, to complete the circuit. Around 160km (100 miles) of driving is involved, which requires a full day for a leisurely tour with time for stops to absorb the views and places of interest.

The disorganised collection of buildings and chalets which is Penhas da Saúde is dominated by the Hotel Quality Inn. It lays no claims to being a village, just a ski resort which is more alive in winter than in summer. Going west on the IC12, which is the main route crossing the park from Covilhã to Seia, the right turn to Manteigas is shortly reached. This road leads almost instantly to the head of the remarkable **Zêzere valley** and for a short distance there are spectacular views down the length of the valley. A lay-by here on this otherwise narrow road provides an opportunity to drink in the views and study the results of an ancient ice flow in carving out this text book U-shape valley. On the final-right hand bend before entering the valley proper, there is a well equipped picnic site with wooden tables beneath the trees and a refreshment bar in season, all tucked away in a fold of the hills on the left and totally invisible from the road. As the valley lies essentially on a north–south line, the lighting varies rapidly throughout the day and the heavy shadows down the right hillside all too soon become shadows on the opposite side; however, it is well lit around midday. The valley takes its name from the River Zêzere which arises here in the Serra da Estrela and flows south, becoming quite a major river before eventually flowing into the Tagus.

A rural scene near Manteigas, the town which lends its name to butter in Portuguese

Once in the valley, the road follows down the right shoulder and there is little opportunity to stop unless the traffic is very light, but there is a succession of interesting cameos presented by the summer farming activities. Seen on the valley bottom here are the stone-built thatched shelters, *casais,* which are peculiar to the park area, and you may glimpse one of the special breed of dog used by the shepherds. This Serra da Estrela mountain dog, as it is called, is a large fearsome animal, usually with a long-haired thick coat and said to be bred from wolves. Unlike many shepherd's dogs, it is relatively docile but that does not mean it can be treated like a pet! Towards the end of the valley look for a sign off right to **Poço do Inferno**, a mountain waterfall which is at its most spectacular when frozen in winter or when carrying the snow melt in spring. In summer it is frankly disappointing.

Manteigas, spreading down the hillside, is the first village reached but apart from its general ambience it offers little reason to stop, except perhaps to collect information from the park office. It is surprisingly short of hotels, except for Hotel Manteigas next to the spa, but it does have three pensions. The town is famous for its dairy products, especially butter as its name implies, and trout fresh from the river.

The road out of Manteigas towards Gouveia and Seia climbs in a spectacular manner gaining height at the expense of distance and when Pousada de S. Lourenço is eventually reached 13km (8 miles) later, Manteigas is still in view far below and looks to be around 2km (1 mile) away as the crow flies. Dramatic views enliven the drive virtually all the way to Gouveia.

Gouveia has grown to a reasonable size as a provincial town. Its Thursday market and a park information office may be reasons to stop; otherwise it is enough to catch glimpses of the town's good solid buildings and main church with its façade decorated in *azulejo* tiles as you drive through. From here head north along the main IC6 (EN17) to pick up signs for Linhares.

Set on the slopes of the Serra da Estrela overlooking the wide Mondego valley, atmospheric **Linhares**, once important on the stage of history, has been left in isolation somewhere back in an earlier century as events moved on. Cobbled alleyways between the solid stone houses lead uphill to a castle clinging hard to a granite crag. The story of the castle is lost in uncertainties ,but it seems to have played a role in establishing the kingdom and was mightily reinforced by that indefatigable castle builder Dom Dinis (1279–1325). As the castle faded in importance and life became more peaceful, the villagers moved from inside the walls to resettle outside. Two towers and extensive walls remain intact and some restoration work is in hand. The parish church, Igreja Matriz, was extensively rebuilt in 1743 and has a simple interior with a Baroque gilded retable. Its surprise element is three paintings by one of Portugal's most famous painters, Groã Vasco. Old ladies in black and donkeys are all part of the enduring appeal of Linhares. On leaving the village, watch out for the granite slabs of an old Roman road.

Return south down the IC6 as far as Seia to prepare for the most dramatic route of all crossing the highest point of Serra da Estrela en route back to Penhas da Saúde. Just 5km outside Seia, the route passes the modern

Albergaria Senhora do Espinheiro before arriving at **Sabugueiro**. Situated at an elevation of 1050m and claiming to be the highest village in Portugal, Sabugueiro is very touristy and keen to flag down passing motorists to sell them fur and leather goods from its art and craft shops. From here the dramatic landscape steadily takes over, and when the trees are all left behind there seems at times nothing left to hold the road against the side of the mountain. Lagoa Comprida, a large dam passed on the upward climb, succeeds in being a tourist attraction and is equipped with a shop and café, open in season. The summit at **Torre** greets you with barren, hostile scenery on a sweeping scale. Bleak, grey granite dominates the landscape all around making the presence of a hospitable café all the more welcome. It is said that Dom João VI (1816–26) ordered a tower to be built 8m high to ensure the mountain reached a total of 2000m. On a fine day the views from here are as sweeping as any in Portugal. On leaving the summit towards Penhas da Saúde, watch out for the shrine and giant sculpture cut into the dark rock at Covão de Boi. Soon after is the road junction for Zêzere valley and beyond that it is back to Penhas da Saúde where this tour started.

Viseu

If city life calls as a change from mountain air, then Viseu is quickly reached along the IP5 (EN16) joined at the north end of the Serra da Estrela. Set amidst forested hills on the banks of the River Pavia, Viseu is an episcopal city of ancient origin and the capital of the Beira Alta region. Life began here as a *castro* back in Roman times and possibly even before, and it has been popu-lated by various invaders briefly or otherwise – over the years, including the Moors. Much of the town's fine architecture and places of interest are found within the old town buried in the heart of the new. This is the place to start, in the large cathedral square which also contains the Misericórdia church and the Bishop's Palace, now the Grão Vasco museum. The **cathedral**'s twin-towered façade in dull granite holds no promise, but the inside is far more elegant, particularly the rope motif carved in the stone of the vaulting and the painted ceiling. A lot of rebuilding was undertaken between the 16th and 18th centuries leaving a mixture of styles. If the vault is Manueline, there are also Gothic influences around and Baroque in some of the carved and gilded retables. The main retable was replaced in 1730 – the paintings by Grão Vasco from the original are kept in the museum.

Opposite the cathedral, and with a much more attractive Rococo façade in granite and white, is the **Misericórdia**. Built in the 16th century by Jorge de Ataíde originally as a small hermitage, it was enlarged much later in neoclassical style. Next to the cathedral is the **Grão Vasco museum** in the former Bishop's Palace. Grão Vasco (Great Vasco), or Vasco Fernandes (c 1475–1541) to use his proper name, is recognised as one of Portugal's most important painters. He bought a house in Viseu in 1512 and lived there until his death. Much of his work is displayed on the second floor of

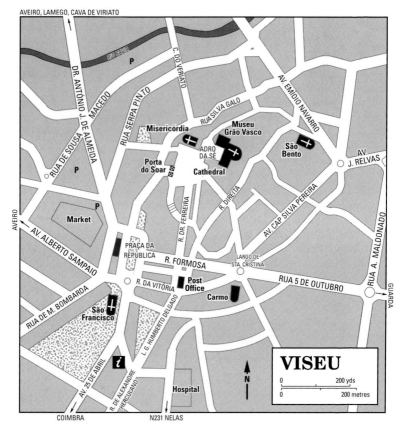

the museum along with that of other masters of his school of painting.

To the south of the cathedral square is a warren of small streets teeming with life. Wander first to the west, which leads to Porta do Soar, one of the town's original gates. South from here heads into Praça da República, or Rossio, which has a long wall attractively covered in blue and white *azulejos*. The tourist office is located a little further down the broad Avenida 25 Abril, on the right.

Touring to the north-east of Serra da Estrela

The villages of Trancoso, Almeida, and Castelo Mendo offer a feast of castles and medieval images and all can be visited in a one-day-long tour following scenic routes. Starting from the north end of the Serra da Estrela again, use the IP5 to head east towards Spain. Castelo Mendo lies just south of this road, not too far from the Spanish border.

Castelo Mendo

After serving the country as a frontier post for almost two millennia, Castelo Mendo is a forgotten town swathed in an air of mystery and now relying on EU money to repave its dirt and cobbled streets. Its location attracted settlers from Celtic times and when the Romans arrived they were greeted with fortifications involving three lines of walls. Alani, Vandals, Goths and Moors followed each other in succession, all coveting this well fortified settlement. After the reconquest by the Christians, it was Don Sancho I (1185–1211) who, finding the castle ruined and abandoned, decided to reconstruct the defences and resettle the town which was well enough established by 1229 for Dom Sancho II to grant a franchise. This franchise gave the right to hold a fair three times a year, at Easter and on the feasts of St John and St Michael, indicating the importance placed on sustaining this settlement. Dom Dinis (1279–1325) came along to improve the fortifications with the addition of town walls entered by six gates, three of which can still be seen. It remained garrisoned but suffered during later wars, including the Peninsular War, after which it was all but abandoned.

On the immediate approach to the town, by the church, there are some mysterious granite crosses mounted on and around granite boulders. Some have stones carefully placed around them as if for some kind of ritual worship. The village is entered through a gate flanked by two stout square towers, remnants of the old town wall. Ancient Celtic granite pigs, one each side, guard the gateway; both are headless and badly scratched by passing motorised traffic. It is said that it was customary to cut the ears of these stone beasts to prevent them frightening passing animals. A medieval atmosphere pervades the narrow streets of the village which hide one or two attractive 17th-century houses. To the south, the highest part, is the castle, of which only parts of the walls and the ruins of castle buildings remain.

Almeida

Roads run fairly straight through this dry, inhospitable and boulder-strewn landscape and the drive northwards to Almeida is quickly accomplished. Sitting within a huge star of robust 18th-century walls, Almeida is one of the most highly fortified border towns in Portugal. This piece of territory, regarded as the key to the Ribacôa (the lands around the River Côa), has been fought over repeatedly by a variety of invaders from the time of the Moors onwards and its history is littered with conquests and reconquests. Originally settled by the Romans, its location was moved slightly by the Moors when they built the first castle. This fell to the Leónese in 1039, only to be recovered by the Moors in 1071. It was back in Leónese hands when the Portuguese wrested it from them for a time but it was not until 1297, under Dom Dinis, that the Leónese were finally ousted. A succession of Portuguese kings spent money reinforcing the castle, including Dom Fernando (1367–83) who proposed it as a base for the conquest of Castile. The only result was that the Castilians

Celtic Pigs and Medieval Pillories

In this part of Portugal, history is written in great tablets of granite. No monuments are more intriguing than the granite pigs found particularly in the Trás-os-Montes region and other parts settled by the Celts. The Celts, it seems, were superstitious people who believed that spirits were everywhere – in trees, unusual rock shapes, springs and animals. It was not a question of mythical animals, but the real creatures encountered in everyday life, maybe animals they hunted and admired. This may have been the case with the wild boar, once prolific in the mountains of this region, which the Celts equated with power and strength, endowed with spirits and identified with the Celtic goddess Diana Arduinna. Celtic deities were bewildering in their number, without organisation, the majority probably very local. Curiously, however, Diana was also the Roman goddess of the hunt. The boar achieved some significance with the Celts in other parts of Europe, as indicated by relics found elsewhere. A bronze shield found in England was embellished with a stylised rendering of a boar and a Celtic helmet found in Hungary was adorned with a bronze boar.

A *pelourinho* (pillory), in granite stands in almost every town and village throughout Portugal. It symbolised the right granted to the town to dispense justice and was accordingly built near to the centre of authority, the church, monastery or town hall. Where it was used for justice, the unfortunate criminal was chained either to the cross at the top or to hooks provided for whatever punishment was to be meted out. Most were built from the 13th century onwards and many moved in design away from the strictly functional to become an expression of art. *Pelourinhos* are seen in a wide variety of designs, even with twisted columns, and many bear personal motifs or sometimes a coat of arms. Some of the pillories seen in the northern villages, such as the one in Soajo, look older than medieval; the mysterious smiling face on the Soajo *pelourinho* may hold some other symbolism.

twice took the castle, which was recovered eventually by Dom João I in 1386 following the defeat of the Castilians in the decisive Battle of Aljubarrota in the previous year.

Work on the present form of the **fortress** started in 1641. It was in Spanish hands for a time around 1762, then more rebuilding followed, now on a Vaubanesque plan, and it rapidly emerged as one of Portugal's most strongly defended towns with cannon embrasures, flanks of bastions and a fortified perimeter 2.5km (1.5 miles) long. State of the art for the period, it enclosed parade grounds, guard rooms, field hospitals and covered roads. Almeida played a key role in events during the course of the Peninsular War (1807–10). It was taken over by the French under General Junot at the start of the war in 1807 and relinquished under the Treaty of Sintra (August 1808), when the French were allowed to withdraw unopposed. Napoleon's troops returned in 1810, led by Masséna, and attacked the fort. Unluckily for the Portuguese, a French shell lit a powder trail from a damaged keg just taken from the magazine in the main church. The explosion killed 500 Portuguese and, with the walls breached in ten places by the explosion, surrender to the French was the only option. Months later the Duke of Wellington, after his famous victory at Torres Vedras, surrounded the fortress only to have the French troops melt away under the cover of darkness.

Almeida has slowly faded into insignificance and is now nothing more than a peaceful town in the middle of inhospitable country, but its magnificent defences are still there and seem as strong as ever. Walls within walls, gates, bastions – this fort is one to thrill students of military architecture. Otherwise there is little to do except admire the fortifications and enjoy the atmosphere of this pretty village hidden within the old walls. There is a new *pousada, Pousada da Senhora das Neves.*

Some slight backtracking is needed to move on to the next port of call, Trancoso, reached via Pinhel. There is little to see in Pinhel, except for a couple of towers left from its fortified days. The alternative, if time allows, is to head north from Almeida to the atmospheric town of Castelo Rodrigo before returning south via Pinhel to reach Trancoso. Little remains of the castle and walls of medieval Castelo Roderigo but enough to lend character and beauty to the old town. Portugal's latest national monument, the Archaeological Park of the Valley of Coa, lies a little further north. A 19km (12 mile) stretch of the remote Coa Valley has recently revealed a treasure of Palaeolithic rock art. To view these 20,000-year-old engravings, head up the EN322 then EN222 in the direction of Vila Nova de Foz Coa as far as Castelho Melhor. A visitors' centre here offers guided tours of the main sites.

Trancoso

Although it is now a sizeable town of some 16,000 inhabitants, spread well beyond its original boundaries, most of the interest lies within the ring of medieval walls. Like many of the fortified towns in the area, Trancoso has witnessed a succession of landlords from the Celts onwards. It was Dom Dinis who fortified the town, although the castle itself is of Moorish origins. Dom Dinis took an obvious liking to the place since he chose to marry the 12-year-old Isabel of Aragón here in 1282, although they chose Leiria as their main residence. Dona Isabel proved to be the perfect loving wife; she later became known as Saint Isabel after the Miracle of the Roses. During her lifetime the king happily showered her with gifts including the towns of Trancoso, Leiria, Abrantes, Porto de Mós and Óbidos.

The town is associated with a number of events which have been written into history for one reason or another. It was here that the cobbler known as

Bandarra, recognised locally as a prophet, composed *Trovas* (c 1580), which described the return of Dom Sebastião and gave impetus to the messianic cult of Sebastianism. A large **Jewish quarter** thrived for a time in the Middle Ages, until the Inquisition became active here early in the 17th century. The houses are still to be seen, most of them with two doorways: a larger one for trade and a narrower, personal door on the upper floor for the family.

Enquire at Turismo (just outside the gateway into the old town), about entry into the **castle**, which is normally opened only on request, and for a town map to locate the points of interest within the spider's web of narrow streets. Much of Trancoso's fascination lies in its medieval atmosphere and monuments like the Romanesque Chapel of Santa Luzia and the pillory in Largo Pelourinho.

The route south from here back to Serra da Estrela leads past another walled town with castle, **Celorico da Beira**, which is worth a stop only if time allows. If the castle is closed, a key is available at the Câmera Municipal.

Touring west and south

This tour fully captures the sense of history in this wilderness of a border country, which played such an important role in the defence of Portugal throughout the Middle Ages. Five fortified villages are visited, Belmonte, Sortelha, Sabugal, Monsanto and Idanha a Velha, all of which suffered the same fate the moment their role was complete – neglect. If at all possible, the scenic run between Manteigas and Belmonte is worth including even if it means a diversion.

Belmonte

Belmonte is the birthplace of Pedro Álvares Cabral (1467–1526), the discoverer of Brazil, and the history of the town since then has been dominated by the Cabral family. There is a statue of Pedro Álvares Cabral himself in the square, and the church where he was baptised, the Romanesque **São Tiago**, stands on the hill by the castle. The church contains a small museum of some limited finds made in the castle grounds including buckles, knives, coins and some pottery. More importantly, the church contains the Chapel of the Cabral family with tombs of some of the family members who held title in the town. Apart from Pedro, many of the family demonstrated unusual qualities and gave their lives in the service of their country. Particularly famous was Fernão Cabral, one of the forebears of the famous navigator, who was an *alcaide* of the castle and a man of huge stature and enormous strength who became known as the Giant of the Beiras.

Head south out of Belmonte to pick up the N18-3 which joins the N233 before reaching Sabugal.

An unchanging lifestyle, seen here in the old streets around Sabugal castle

Sabugal

Dominated by its imposing medieval castle, Sabugal sits on a low hill on the banks of the River Côa. As noble as the **castle** seems from the outside with its strong battlemented walls and robust square towers, there is nothing to see inside, except the menagem (the keep). The inner buildings, which had been partially demolished by locals reusing the stone to build their own houses, were cleared sometime after the law of 1846 forbidding burials in churches, and the castle was then used as a cemetery. When the castle was declared a National Monument around 1950, the cemetery was moved and the walls restored. While the 39 steps leading up to the ramparts benefit from a handrail, the ramparts themselves are unprotected, although they are quite wide and offer good views over the castle wall down onto the town and over the river. Keen eyes will pick out an interesting low bridge over the river made of huge stone slabs. This is used by the local women to get to a spot on the far river bank which they favour for washing clothes. Inside the castle, the tall menagem tower is open to visitors with legs strong enough to climb the many steps inside.

Centuries-old granite houses are clustered around the castle walls and in the alleyways between, where children play while grannies work on their lace. The line of walls which went around the town no longer exists except for one of the gateways together with the Torre do Relôgio.

From Sabugal, Sortelha is signposted off down a minor road which is comfortable to drive and offers uncompromising views of this harsh granite countryside.

Sortelha

Perched on a huge heap of granite, Sortelha **castle** is endowed with a rugged beauty unrivalled anywhere except perhaps by Monsanto. A handful of houses lie within the castle walls, welded and melded around granite boulders, and many of them still occupied. A 16th-century pillory stands by the castle entrance where steps lead up onto the walls. Extensive views over a boulder-strewn landscape underline the defensive role of this castle recognised by successive Portuguese kings from Dom Sancho I onwards, first against the Moors, later against the Castilians and even against the French in the Peninsular War.

Wandering the village is an adventure in itself, using the footsteps cut into the granite boulders to make onward progress around the alleyways. This is one of the lesser known and visited fortified villages with facilities restricted to a single bar. Perhaps for these reasons it is one of the most atmospheric.

From here, backtrack to Sabugal and then head south on the N233 to Penamacor to pick up signs for Monsanto. Penamacor itself has a castle but it is barely worth stopping to see.

Granite dominates the scenery around Sortelha

Monsanto

The modern town of Relvo spreads around the lower slopes, while brooding old Monsanto sits on top of Mons Sanctus (Sacred Mountain) at an elevation of some 758m and crowned with a castle. Granite dominates on this craggy hilltop; the houses are built from it, welded to it and surrounded by it. Likewise the castle is a remarkable blend of man and nature, where a rugged defensive structure of huge granite blocks weaves between natural rock features to produce something strong and impenetrable.

There is an opportunity to park fairly high up the mountain but this still leaves some walking to reach the castle on the summit. Narrow cobbled streets full of old granite houses lead the way towards the top. The price of modernity in Monsanto, and other similar ancient villages, is a network of electricity cables across the streets, a forest of aerials on roofs and now satellite dishes on walls. There are still odd corners free of these intrusions to perpetuate the romance of how it once looked and to kindle a sense of wonder. Before entering the castle you encounter the shell of the Romanesque Chapel of São Miguel with some rock-hewn graves nearby, then inside there are courtyards, arches and walls strewn between boulders to see, steps to climb and ramparts to walk. It is a very atmospheric ruin and views alone make the climb worthwhile.

It is a relatively short onward journey of 16km (10 miles) from Monsanto south to Idanha-a-Velha.

Idanha-a-Velha

This charming backwater of a place built in honey-toned granite has some unexpectedly strong historical connections. Originally a Celtic settlement, it was taken over by the Romans and developed into one of the most opulent of Lusitanian towns, known as Egitania. Relics from this period are still around. The legendary Wamba, elected king of the Goths in 672, is claimed to have been born here, and it was the seat of a bishopric until the arrival of the Moors.

The next pleasant surprise is the model of quiet efficiency which the town uses to guide its small but steady flow of visitors around. An arrow on the wall observed on entering the village indicates the start of an archaeological circuit which leads to all the major historical points of interest and provides on-site information in both Portuguese and English. To be seen along the way is **Templars Tower** built on the site of an earlier Roman temple, an olive press where the granite millstones were operated by a donkey in harness, the **south gate** opened in the 4th-century Roman wall by the Visigoths in the 9th century, an ancient **Basilica** full of Roman inscriptions which is Visogothic in part, and the **north gate** which originally had three arches. There are extensive stretches of the original town wall in this area which is currently undergoing further archaeological exploration. Museum exhibits in the Chapel of **São Sebastião** add a little more substance to the historical importance of this tiny village. Two other things to see are the **Roman bridge** over the River Ponsul and the ancient **necropolis** near the entrance to the village. Here the sign points down the road but look out for a sloping path leading up the right-hand bank into the field within a few metres – easy to miss.

From here the easiest way back to the Serra da Estrela region is via Fundão which provides an opportunity to look at Covilhã.

Covilhã

Steeply terraced down the hillside, Covilhã has enjoyed a natural progression over the centuries from Roman town to market town in the Middle Ages, through textiles to important industrial town; it still trades heavily in wool. Apart from wonderful views of the mountains, there is not too much to see in the town itself, although the Romanesque chapel of São Martinho e Calvário in the lower town is worth a visit. It is a good place for shopping, with several giant supermarkets (almost too many) recently opening branches, and if you are running out of film or the camera needs new batteries, this is the best place to look.

From here the EN18 leads steadily south towards Portalegre which is the gateway to the northern section of Alto Alentejo, the next section of the country to be explored.

Practical Information

Hotels and Restaurants

ON SERRA DA ESTRELA

Albergaria Berne, Bairro Santo António, Manteigas (tel. 075 981 351). This four-star *albergaria* with 17 rooms has been recently improved and upgraded. **Albergaria Senhora do Espinheiro** (tel. 038 22 073). Located 5km (3 miles) east of Seia, this comfortable four-star hotel with 23 rooms is quietly positioned.

Pousada de S. Lourenço, Penhas Douradas, Manteigas (tel. 075 982 450). Opened in 1980 with 22 rooms, this occupies another superb mountain location, again with a good restaurant.

Quality Inn, Penhas da Saúde (tel. 075 313 809). Previously known as Hotel Serra da Estrela, this comfortable three-star hotel offers 38 rooms and is ideally located high in the mountains. It also has an excellent restaurant open to non-residents.

Residencial Estrela, Rua Dr Sobral, 5, Manteigas (tel. 075 981 288). A good value two-star establishment with 22 rooms.

The best restaurants on the mountain are found in the hotels, but for cheaper eating head for the pensions in Manteigas, most of which have restaurants.

OFF THE SERRA DA ESTRELA

The following hotels are located either on the skirts of the mountain or in nearby villages.

BELMONTE

Hotel Belsol, Quinta do Rio (tel. 075 912 206). An attractive two-star hotel with good facilities, including a restaurant.

COVILHÃ

Hotel Turismo da Covilhã, Acesso à Variante (tel. 075 323 843). Modern, pleasantly furnished three-star hotel with excellent facilities including sauna, jacuzzi, squash court, restaurant and coffee shop. Situated on the eastern edge of town.

Residencial Solnev, Rua Visconde de Corsicada, 126 (tel. 075 323 001). Inexpensive three-star *residencial*, 34 rooms, in the heart of town and with a good restaurant.

The best eating places in Covilhã are those associated with hotels and residencials of which there are a number.

GOUVEIA

Casa da Capela, Rio Torto (tel 038 46 423). One apartment and two rooms in a delightful 18th-century house just 7km (4 miles) south of Gouveia.

Hotel de Gouveia, Av. 1 de Maio (tel. 038 491 010). Two-star hotel with 31 rooms and a restaurant.

MONSANTO
Pousada em Monsanto (tel. 077 32 425). Integrated into the village, this granite-built *pousada* offers 10 rooms and a restaurant.

SEIA
Casa das Tílias, São Romão (tel. 038 20 055). Actually located within the Natural Park, this 19th-century manor is quietly located within its own grounds and offers six rooms to guests.
Hotel Camelo, Rua 1 de Maio (tel. 038 25 555). A fairly large three-star hotel with 56 rooms and good facilities, including a restaurant.

Places of Interest

Museu de Grão-Vasco,Viseu, open 9.30am–12.30pm and 2pm–5pm, closed Mondays.
Serra da Estrela Natural Park Offices
MANTEIGAS Rua 1 de Maio (tel. 075 982 382).
GOUVEIA Rua dos Bombeiros Voluntários, 8 (tel. 038 42 411).
SEIA: Praça da República, 28 (tel. 038 255 506).

Tourist Offices

Regional Tourist Office
Praça da Município, Covilhã (tel. 075 322 170).
Tourism Posts
BELMONTE Praça da República (tel. 075 911 488).
FUNDÃO Av. da Liberdade (tel. 075 52 770).
GOUVEIA Av. dos Bombeiros Voluntários (tel. 038 42 185).
GUARDO Largo da Sé (tel. 071 222 251).
MANTEIGAS Rua Dr José Carvalho, 2 (tel. 075 981 129).
PENAMACOR Av. 25 de Abril (tel. 077 94 316).
SEIA: Largo do Mercado (tel. 038 22 272).
VISEU: Av. Gulbenkian (tel. 032 422 014).

11. ALTO ALENTEJO NORTH

Not yet the sweeping plains of Alentejo dotted with spreading oak trees, this northern part has its own distinctive landscape, especially around the Parque Natural da Serra de São Mamede. Portalegre is not just the capital of the region but also the hub of the road system, which makes it a good base for exploring this lesser known area. Lesser known it may be but it includes two of Portugal's most beautiful walled towns, Marvão and Castelo de Vide, once vital in the defence of the realm, equally vital now in attracting visitors to the region. Elvas is the other major town visited. This could with equal facility have been included in the following chapter, along with Estremoz, but its close proximity to Campo Maior makes it a natural extension of this tour. Fascinating landscapes, Roman remains, blue and white painted Alentejana houses, huge chimneys and yet more castles weave a rich background tapestry to this beautiful and little explored part of Portugal.

Portalegre

Perched on the lower, western slopes of the Serra de São Mamede, busy Portalegre has long since expanded beyond the bounds of its **castle**. The Romans settled here and fortified their town but it is not thought there was any further serious castle building until the advent of Dom Dinis (1279–1325). There was a bit of family trouble at that time involving Dom Dinis and his brother. Their father, Dom Afonso III, had given Infante Afonso charge of Portalegre, Marvão, Castelo de Vide and Arronches. Dom Dinis in the meantime was too busy building castles here, there and everywhere to worry much, but he did grow concerned when Infante Afonso's three daughters all married Castilian noblemen. Fearing that these important border towns might pass through inheritance to the enemy, he laid siege to Portalegre, Arronches and Marvão and forced his brother to capitulate. In the agreement which followed, Dom Dinis gained control of the three border towns, giving his brother Óbidos and Sintra in exchange.

In its final form, the castle walls were strengthened by 12 towers and entered through eight gates. Today, apart from the keep with its Gothic windows on top of the hill, there is little left to see although some of the gateways have been incorporated into the town and can be seen arched between the houses. Portalegre found a new prosperity in textiles in the 17th and 18th centuries and these boom years left a legacy of now faded mansions. One of the most inescapable features of the town are the tall twin chimneys of the cork factory, started originally by the Robinson family from England. Part of the factory is shortly to be converted into a museum.

In spite of its size, there is not too much to see in town; the twin-towered **cathedral** makes a good starting point for a sightseeing tour. Portalegre has been an episcopal city since 1545. However, its cathedral, dedicated to Nossa Senhora da Assunção, only started to take shape in 1556 under the first bishop, Julião de Alva, and much of the present building is 18th century. The three-aisled interior lacks nothing in space, emphasised by the rib-vaulted ceiling set on granite columns which were plastered during the 18th-century renovation work. There are so many side chapels that the church almost appears to have five aisles and many of these chapels have Baroque altarpieces with paintings by Portuguese artists. Also of interest are the painted ceiling in the chancel and the blue and white *azulejo* tiles in the sacristy depicting the Flight from Egypt. Next to the cathedral is the **municipal museum** installed in the former Episcopal Palace and Diocesan Seminary, with a collection of fans, silver snuffboxes, pieces of furniture and, above all, a wealth of religious art from the 16th century onwards. The finest surviving monument is the 16th-century **Convent of Nossa Senhora da Conceição**, also known as São Bernardo monastery. It is occupied by the military for use as a training school, but they normally respond kindly to requests to look around. Inside the church is the tomb of the founder, Jorge de Melo, made from Estremoz marble and thought to be the work of the famous Nicolas Chanterène. For something very different, join one of the twice-daily (10am and 4pm) tours of the **Tapestry Factory** which occupies a former 17th-century Jesuit Convent, just a short walk from Rossio square.

Tourist offices around the country are usually good but they do vary greatly in the help they offer. The office at Portalegre is particularly sleepy and visitors arriving without accommodation should not rely on finding it open. There is a hotel in town, the *Dom João III*, which looks as austere as a barracks. More cheerful accommodation can be had out of town.

Touring the Parque Natural da Serra de São Mamede

These mountains are the highest in the country south of the River Tagus and reach an altitude of 1025m. Lying within the park boundaries are both Marvão and Castelo de Vide, which are included in this tour along with the highest peak, a Roman bridge and a host of charming villages.

Start out from a road at the southern end of Portalegre signposted simply 'Serras'. At first the road climbs up alongside the town but Portalegre is left behind as soon as the top of the hill is reached. Salão Frio is barely

N

0   5 miles
0   10 kms

Castle / fort
Cave
Site of special interest

CASTELO
BRANCO

IP2

18

364   Nisa

IP2

Castelo
de Vide

Alpalhão

Marvão

SPAIN

IP2   359

823m

Serra de S. Mamede

Flor da Rosa

IC13   119

Crato

PORTALEGRE

Alegrete

Ponte de Sor

Alter do
Chão

18

246

Esperança

'Penturas Rupestris'
(cave painting)

Arronches

Ouguela

Fronteira

Torre de
Palma

Monforte

371

Avis

Santa
Eulália

Campo
Maior

Sousel

IP2

Elvas

IC10   Estremoz   4   IP7

Borba

Arraiolos   18   Vila Viçosa

254

SPAIN

Redondo

ÉVORA   IP2   18

Monsaraz

Reguengos
de Monsaraz   Mourão

noticeable as a village but it does have a camp site and *Zé Maria,* an excellent local restaurant. Notice the road left here which is used in the onward route after first visiting **Pico São Mamede**, the highest peak. Stay ahead for the moment but travellers looking for accommodation might note the little sign on the left for O Pomar. This is the home of Ros and John Poulton, interesting and charming hosts from Kenya, who have rooms to let in their delightfully situated residence. Just past here is another good local restaurant, *A Lareira* (The Fireplace). Turn left at the fork and follow signs to S. Mamede and from here the peak is quickly reached. As usual for high peaks in this country, it bristles with aerials but a brief amble around to the left leads to a fine viewpoint from where much of the park area can be surveyed, including Marvão.

Return by the same route to Salão Frio but now turn right and shortly a clutch of pretty electric-blue and white houses, all neat and trim, announce the village of **Monte Carvalho**. Not a village of great merit or note but, set deep in the countryside, it will be hard to pass for those seeking tranquillity. Beyond here the main Portalegre road is reached where a right turn leads in the direction of Marvão. When the main junction is reached at Portagem, turn left but prepare to turn right almost immediately to visit the **Roman bridge**. Now a popular picnic spot with the locals, table facilities have been provided and the river dammed to make a swimming pool. On the Spanish side of the bridge is an old keep which once served as the toll house.

Marvão

From the Roman bridge at Portagem it is just a short hop to Marvão which is well in view long before it is reached. Perched high on a granite escarpment at an elevation of 950m, Marvão looks totally invincible to invaders. However, these days no efforts are made to repel visitors, who are encouraged to park their steeds outside the town and proceed on foot.

Although the Romans were around this area, certainly in the valley below, there is nothing to suggest they occupied the site of Marvão and equally there is only folkloric evidence to suggest it was settled by the Visigoths. Its history starts uncertainly around 1166 when it was recovered from the Moors and more certainly in 1226 when it was repopulated and granted a charter by Dom Sancho II. Whatever its state at this time, the **castle** was significantly rebuilt by Dom Dinis into a powerful fortification, but only after he had regained control from his brother following family problems (related in the history of Portalegre castle earlier). In 1641 when Portugal was struggling to overthrow Spanish rule and restore her own monarchy, the castle fell to the Spanish and was not recovered until 1664. Further restoration was required after the devastating 1755 earthquake and the castle was finally called into action again to repel the French in 1808 during the Peninsular War.

The castle has three lines of defences. First encountered is the outer wall encircling the whole town. Within is a second line of walls strengthened by towers which protect the inner castle comprising a keep and associated buildings. Bastions and artillery platforms were added in the 17th century to

The magnificent setting of Marvão castle

protect the eastern side which has the weaker natural defences. There is a huge water cistern in the castle, approached down steps and illuminated,

Castles in Portugal

As a country that has been a battleground over millennia, castles are firmly woven into the fabric and history of Portugal. Social organisation in the form of *castros* (fortified hilltop settlements) appeared with the Celts around 700–600 BC. Many *castros* have been discovered in the north, particularly around the Minho where excavations have revealed whole fortified villages, or *citânias*. The Romans adopted and strengthened some of the *castros*, and more conquerors in the form of the Visigoths and the Moors underlined the continual need for strongholds. By the 11th century Portugal was emerging as a nation and many of the earlier forts and castles, particularly those strategically placed near its borders and along the coast, were fortified to the best standards of the day. Spurred on by the fear of Castilian domination, the pace of castle renovation and rebuilding quickened with the arrival of the energetic Dom Dinis on the throne towards the end of the 13th century. Castle after castle was built or rebuilt and towns fortified in a broad defensive belt around borders most under threat and his son Dom Afonso IV carried on the same strategy. Modification and modernisation of castles carried on through to the 18th and 19th centuries.

Central to a castle was a principle tower, a **keep**, which was the ultimate defensive position. It was also used as an emergency or even permanent residence and often contained the public treasury, placed there for safety. Military appointments sometimes went to a local nobleman who was appointed the *alcaide* (captain), a position that often became hereditary. If the nobleman was particularly powerful and landed, then the appointment might become *alcaide-mor* (captain major). The *alcaide* was responsible for the management and maintenance of his castle and other fortifications in the region, for enlisting men, collecting rent, taxes and fines, as well as paying a tribute to the king.

Outside the keep lay the garrison, protected by the castle walls and **ramparts**. In their present day meaning of the top of the wall, or the path around the top encircling the enclosure, ramparts were an essential element for providing sentries with a high and commanding viewpoint, allowing access to towers and offering a protected firing position down on the enemy. The thickness of the walls determined the width of the ramparts, but where good width was provided it allowed easy and quicker access for archers to assume position and for the movement of defensive engines. Access was normally by stone steps set against the wall. Where the walls were thinner, the ramparts were often constructed of wood, rather like a long platform. The introduction of cannons in the 16th century necessitated some changes in design, leading to thicker walls and wider ramparts with access by wide ramps rather than steps.

Towers were also built into the castle walls as buttresses or simply as defence for long stretches of wall. From the 12th century towers were predominantly square, but prismatic angle towers offering a greater range of firing positions started to appear in the 14th century. Angled towers had a distinct drawback: destruction of a corner by the enemy led to the collapse of two adjacent walls, seriously weakening defences. Recognition of this weakness led to the building of cylindrical corner towers around the 15th and 16th centuries. Walls were castellated for the protection of the sentries or archers, and the **battlements** acquired various forms – typically square or chamfered in Portugal – and sometimes included arrow slits. From the 14th century onwards, the merlons were widened and the spaces between often made with a downward slope to assist the launching of stones or boiling liquid onto the enemy. Later, when cannons arrived, these spaces were adapted and shaped for guns, or special embrasures were incorporated in the parapet.

Strongly constructed **balconies** were often used as an element of vertical defence and they are seen typically at a high position on the keep or sometimes on the castle walls. They were often provided with a hole in the floor through which boiling liquids could be poured. Brackets, or corbels, supported the balconies which themselves became a decorative element. A later development was the **bartizan**, a small enclosed tower built at the angle of the castle walls; it was more frequently used on forts which lacked a keep or a tall tower. The bartizan provided a sheltered and protected lookout point for a sentry, usually just big enough to enclose a standing soldier. Architects had a field day with bartizans, and many amongst the varied designs are decorative and attractive while still wholly practical.

Doors or gateways into the castle called for special defensive precautions, often resulting in two offset entrances with a space or courtyard between which could be used to trap and attack intruders. Ironwork, plate and bars were used to strengthen the doors against attack by battering rams and later an iron portcullis was introduced. Drawbridges too were part of the defensive system used from the Middle Ages onwards.

Gradually, when artillery had finally replaced archers, the castle evolved into a fortress of simpler design, more suited to modern weapons. The high tower was no longer appropriate. Now bastions were built into the angles of the fortress walls allowing fire to the flanks along the face of the main fortress wall.

Central Portugal is rich in castle remains, some still in good heart, others in sad decay, but all having experienced the thick of battle. Their mute stones could tell of heroic deeds, of death and starvation; as it is they tell a tale of survival, of the emergence of a nation and of their own redundancy.

which is said to store enough water to supply the town for more than six months. It must be added that the population is less than 1000. This is an open castle which is fun to wander around, if it is not plagued by the swarms of earwigs it suffers in late summer. Next to the castle is a small but interesting **museum** located in a church, which houses bits and pieces from early periods including the Iron and Bronze Ages and from the Roman era, as well as the inevitable religious artefacts. One room gives information on local dolmens and menhirs.

Walking around the outer walls provides some interesting and different viewpoints of the town, which is a delightful muddle of narrow cobbled streets, whitewashed houses and flowerpots. Hidden within the streets and on the road which leads in from the entrance, are a number of shops and bars, including a handicraft shop which sells only produce of the village; this includes pottery, jewellery, honey, jam and even perfume. Surprising as it might seem, there is some accommodation available in town including a *pousada* and the attractive *Dom Dinis* pension.

Just a short distance down the access road from the entrance to the town is the Monastery of **Nossa Senhora de Estrêla** which now houses the Misericórdia hospital. Its origins are more interesting than the church itself. Folklore has it that when the Visigoths were fleeing from the Moors, they hid a small statue of the Virgin which remained undiscovered for 400 years, until a bright star led a shepherd to the spot. A chapel built there was transformed in 1448 when the Franciscans were allowed to found a small monastery. Our Lady of the Star was in the thick of many battles and there are countless tales of her intervention.

The next destination, Castelo de Vide at the northern end of the Serra de São Mamede, is quickly reached from here.

Castelo de Vide

Much larger than Marvão with a population around 4500, Castelo de Vide is no less beautiful.

The medieval upper town has 14th- to 16th-century white houses, often with Gothic portals, crowding the cobbled streets around the castle, while the lower town has crystal-white houses of the 17th and 18th centuries. It takes little imagination in some of these streets to be cast back into the Middle Ages – give or take a few wires and cables, they have hardly changed.

The town was occupied by the Romans around AD 44, and their military road connecting Mérida, the capital of Lusitania, to the western coast of the peninsula, ran through the valley. Roman generals were believed to have built the first fortifications which were destroyed by the Vandals in the 5th century; the Moors arrived in the 8th century and probably rebuilt the defences. Knowledge of the town's history becomes a little more certain from 1180 when Portugal's first king, Dom Afonso Henriques, granted the town a charter. Once Dom Dinis had recovered the town from his brother Afonso by a swap arrangement involving Óbidos and Sintra and other towns away from the

Attractive Castelo de Vide still keeps watch over the medieval town

border country, he ordered major work to commence on the castle. This was continued by Afonso IV and Pedro I. The castle was involved in a swap for a second time when Dom Fernando gave it to the Order of Christ in exchange for Castro Marim. Castelo de Vide was involved in all the same scrapes and skirmishes as Marvão right up until the Peninsular War in the early 19th century.

Elegant Praça Dom Pedro V at the hub of the modern town is a good place to absorb the atmosphere, perhaps from one of the café tables, before setting out on a walking tour of the old quarters. There are many fine buildings in the square including the town hall and the Torres Palácio, now a hospital, which was the birthplace in 1780 of the statesman Mousinho da Silveira. Set off by passing the rear of Igreja de Santa Maria da Devesa and entering Rua de Santa Maria. Flower-decked houses with iron balconies and granite doorways huddle along the steep narrow streets leading up to the old town which is entered through an arched doorway in the walls. Inside there are more white-washed houses, some with Gothic doorways, crowding the narrow, cobbled streets, full of flowers and cared for with pride. The medieval town within the walls here preserves such an ancient atmosphere that it is far more interesting than the castle itself. Entrance to the **castle** is free but it does have opening hours (see page 200). The keep, which was badly damaged in an explosion in 1705, is reached by walking across the roof of the large *cryptoporticus*-like building on the left on entering. There is not a great deal to see since a lot of the castle is in a poor state of repair although the walls are still intact.

On completing a tour of the old town, leave through the same gate but now turn left towards the old Jewish quarter to find the old **synagogue**, located just off left near the top of the delightful Rua da Fonte. Descend ahead down the cobbled and flower-fringed Rua da Fonte to reach an irregular square containing the well-worn and fascinating Renaissance covered fountain, Fonte de Vila. Heading further down back to the square completes the circuit.

Local handicraft shops offer something a little different in pottery dolls and cork dolls alongside the more usual embroidery and woodwork, but if shopping therapy is failing to revive you, head for the café to try some local cakes. Either *boleima* (bread cake with apple) or *bolo de castanha* (chestnut cake) with a coffee should restore sufficient energy for the drive back to base.

Destinations south

A southern tour usefully incorporates a number of smaller places of interest although Elvas remains the focal point and requires the most time. On the way down, there is a side trip to Esperança to see some cave paintings before the fortress town of Campo Maior is reached, and there is the option of a further side trip to medieval Ouguela before pressing on to Elvas for the main feast. On the return Monforte awaits and nearby is Torre de Palma, a surprisingly large Roman site.

Head south out of Portalegre and take the road signposted Arronches and Campo Maior. For a diversion to see the prehistoric cave paintings, turn left at Arronches heading for the village of **Esperança**, and on reaching the village follow signs for 'Penturas Rupestris'. This leads to the cave, which lies about 3km (2 miles) outside the village. Now with faded colours, the paintings are not immediately obvious, but when the eyes adjust quite a number of them can be picked out on the rock face. Return to Arronches and continue to Campo Maior.

Campo Maior

Keep following the 'Castelo' signs through the narrow streets of this large agri-cultural town to follow the **castle** walls around to the entrance. The houses of unusual design against the castle walls were originally the garrison quarters and are still used as dwellings. They are supported along the front by a strong sloping buttress interrupted by bold arches which form the doorways into the houses.

Like many of the settlements in this region, Campo Maior's early history is uncertain. After the reconquest from the Moors by the Christians, it passed into Spanish hands for a time and it was not until 1297 that it reverted to Portugal under the Treaty of Alcañices, by which Castile recognised the defin-itive borders of Portugal. Dom Dinis (1279–1325) wasted no time in rebuilding the castle into a major stronghold to defend one of the more tempting invasion routes from Spain. Later kings, particularly Dom João II and Dom Manuel, introduced further modifications and improvement and reduced the town in size so that all could live within the castle walls. In the turmoil which followed the death of Dom Fernando in 1383 and the end of the first dynasty, Campo Maior, like many other towns and nobles, took the side of Dom Fernando's daughter Beatriz, and Castile. It was not until 1388, three years after the issue of succession had effectively been settled by the defeat of the Castilians at the Battle of Aljubarrota, that Dom João I was able to recapture the castle.

A furious spell of serious rebuilding took place in 1640 when Portugal revolted against Spanish domination. The castle was completely remodelled into a fort with the aid of Frenchman, Nicolas de Langres. New lines of walls were added, with bastions and ravelins to raise the fortifications to state of the art for the period. This fort was no stranger to military action, but it faced its biggest test when attacked by a huge Spanish force in 1712 during the War of Spanish Succession and survived 36 days of siege. This action left many dead but it was not as destructive as the natural disaster of 1732 when a bolt of lightening struck the keep housing the powder magazine. The resulting explo-sion wounded and killed 1500 people and the castle and town were left in ruins. Dom João IV ordered the fort to be rebuilt and it was to see yet further military action before slipping into redundancy.

Inside the castle walls there is a large area to wander around although not too many buildings to inspect. Walking the ramparts around the walls does give a spectacular view down over this expanding town and the prominent parish church. Those looking for a more chilling experience could head for the parish church to inspect the adjacent **Capela dos Ossos**, decorated with human bones, rather like the one in Évora (see page 215).

Ouguela

Just 8km (5 miles) over the plains to the north, close to the Spanish border, lies the medieval town of Ouguela. Sitting on the only rise in these parts and still enclosed within heavy walls, with goats occupying the moat, Ouguela is another of those small towns which has been left behind by time and drips with medieval atmosphere. Originally a Roman settlement called Budua, it was later occupied by the Visigoths and then the Moors. After that its history broadly parallels that of nearby Campo Maior. Within the walls now are the garrison quarters and the governor's residence in ruins, mixed with trimly kept whitewashed houses. Built into the wall of the castle, but opening outside, is the parish church of Nossa Senhora da Graça.

Elvas

Busy Elvas is a lively frontier town which still lives within its star-shaped fortified walls. It draws a steady stream of visitors to see the castle and the Graça fort, the towering aqueduct bringing water from Amoreira, the cathedral and some of its other churches. The road from Campo Maior enters the town through São Vicente gate and keeping more or less straight ahead brings you to Praça da República at the heart of the town, which has a reasonable but still inadequate amount of parking space.

Dolmens and menhirs in the locality tell of early civilisations, but the Moors were along by 714 to take the town and build a castle. They stayed for 500 years until it was eventually recovered by the Christians in 1230. A legacy of the Moors is seen in some of the street names beginning with al-, like Alcaiza, Almocovar and Alcamin. Three lines of walls at one time fortified the town, but the inner ones have been absorbed by the town and some of the old gateways now form graceful arches between the houses. With the close proximity of the Spanish town of Badajoz, the need for powerful defences was recognised from the beginning and the almost constant modernisation over the centuries with ramparts, bastions and moats converted the town into one of the strongest fortresses in the country.

After withstanding many skirmishes with the Spanish, the town succumbed to bribery by the Spanish Philip II in 1580 and turned itself over for a payment of money. The inhabitants redeemed themselves 60 years later when the opportunity arose to throw off the Spanish yoke. Elvas became an important base during the Peninsular War: it was from here that Wellington launched his successful assaults on Badejoz in 1811 and 1812.

Praça da República is a good place to start a tour of the narrow streets of the old town, and the first stop is the tourist office here to pick up a street plan. At the top of the square is the old cathedral, now the church of **Nossa**

Elvas: the tiny Largo de Santa Clara provides the setting for a 16th-century pillory

Senhora da Assunção. Elvas was the seat of the diocese in 1570 but lost its episcopal status in 1881. The present Manueline-style church was started around 1517 by the architect Francisco de Arruda on the site of an earlier Gothic church and the first mass was celebrated in 1535. The interior is divided into three aisles with the central one higher than the side aisles. *Azulejo* tiles in blue and yellow on a white ground (17th-century) decorate the nave and the sacristy.

Perhaps a more interesting church is the small, octagonal **Nossa Senhora da Consolação** just behind, which is built on the plan of a Templars' church. Do not be deceived by its plain exterior – the interior is quite sumptuous. It was built in 1543, but altered in 1659 and again in 1676. The cupola is supported by eight simple Tuscan columns which, like the vaults and archi-trave, are richly painted, the rest of the surfaces being covered with *azulejo* tiles of the mid-17th century. Behind this church lies the tiny triangular Largo de Santa Clara, where there is a 16th-century marble pillory and, in one corner, an old archway beneath a loggia which is one of the few remnants of the 10th-century Moorish wall. Following through the arch leads to the castle which does not offer too much excitement, apart from the handicraft shop now installed in one of the buildings. Here is the place to learn about the old craft of paper lacework used for kitchen shelves and for decoration in reli-gious festivals, and to see some examples. This craft was started by the Dominican nuns of Nossa Senhora da Consolação who packed boxes of sugar plums and covered each full box with a handmade lace napkin. The industry came to an end when the convent closed, but the art has now been resurrected by the ladies of Elvas.

Lying outside the city walls on the western side, in the São Francisco Valley, is the towering **Amoreira aqueduct**. This 7km (4.5 miles) of ducting which first brought water to the fountain in Largo da Misericórdia in 1622 actually took 125 years to build. While it can hardly claim to be the world's prettiest aqueduct, the 1132m stretch crossing the São Francisco Valley which piles arch upon arch to a height of 31m is at least impressive. It has now been elevated to the status of a national monument. There are two more forts asso-ciated with Elvas, **Forte de Santa Luzia** to the south, which can only be viewed from the outside, and **Forte da Graça** to the north, which can be viewed by arrangement with the tourist office (though they usually require advance notice to make arrangements).

Leave Elvas by the Portalegre road which leads first through the small village of São Vicente – where fat chimneys dominate tiny houses – to reach Santa Eulália which, in spite of its small size, boasts a bullring. From here follow signs through rolling countryside to the fortress town of Monforte. Although the town has its picturesque corners with some typically Alentejana houses, not enough remains now of the castle built in 1309 to make a stop worthwhile. Continue on the Alter do Chão road over a medieval bridge and through a shallow valley dotted with small chapels. Just 3km (1.9 miles) along this road watch for the sign on the left to 'Ruinas'. It is a further 2km (1.25 miles) down tracks before the Roman ruins of Torre de Palma are reached.

Torre de Palma

While this is the site of a very large **Roman villa**, possibly the largest on the Iberian Peninsula, there is little to see above ground and it really is one for history buffs. There is a caretaker, who normally presses a site plan of the main section onto visitors; the information is in Portuguese, but the plan is useful nevertheless. The villa was occupied from the 2nd through to the 5th centuries AD and included an elaborate house with two bath complexes, workshops for producing olive oil and other goods, and several still unidentified rooms. Excavations are ongoing and many of the mosaics unearthed are now covered for protection.

Just inside the entrance to the site, before the house complex is reached, are the remains of an early Christian **basilica** and **cemetery** complex. Excavations have shown that a Roman temple existed originally beneath the east end of this 4th-century church.

Return to the main road and continue on to Alter do Chão.

Alter do Chão

Dom Dinis (1279–1325) was fond of Alter do Chão and visited the town frequently, granting it many privileges. Dom João V was equally fond of it and, in 1748, the town was made the royal stud farm. Andalucian horses were imported and bred to produce eventually a highly sought-after Lusitanian breed. The stud remained with the House of Bragança until it was taken over by the state in 1910 on the collapse of the monarchy. It is the **Coudelaria de Alter-Real** stud, lying 3km (2 miles) out of town, that is Alter do Chão's main attraction.

There is also a **castle** to see, standing alone right in the centre of town. According to the plaque, it was built on the instruction of Dom Pedro I on 22 September 1359. Perhaps it was built at night, or the architect simply gave free rein to his expression, for the result is an irregular pentagon with three rectangular and two cylindrical towers. Look amongst the whitewashed houses of the village for the beautiful 16th-century fountain made from Estremoz marble.

From here the return route to Portalegre passes through Crato, another town with a 13th-century fortress, overgrown and neglected and only worth a stop if time allows.

The route south to Évora leaves behind the hills of Serra de São Mamede for the wide open plains and unique landscape of southern Alto Alentejo.

Practical Information

Hotels and Restaurants

PORTALEGRE
Hotel Dom João III, Av. da Liberdade (tel. 045 21193). Rather austere three-star hotel with 56 rooms. Facilities include a restaurant.
Guest House O Pomar, Estrada da Serra (tel. 045 25 720). Two double rooms available in a homely private house delightfully situated amongst the olive trees.
Pensão Alto Alentejo, Rua 19 de Junho, 59 (tel. 045 22 290). Situated near the cathedral, this inexpensive pension offers nine rooms, basic but clean.
Quinta das Varandas, Serra de São Mamede (tel. 045 28 883). Part of the Turismo Rural scheme, this refurbished manor house offering five rooms is situated within the natural park.
A Lareira, Estrada da Serra. Good Portuguese food; inexpensive/moderate.
O Cortiço, Rua Dom Nuno Alvares Pereira, 17 (tel. 045 22 176). Typically large Portuguese portions, well favoured by the locals and cheap.
Restaurant O Abrigo, Rua de Elvas, 74 (tel. 045 22 778). Good food in a pleasant atmosphere and inexpensive.
Zé Maria, Estrada da Serra, Salão Frio. Expect only typical Portuguese dishes in this locally popular restaurant; inexpensive.

CASTELO DE VIDE
Hotel Sol e Serra, Estrada da São Vicente (tel. 045 91 301). Modern, tourist style three-star hotel with good facilities including swimming pool and restaurant. Most of the 51 rooms have balconies.
Residencial A. Xinxel, Largo de Poço Novo, 5 (tel. 045 91 406). Fairly recently opened, expect spartan but clean rooms and a dining room tiled in blue and white *azulejos*.
Residencial Casa do Parque, Av. da Armenha, 37 (tel. 045 91 250). Three-star *residencial* offering 24 rooms but limited facilities.
Marinho's Restaurant, Volta do Penedo, 10 (tel. 045 91 408). Typical Portugues dishes served at a moderate price.

ELVAS
Hotel D. Luís, Av. de Badajoz (tel. 068 622 756). Large three-star hotel with restaurant.
Pousada de Santa Lucia (tel. 068 622 194). Located in the town, this modern building provides 15 rooms and a suite.
Restaurant O Aqueduto, Av. da Piedade (tel. 068 63 676). Good stone-floor atmosphere, menu includes a good range of fish dishes as well as meat; moderate.

MARVÃO
Pensão Dom Dinis (tel. 045 93 236). A very comfortable three-star pension well situated in town.

Corn drying in the sun outside a farmhouse at Portagem

Pousada de Santa Maria (tel. 045 93 201). Two of the larger village houses were converted in 1976 into a *pousada* which now offers 28 rooms and one suite.

Residential Sever, Portagem (tel. 045 93 318). A three-star *residencial* offering 15 rooms.

Marvão has a very limited choice of restaurants. There is always the pousada but it is very expensive; or try **Restaurant Veranda do Alentejo** in Largo do Pelourinho.

Places of Interest

ALTER DO CHÃO Coudelaria de Alter-Real stud farm, open 9am–5pm.

CASTELO DE VIDE Castle, open summer 9.30am–12.30pm and 2pm–8pm; winter 10am–12.30pm and 2pm–5.30pm.

CAMPO MAIOR castle, open 9am–12.30pm and 2pm–5pm.

ELVAS castle, open 9am–1pm and 3pm–6pm, closed Thursdays.

PORTALEGRE Municipal museum, open 9.30am–12.30pm and 2pm–6pm.

MARVÃO Museum, open 9am–12.30pm and 2pm–5.30pm.

Tourist Offices

ALTER DO CHÃO Câmera Municipal (tel. 045 62 454).

CAMPO MAIOR Câmera Municipal (tel. 045 686 104).

CASTELO DE VIDE Rua Bartolomeu Àlvares da Santa, 81 (tel. 045 91 361).

ELVAS Praça da República (tel. 068 622 236).

MARVÃO Rua de Matos de Magahães (tel. 045 93 226).

PORTALEGRE Estrada da Santana, 25 (tel. 04521 815) and Galeria Municipal, Rossio.

12. SOUTHERN ALTO ALENTEJO

First impressions of this part of Alto Alentejo might easily be of a peaceful, empty landscape of gently rolling cornfields dotted with flat-topped oak trees stretching endlessly mile after mile and broken only by farmsteads here and there. Arising out of nowhere are the towns which formed the front line of the country's defence against the old enemy, Spain. Alto Alentejo bristles with them, and with walled villages and castles where the echoes of history rumble around the old streets and shadowy figures flit along the castle ramparts – usually visitors these days. The past beckons everywhere in Estremoz, Vila Viçosa, Monsaraz and Mourão, but nowhere more strongly than in Évora, and these towns are as rich in culture as any in the country. To discover Alentejo takes time and is a little like opening a well-wrapped parcel: take away the medieval layer to reveal an Islamic wrapping, remove that to see the Visigoth layer and undo that to find an inspired Roman civilisation which left an indelible mark.

Southern Alto Alentejo offers more in accommodation than Baixo Alentejo but it still fails to meet the demand in summer, which makes touring without advance bookings risky in high season. There is another very good reason for avoiding high summer – it gets very hot just as it gets cold in winter. Évora, roughly 150km (94 miles) from Lisbon, makes an ideal base for touring the region and most places of interest lie within an easy day's driving. Estremoz would not be as convenient geographically, but does have the very tempting 30-roomed Pousada da Rainha Santa Isabel located in a 13th-century castle with antique furnishings of the period.

Évora

Historic Évora, which attracts more visitors than anywhere else in Alentejo, is a place of culture listed now by UNESCO as a World Heritage site. It has taken a long time to acquire this status, and farmers in the megalithic period would not have appreciated that they laid the foundation stones for it in the form of the menhirs and dolmens still around. The Celts were here, the Carthaginians passed through, but the first to leave a real mark were the

Romans. Lusitani tribes put up fierce resistance, especially further north, but by 60 BC Julius Caesar had set up colonies in the area at Pax Julia (Beja), Myrtilis (Mértola) and Ebora (Évora). Southern Portugal was culturally advanced before Julius Caesar's men arrived and it is likely that the Greeks and Phoenicians had already introduced some crops, including olives, although the Romans are generally credited with bringing vines, wheat and olives with them. Many of these crops were farmed around Évora on *latifúndios*, massive agricultural estates which employed large numbers of labourers with no stake in the land. That system introduced by the Romans is more or less still in place today and Alentejo is the only province in Portugal which has large farms under single ownership. The Visigoths followed the Romans early in the 5th century but their footprints have faded. Islamic forces took over in 714 and Évora continued to flourish, largely under the Ibn Wazir family. Gerald the Fearless (Geraldo Sem-Pavor), an outlaw knight, staged a surprise attack in 1165 to take the town from the Moors. At night time, he drove spears into the outside wall to make a ladder, enabling him to climb in and open the doors to the waiting Portuguese. In so doing he regained the favour of the king, Dom Afonso Henrique. Évora remained a cultural centre favoured by the first two dynasties of Portuguese kings and the Cortes was occasionally summoned here. The city attracted scholars and artists from far and wide and a Jesuit college was founded in 1559 by Cardinal Dom Henrique, who later became king. During this period it grew to become the most important city in the country after Lisbon. Spanish rule in Portugal at the end of the 16th century marked the start of a gradual decline for Évora, though it was here, in 1637, that the first serious resistance to Spanish domination occurred. In 1759, the Marquês de Pombal closed the Jesuit college and in 1808, during the Peninsular War, the town fell to the French forces of General Loison and was brutally sacked. The legacy of this rich and varied history is a collection of fine monuments which is bringing back some prosperity to the town through tourism.

The Town

Full of Moorish alleys, fine 16th-century granite and whitewashed buildings, wrought-iron balconies and arcaded walkways, the old walled town of Évora sits on a low rise and is still home to thousands, although the city has long since expanded beyond its medieval boundaries. The town plan could have been inspired by a spider's web with all roads leading to the centre, and it is around the centre that most of the interesting monuments are to be found. Évora is one of those places which runs away with time: set aside at a least a full day and expect to explore on foot.

Praça do Giraldo is the hub of the city if not quite the centre, and a good place to start a tour if only to pick up a street map at Turismo. A huge 16th-century fountain dominates one end of this spacious square, more or less in front of the Renaissance-style Igreja São Antão built in 1557, whilst the northeast side is pleasingly arcaded. Parasol-shaded tables from nearby cafés are set out in the centre in summer adding to the atmosphere. Rising out of the arcaded side of the square is Rua de 5 Outubro which leads up the hill to the cathedral and the Roman temple. A clutch of tourist souvenir shops line the route selling anything from wall plaques to pottery, carpets and items in cork; eye-catching for its difference is the Egyptian shop. Turn right at the top of the street for the granite **cathedral** with its ill-matched, square twin towers.

This grand Romanesque-Gothic structure, one of the finest cathedrals in southern Portugal, was built in 1186, possibly on the site of an earlier mosque, and dedicated to St Mary in 1204. The façade is fascinating, as the two Romanesque towers share no architectural features except for matching Gothic windows each side of the door. The buttressed bell tower has a clock face and is capped by a cone surrounded by a series of turrets similar to those seen on the converted mosque at Mértola, while the other tower has six irregularly placed facing windows and is topped by a single large cone covered in blue tiles. Each of the towers is as sturdy as a castle keep, which reflects the role of the church in protecting the people in the troubled times of the early Middle Ages. Between the towers, the deeply recessed porch protects the figures of the twelve apostles carved by a local sculptor in the first half of the 14th century. The interior is distinctly Gothic, with three soaring naves and a vaulted roof from which hang mighty chandeliers supported by rosary-like chains. Both the choir and the high altar were remodelled by the German J. F. Ludovice (the architect of Mafra) in the early part of the 18th century. Polychrome marble features strongly in the chancel and especially noticeable are the beautiful columns. A small entrance charge is made for both the cloisters and the Museum of Sacred Art located in the bell tower. The museum is abundantly and richly furnished with religious artefacts, ecclesiastical vestments and jewel-encrusted gold and silver chalices and crucifixes from the treasury – altogether a sobering display of wealth which raises more questions than answers.

The nearby archbishop's palace now holds the excellent **Museu Municipal**. Ornate doorways and windows from the original royal palace of Dom Manuel and the royal church of St Francis have been cleverly incorporated into the structure and form part of the exhibits. The central courtyard has a display of stonework from the Roman and medieval periods, whilst the ground floor Renaissance room has work by the French sculptor Nicolas Chanterène including some especially delicate marble pillars from the Paraiso monastery and the tomb of Álvaro da Costa. Chantarène worked in Évora for a period in the 1530s. Upstairs, the collection of 15th- and 16th-century paintings by Flemish and Portuguese artists easily outshines the period furniture.

Beyond the museum lies Portugal's best preserved Roman monument, the **Temple of Diana**. It was built in the 2nd or 3rd century AD and, while its actual dedication is not known, popularly assigned to Diana. Most of the podium remains but only the north end of the colonnade which once surrounded the temple still stands. Corinthian capitals carved from Estremoz marble grace granite columns (which have 12 rather than the more usual 24

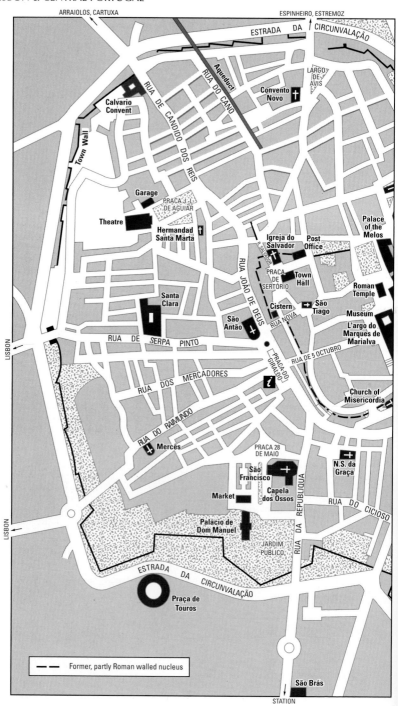

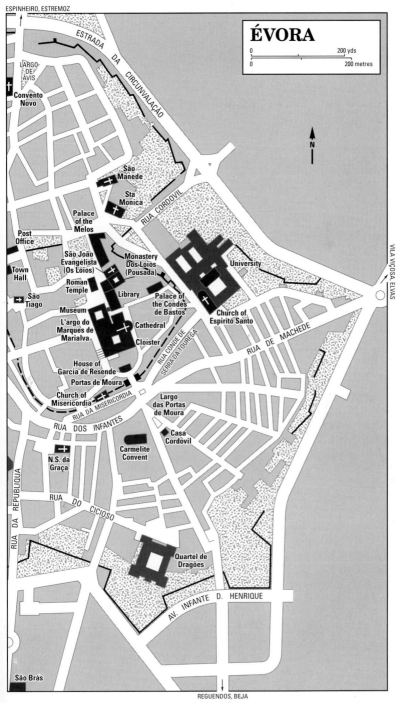

ÉVORA

0   200 yds
0   200 metres

N

ESPINHEIRO, ESTREMOZ

ESTRADA DA CIRCUNVALAÇÃO

LARGO DE AVIS

Convento Novo

São Manede

Sta Monica

RUA CORDOVIL

Palace of the Melos

Post Office

São João Evangelista (Os Lóios)

Monastery Dos Lóios (Pousada)

University

Town Hall

Roman Temple

Library

São Tiago

Museum

Palace of the Condes de Bastos

Church of Espirito Santo

L'argo do Marques de Marialva

Cathedral

Cloister

RUA CONDE DE SERRA DA TOUREGA

RUA DE MACHEDE

House of Garcia de Resende

Portas de Moura

Church of Misericordia

RUA DA MISERICORDIA

Largo das Portas de Moura

RUA DOS INFANTES

Casa Cordovil

N.S. da Graça

Carmelite Convent

RUA DA REPUBLICA

RUA DO CICIOSO

Quartel de Dragões

AV. INFANTE D. HENRIQUE

São Brás

VILA VIÇOSA, ELVAS

REGUENDOS, BEJA

213

flutes) and all are in a remarkable state of preservation. The temple was apparently used as a slaughterhouse until late in the 19th century and this may have helped with its preservation by preventing the stone being removed for other building projects. Adjacent to the temple lies the rather grand Pousada dos Lóios occupying the 15th-century **Monastery dos Lóios**, which is believed to have been built by the nobleman Rodrigo Afonso de Melo on the foundations of Évora castle, destroyed in 1385. In restoration, the chapter hall was converted into a restaurant opening on to the cloisters and many of the most elegant features of the former building, like a splendid Manueline arch, have been carefully retained. Visitors enquiring at reception are usually permitted to look around between meal times. Next to the *pousada* is the associated **Igreja São João Evangelista** which houses tombs of the de Melos family. Although a small charge is made for entry, it offers an opportunity to see 18th-century *azulejo* tiles painted by the master himself, António de Oliveira Bernardes, illustrating the life of St Laurence Justinian, patriarch of Venice. Squeezed between the church and the old Palace of the Melos (also known as the Cadavals) is the Jardim do Paço with its café/restaurant.

Walking past the old palace and turning right into Rua de Menino Jesus gives a view of the robust medieval walls and tower now built into the old palace. Parts of the wall that run through the small garden known as Largo das Colegias are considered to be original 1st-century Roman, although reinforced by the Visigoths some centuries later. Above the wall here can be seen the palace of the Dukes of Bastos where the kings lived when resident in Évora. Across the main road at the bottom is the modern **university**, which occupies a group of buildings originally built for the Jesuit college in 1559, and is regarded as one of the oldest universities in the world. It was closed down in 1759, when the Marquês de Pombal revenged himself by expelling the Jesuits from the country after they blamed him for the great earthquake of 1755 which effectively destroyed Lisbon and devastated large areas of the south. The university was re-established by parliamentary decree only in 1979. Turn left round the corner of the buildings to find the entrance to the Cloister of Studies which is well worth a moment or two. It is enclosed by a two tier-arcade supported by marble columns, and within the arcades are the classrooms, each identified by a tile on the outer wall indicating the subject taught.

From the university take the Rua do Conde de Serra de Tourega to pass around the hilltop back in the general direction of Praça do Giraldo. To the right, at the end of this road, are the sturdy twin towers of Portas de Moura, a former gateway to the medieval town. To the left is the rectangular Largo das Portas de Moura with an attractive spherical fountain in white marble built in 1559, and also to the south is the private 16th-century Casa Cordovil, eye-catching for its graceful horseshoe-shaped Moorish arches on slender columns. Still continuing towards Praça do Giraldo, along Rua da Misericórdia, look for a left turn into Rua da República to find **Igreja de São Francisco**. So many royal weddings took place here in the Middle Ages that it became dubbed the Royal Church of St Francis. Its architectural style draws on elements from the late Gothic and early Manueline with more than a touch of the Moorish, like the roof cones which here have the Manueline twist. It was built between 1460 and 1510, with a fine Manueline doorway which embraces the symbols of Dom João II (a pelican) and Dom Manuel I (an armilliary globe). The main attraction for visitors here is the macabre 17th-century **Capela dos Ossos** (the Chapel of the Bones), the walls of which are entirely covered with the bones and skulls of Franciscan monks exhumed from a nearby cemetery. A Latin inscription over the door warns: 'The bones here are waiting for yours.'

Évora seems to overflow with fine buildings from the 15th to 17th centuries, and if cultural overload has not yet taken its toll, the 16th-century **Palacio de Dom Manuel** in the park to the south is close by and worth a few moments. Originally a Franciscan monastery, it became the residence of kings, used by Manuel I, João III and Sebastião as well as the Castilian kings, who changed much of the structure of the original building. Now just one restored wing remains since the rest of the original palace was completely destroyed by fire in 1916. Like many of Évora's buildings, it combines Moorish, Manueline and Renaissance influences.

Around Évora

Surrounding Évora are a number of small fortified towns full of medieval character. All are within easy reach and, with a little planning, a number of these towns can be incorporated into a day's tour. Allow more time if the scattering of megalithic monuments around the area have high priority. There are some 25 recognised megalithic sites of dolmens, cromlechs, necropolises and menhirs, many of which have been declared National Monuments, and all are included in an excellent guide which details their location, published by the Câmera Municipal de Évora and available in English through Turismo. There are other sites besides and one or two of these are included or indicated in the tours described here. The first tour heads out on the eastern side of Évora taking in Évora Monte, Estremoz, Vila Viçosa, Alandroal, Reguengos de Monsaraz, Monsaraz and Mourão before returning to base. It is a tour rich in scenery, sites and history, but if time runs out distances are not so great and it is easy enough to return to Évora and pick up the tour again the next day.

Évora Monte

The EN18 out to Estremoz, signed off the ring road which basically circles the old medieval walls, quickly plunges into the cork oak-covered rolling hills which characterise the scenery in this corner of Alentejo. Medieval Évora Monte, dominated by its **castle**, lies up on the left, a short drive from the modern village. This easily defended steep hill, rising to 474m, has witnessed settlement from very early days and was crowned by a castle in Moorish times. This was restored by Afonso III and, with this part of the country in a state of near permanent warfare at that time, Dom Dinis continued with restoration and enlargement. He also enclosed a triangular section of the hilltop with sturdy town walls which still exist almost intact today. A violent earthquake in 1531 caused the collapse of the castle and part of the walls, but everything was immediately repaired and the angles of the walls were reinforced by cylindrical towers. Unfortunately, in recent restoration work the castle has been cement rendered, which entirely destroys its ancient appearance. There is not much to see inside the castle, although vaulted rooms on all three floors are open, but it is worth the climb to the top for the extensive views encompassing both Évora and Estremoz. Near to the castle, in Rua Direita, stands a house marked by a plaque where a treaty was signed on 26 May 1834 to end the civil war known as the War of the Brothers, between Pedro and Miguel. Miguel was forced into abdication and exile, paving the way for his niece Maria to become Queen of Portugal.

Estremoz

Estremoz, best known for its marble, is quickly reached from Évora Monte. It lies on chalky land containing zones of marble, which is extracted from the ground in the manner of open-cast mining, creating deep pits which can be seen in areas just outside the town. This fine-quality marble, worked also by the Romans, provides the main source of wealth for the area. Local clay is available too and has created a strong tradition in pottery; the best place to buy it is on the main square, Rossio, in the lower town, especially at the Saturday market. When Estremoz finally returned to Portuguese hands after the Moorish occupation, Dom Dinis walled the town, enlarged the castle and built himself a residence, now a *pousada*. The imposing square keep is often called **Torre das Três Coroas** (Tower of the Three Crowns), since it is believed to have been built during the reigns of Afonso III, Dinis and Afonso IV. Rising to a height of 27m, it is crowned with Moorish battlements terminating in pyramids and fitted with Gothic angled balconies.

Rossio, the main square, lies at the heart of the lower town which straggles out to one side of the old walled town. Surrounded by cafés, restaurants, shops and two convents, the square is always full of atmosphere but comes fully to life on a Saturday when the **market** comes to town. There is always pottery on sale no matter which day, for some of the pottery stalls seem to have taken up permanent residence here. Of the two convents, one is now the town hall and the other, once of the Order of Malta with two cloisters and a church, became the Misericórdia in 1880. Next to this church, at No. 62, is the **Museu Rural**, an excellent ethnographical museum with the life and lifestyle of the people depicted in miniature by models made in straw, cork, wood and metal, with some of the actual genuine artefacts also on display.

The old upper town is reached along a steep rising alley out of Rossio square on the opposite side to the museum. Abutting the Tower of the Three Crowns is part of the **palace** where Dom Dinis and Rainha Isabel lived for much of their lives. It was damaged by explosion in 1698, rebuilt by João V

The Story of Cork

The cork oak, *Quercus suber*, grows in coastal regions around the western half of the Mediterranean including the north African coast. It is dominant in Portugal and especially so in Alentejo which is home to around one-third of the world's oak trees. Annual cork production from Alentejo alone is sufficient to meet about half of the world's requirements and is a major export earner for the country.

Growing cork is not for the impatient. On the poor, acid soils of Portugal, it takes around 25 years for a tree to reach the stage where cork can be taken, but the slower the growth, the better the quality of the cork. The local pigs don't mind how long the oaks take to grow providing that the acorns keep falling – acorns, black pigs and Alentejo are inseparable. It is not just the cork oak that feeds the pigs; another extensively grown oak, *Quercus ilex*, produces much appreciated, sweet acorns. Both these oak trees are pruned to create a flat, spreading crown which provides plenty of shade for animals from the burning heat of the summer sun.

Cutting the cork is done in the height of summer when the gnarled, dull grey outer bark is easier to strip. Sharp axes are used to make first a horizontal incision around the circumference then vertical slits to enable the bark to be peeled off, first from the trunk then from the lower part of the branches. Provided that the outer cork layer, only is taken and the inner cambium is left intact, the tree suffers no permanent damage and sets about the task of replacing its outer cork layer, which takes around nine or ten years. Freshly stripped boles take on a wonderful wine-red hue which makes the cork oak easily identified even by the layperson, although the colour fades over the years as the cork grows again. A single number painted on a tree identifies the year in which the cork was taken, and where two such numbers are found on different parts of the tree, it indicates separate cropping by the farmer to regulate cash flow.

A single cutting can yield anything from (20 to 45kg). After removal from the tree the curved sheets are sorted, stacked and left in the sun to dry for several months, until the fatty substances which fill the millions of air cells have all been dried off. After boiling in water, the then flexible sheets are flattened and again dried in the sun. Not all cork is of the same quality – virgin cork from the first cutting, for example, is not as good – so all the cork needs to be graded for various applications. Low-grade material and cork waste is used for making composite cork board or for wall insulation, while better-quality cork goes to make bottle stoppers for the wine industry, filters for cigarettes, sound insulation in studios, shuttlecocks and a whole host of other applications.

and further restored in 1970 to house the Pousada Rainha Santa Isabel. It has 30 rooms and three suites all luxuriously furnished in 12th- and 13th-century style but with a 20th-century swimming pool! Isabel died here in 1336 – the room in which she died has been converted into a small chapel. She freely spent her husband's money helping the poor and needy and founding hospitals and orphanages. Dom Dinis was not altogether too pleased with his wife's largess at his expense and forbade her to continue. Seeing her walk out one evening on one of her mercy missions with something beneath her cape which he knew to be bread, he challenged her to reveal it to him. 'It is only roses,' she replied, opening her cloak to show him, and sure enough the loaves had turned into roses. Through her good works and the 'Miracle of the Roses' she became a saint in her own lifetime. Ask at reception to see the chapel which has walls lined with blue and white *azulejos* depicting the miracle performed by the queen. Across the road, in the old Hospicio de Caridade, is the **municipal museum** housing a whole host of exhibits including stelae, a reconstructed kitchen, furniture and a collection of painted ceramic figures.

From Estremoz the route starts to circle around to the south to take in Borba, Vila Viçosa and Redondo. Dazzling white **Borba** seems to be built of marble. It has the ruins of a medieval castle and a collection of buildings from the 16th to 18th centuries, but none with the grandeur seen in the more illustrious towns in this area. Marble quarries dominate and there is no escape until Vila Viçosa is reached.

Vila Viçosa

The peaceful broad streets lined with orange and lemon trees give no hint now of the drama which has unfolded here throughout the centuries, both in the castle and in the Ducal Palace. Strongly favoured by the Dukes of Bragança, Vila Viçosa became home to Jaime, the fourth Duke of Bragança, after his father had been executed for conspiring against the king. He found the castle a bit draughty so, in 1501, he decided to build a new residence. It was here, in 1512, that Duke Jaime stabbed to death his Spanish wife, Leonor, in a fit of unfounded jealousy. Later, with the overthrow of King Philip IV of Spain, the eighth Duke of Bragança was reluctantly persuaded to leave his comfortable life of painting and hunting in Vila Viçosa to ascend the throne in 1640 as Dom João IV. This was the start of the reign of the House of Bragança which lasted until Portugal became a republic in 1910. The palace was also the birthplace of Catherine of Bragança in 1638, and Dom Carlos spent his last night there before his assassination in Lisbon in 1908.

The somewhat austere three-storey building of the **Ducal Palace** seems almost diminished by the huge expanse of the square in front, which also dwarfs the statue of Dom João IV, the eighth duke, on his horse. Guided tours lasting about 45 minutes are laid on in various languages throughout the day, except for lunchtime. Endless rooms contain a rich mixture of furnishings and paintings. One of the first to catch the eye is the painting on the marble staircase depicting the 15th-century Battle of Ceuta, in North Africa, which started Portugal on a trail of discoveries and colonial expansion. English, Flemish and French tapestries hang in the tapestry room; the heady mix continues with Chinese porcelain and Brazilian ebony furniture. It becomes less like a museum tour when the personal rooms of the artistic Dom Carlos and family are reached. Some of the king's paintings still adorn the walls, dresses and suits hang in the wardrobes, and the table is still laid awaiting the return of the king and his son from that fatal last trip to Lisbon. The best is saved until last: the massive kitchens with 2000kg of gleaming copper hanging there in the shape of pans of every description.

On the right of the palace, guarding the entrance to this massive estate, is the famous Manueline gate displaying the knots associated with the House of Bragança. The stables here house yet another **museum**, this time dedicated to coaches. Also in the grounds is a chase enclosed by 18km (11 miles) of walls reserved for royal hunting parties; overall, the estate covers some 21,000 ha of prime hunting ground.

A short walk up the road lined with orange trees opposite the palace leads to the **castle** which is not of special interest, although it is possible to walk in the grounds and on the walls. The moated castle itself is entered from the far side across a drawbridge, through the smaller gate and into a courtyard which now houses a museum devoted to hunting.

Alandroal

It is only a short drive from Vila Viçosa to Alandroal on the skirts of the hilly, rather than mountainous, Serra de Ossa. Alandroal, with its Moorish sounding name, has a coat of arms which proudly declares that it belongs to the house of Avis and the Moorish and Avis connections together have written the main chapters in its history. In contrast to the electric-blue and white used to decorate many houses in Alentejo, this is an ochre and white town, so painted as a protection against the plague. The proof of the pudding is that Alandroal has remained plague free. Blue and white is believed to ward off evil spirits and is probably a legacy of the Muslims who still believe the blue and white eye is a powerful symbol against evil. The old town, its streets well shaded with orange trees and palms, is a pleasant place for strolling although there is not too much to see. A grand marble fountain, Fonte Monumental da Praça, has six heads (only the middle two spout water), and beyond that the **castle** is the next point of call. According to inscriptions left by the founder of the castle, Lourenço Afonso, 9th Master of the Order of São Bento de Avis, the work was started on the order of Dom Dinis in 1294 and finished in 1298. With the Arab Galvo as principal architect, it is not surprising to find Moorish elements, like the pyramid-capped battlements, in the structure. Inside the castle lies Igreja Nossa Senhora de Conceição which was built around the same time as the castle. Walking the battlements opens up good views of the town and the surrounding countryside.

From Alandroal the road divides, which leaves a choice of opting for a quieter life by visiting the small castle town of **Terena** located in rolling plains to the south. This old town essentially consists of two narrow, cobbled streets and a castle, but there is the added attraction of taking lunch on the terrace at *Migas*, perhaps trying the Alentejo pork speciality of *migas*. The other choice is to press on to Redondo. Both routes meet up again at Reguengos de Monsaraz.

Redondo

Very much a pottery town, Redondo is fast expanding and gaining a reputation for its excellent wine. The road from Alandroal joins the EN254 before entering Redondo and this road leads conveniently into the main square, Praça da República, which is the location of Turismo. The town's claim to fame is that it was the headquarters of Viriatus, the intrepid Lusitanian shepherd turned warrior, who caused the invading Romans so much trouble until he was eventually assassinated in 139 BC by three traitorous comrades bribed by the Romans. It is the pottery, the medieval walls and the ruins of the **castle** that attract visitors. The town was fortified by that assiduous castle builder Dom Dinis in 1319, but the castle was sacked by Edmund Earl of Cambridge in 1381 (who dealt out the same treatment at Monsaraz). The English at that time were invited to Portugal under the old Alliance to help defend the frontier during the wars between Dom Fernando and Henry II of Castile. Unfortunately, the troops turned out to be 14th-century forerunners of the 20th-century lager louts. Check the front gate of the castle, Porta do Sol, by all means but do not miss the rear gate, Porta da Ravessa, which gives its name to an excellent wine produced by the Adega Co-operative de Redondo. They produce some nine million litres of wine from 1200 ha of vineyard in modern stainless steel equipment and by the latest techniques.

There is the sight of water as the road from Redondo to Reguengos de Monsaraz crosses the reservoir formed by Barragem da Vigia. Abandon ideas of stopping at Reguengos de Monsaraz, once a prominent wool town and now a leading wine producer; instead, look straight away for the road to the old town of Monsaraz. There is a chance to catch one of the megalithic sites, **Anta do Olival da Pega**, en route. Before Monsaraz is reached and just before the right turn to Horta da Moura, look for a small road off left marked with bollards which starts surfaced but immediately becomes a track. Continue a short distance through the olive grove and park near the sign announcing 'Anta'. This site is a burial chamber with a long corridor, which yielded engraved slate and carved horn pieces when it was first explored.

Monsaraz

Located on a jutting peak above the Guadiana river and firmly enclosed by stout walls, Monsaraz is one of those fairy-tale towns too good to miss. If time allows only one visit to the area then Monsaraz should be considered first. Dolmens and menhirs abound in the region telling of prehistoric settlement by the megalithic builders and in the Iron Age; the Romans and Visigoths

Medieval Monsaraz dominates the surrounding countryside

followed, then the Moors, but they left only faint footprints. Recovered from the Moors in 1167 by Geraldo Sem-Pavor, Monsaraz was given to the Knights

Templar by Dom Sancho II in 1232 as a reward for their help in its recovery; it passed to the Order of Christ in 1319 when the Templars were extinguished. Dom Afonso and then Dom Dinis encouraged repopulation and ordered a castle to be built for the people's protection, which was done in 1310. When the English Earl of Cambridge took up residence, after being invited by Dom Fernando, he and his merry band rebelled on not being paid and rewarded their host by sacking the castle in 1381. This probably made it easier for the Castilians to take it during the Castilian Wars of 1383–85. The castle was recovered from the Castilians almost immediately by Nuno Álvares Pereira, who later became known as the Sainted Constable.

Cobbled Rua Direita leads directly from the town gate to the castle past 16th- and 17th-century whitewashed houses, all with square windows and doors. The parish church, **Igreja Matriz**, stands in the main square, along with the 18th-century **pillory**. Next to it is Turismo which has little to offer in the way of information except for a simple leaflet, but the town is so small it barely needs a plan. The former **Paços de Audiência**, in the same square, houses an exhibition of sacred art which includes mainly vestments but is of limited appeal. At the end of Rua Direita is the compact granite **castle** looking as sturdy as the day it was built. Its battlements invite exploration. Climbing to the top of the keep is not too difficult and is worth it for the views, not just of the houses clustered within the town walls but over the countryside, including the Guadiana river. The upper floor in the keep was once the home of the *alcaidaria*, while the lower floor was earlier a prison then an armoury.

Signs from Monsaraz lead to Mourão which actually lies across the Guadiana river. There is the **Cromlech do Jerez** to visit en route, found by turning down the track opposite the Quinta de Jerez. This is a standing stone believed to be connected with fertility rites; the sacred area around is marked off by smaller stones.

Mourão

Mourão is another fortified border town which was caught up in the sometimes fierce battles along this frontier. Originally the settlement was at Vila Velha nearer the river, probably a Moorish village, but it was deserted for some time after reconquest by the Christians. A new settlement was established on higher ground, and the first **fort** was built in 1226 under Gonçalo Egas, Prior of the Order of St John of Jerusalem. He is believed to have granted the first charter, confirmed by Dom Dinis in 1296. Further reconstruction and enlargement continued, and by the time Dom Sebastião arrived to raise men for his North Africa campaign in the 16th century, the town was large enough to provide 400. The castle and town suffered heavy damage in 1657, during the Wars of Restoration, at the hands of an overwhelming force of Spaniards, but the castle was again restored. Little remains now of even the 17th-century rebuilding except for the walls.

Assuming that further megalithic sites in the area are not to be explored, it is a straight run from Mourão back to Évora through Reguengos de Monsaraz.

Évora to São Cucufate

The prime purpose of the next tour is to visit the extensive Roman remains at São Cucufate, one of the best preserved Roman monuments in Portugal, although Portel and Viana do Alentejo can also be visited en route. Set off by taking the Beja road IP2/EN18 out of Évora and enjoy some of Alentejo's scenery of rolling plains dotted with flat-topped ilex oak. The trees are pruned this way, to the delight of the pigs, to increase the yield of sweet acorns and the area of summer shade, whilst the farmer delights in taking away wood which is ideal for converting into charcoal. Divert off the road for **Portel**, just awakening to tourism, to visit its robust castle. It is unusual in having massive cylindrical angle towers to give greater protection to the walls and most of these still stand. If the castle has no appeal, look in the handicraft shops for the miniatures of traditional Alentejo furniture, a local speciality.

São Cucufate

On reaching Vidigueira, take the Alvito road and look out shortly for signs to São Cucufate, which lies just off the main road to the right. Remarkably for one of the most impressive Roman sites in Portugal, it is unprotected. The substantial remains belong to a **Roman villa** built in the 4th century AD. Excavations have shown previous buildings existed, starting with a villa built in the 1st century which was rebuilt early in the 2nd century around a peristyle but destroyed by the construction of the present building. The villa was used as a monastery until the 16th century, and may even have been used in Moorish times, which accounts for its remarkable state of preservation, despite the monk's having destroyed certain outbuildings to use the ground as a cemetery.

The villa was a rectangular structure of two storeys, with the lower vaulted floor used by the domestic servants and as a storeroom and the upper one to house the family. Just enough evidence remains upstairs to trace the room plan. The façade had a long terrace served by three stairways which opened on to a garden. Some of the original work stopped at foundation level. It is thought the building may never have been completed to plan and that the earlier 2nd-century baths were adapted. On the edge of the villa is a temple very similar to the one found at Milreu outside Faro in Algarve. Amazingly, the ruins stand to a considerable height and the brickwork is still in remarkably good condition. Of the ground floor storage area, a *cryptoporticus* can be discerned, although the roof is missing and, unusually, there are no mosaics to be seen. It is thought to have belonged to an unknown family from Pax Julia (Beja).

Viana do Alentejo

Leave São Cucufate to continue via Alvito to Viana do Alentejo. The latter village has a fine heritage in monuments built throughout the Middle Ages, and none more astonishing than the fortified and crenellated Gothic **Igreja Matriz**, which stands within the castle walls and appears to merge with them. It is worth a stop just to see the church's Manueline doorway. Only the ramparts and battlements of the **castle** remain, protected by a round turret at each corner. Just out of town to the east stands the sanctuary of **Nossa Senhora d'Aires**, which has attracted pilgrims through the ages and still does on the fourth Sunday of September every year when the town is authorised to hold a fair.

Évora to Arraiolos

Other interesting trips out of Évora include the one to Arraiolos which is a relatively short distance – 22km (14 miles) – to the north. The main interest here is not so much the monuments, of which it has its fair share including the ruins of a medieval castle and some fine 16th-century buildings, but its **carpets**. Making carpets and rugs is thought to have originated with the Moors. Demand was stimulated amongst the nobility in the 16th and 17th centuries, when the explorers brought back rugs from Persia and India. These were copied to such good effect in an expanding industry here in Arraiolos that the town has been famous ever since, although now the original patterns have been replaced by local designs. Some of the 18th-century work can be seen hanging on the walls of Portugal's famous houses and palaces, like Queluz Palace near Lisbon. Walking the main street will lead you to the carpet shops, some of which have workshops behind. These colourful creations are expensive, but if it is any consolation, they are cheaper to buy here than anywhere else in Portugal. Take a leaf out of William Beckford's book. According to Rose Macaulay in *They went to Portugal*, on a visit to Arraiolos he 'laid in a stock of bright carpets for his journey, lest he should find himself in an uncarpeted room; in the Estremoz pousada he spread them all around his bed, where they made a flaming, exotic appearance and protected his feet from the damp brick floors'.

Évora to Miróbriga

One final suggested excursion is to the Roman site of Miróbriga right over in the west of the province, close to Santiago do Cacém. It could be combined with the São Cucufate tour (see page xxx), particularly if just the two Roman sites were targeted and São Cucufate left for another day. From Évora it is a two-hour rural drive with plenty of Alentejo scenery and no large towns to negotiate. The route starts out south to Viana do Alentejo, then Alvito, before heading west on the EN257 to join the road running south to Ferreira do Alentejo (EN2). From here it is a fairly straight run west on the EN121 with a short right then left dog leg to cross the major IP1/EN262. Just before entering Santiago do Cacém look for the sign left to Miróbriga.

Miróbriga

This extensive site has been fairly well excavated and researched over the years. The first time, in the 19th century, was under the direction of the Bishop of Beja who used the artefacts to enrich his private collection. Further periods of research in 1940 and 1958–78 culminated in an international project involving Portuguese and American archaeologists, who carried out intensive studies in 1981–85. The site was occupied in the Iron Age and the Roman site built on top, which may explain some of the observed anomalies. It lacks a typical Roman urban layout and there is no other known site in close proximity. One view is that from the 3rd century the site was a sanctuary or large pilgrimage centre, with temples dedicated to Aesculapius and Venus. It was also equipped with baths for use by visitors and a hippodrome to provide entertainment during religious festivals. A contrary view regards the temples simply as part of the forum, as is the case with many Roman provincial towns. Unusually, no mosaics have been found on the site.

The site is well laid out with footpaths which lead systematically all round, past houses, the baths with hot and cold sections, through the hostel including dining rooms, to the forum or acropolis, which was also an Iron Age settlement with a temple. The hippodrome is on a separate site about 1km south of the area and is the only one found in Portugal so far. Artefacts from Miróbriga can be seen in the Municipal Museum at Santiago do Cacém.

Just one more area of this central region of Portugal awaits exploration, the Costa Azul below Lisbon, which can be conveniently accommodated on the way back to the capital.

Practical Information

Hotels and Restaurants

Much of the better accommodation in this part of Alto Alentejo is in manor houses of architectural merit in the TURIHAB (TH) scheme normally located well outside town; in *casa rusticas* (rustic houses), generally within the town or close by and part of Turismo Rural (TR); or on an active farming estate in the Agroturismo (AT) scheme. See page 30 for more details.

ALANDROAL
A Chaminé (tel. 068 44 335). Frogs' legs in tomato sauce do not turn up often on menus in Portugal, but here is your opportunity; otherwise stick to the grills which are good.

ALVITO
Pousada do Castelo de Alvito (tel. 084 48 383). The 15th-century fortress has been converted to provide 20 rooms, swimming pool, chapel garden and small amphitheatre.

ESTREMOZ

Monte dos Pensamentos (TR), Estrada da Estação do Ameixial (tel. 068 22 375). Splendid country house 2km (1 mile) outside Estremoz with four rooms.
Pousada Rainha Santa Isabel (tel. 068 22 618). Built into the historic fortress, rooms furnished in 12th- and 13th-century style, swimming pool. Good restaurant.
Restaurant Alentejano (tel. 068 22 834). Wood-panelled dining room above café, good on pork dishes, very reasonable.

ÉVORA

Albergaria Vitorias, Rua Diana de Lis (tel. 066 27 174). Limited facilities in this four-star establishment, no restaurant, 48 rooms.
Casa de Sam Pedro (TH), Quinta de Sam Pedro (tel. 066 27 731). Converted 18th-century manor house 5km (3 miles) outside Évora with three rooms.
Casa de S. Tiago (TH), Largo Alexandre Herculano, 2 (tel. 066 22 686). Located in 16th-century house in the heart of Évora, six rooms.
Estalagem Póquer, Quinta de Vale Vazios, EN114 (tel. 066 31 473). Four-star hotel with just 15 rooms but good facilities, including restaurant, swimming pool and tennis.
Évorahotel, Quinta do Cruzeiro (tel. 066 734 800). A large three-star hotel with full facilities including restaurant, swimming pools and tennis.
Hotel Ibis, Quinta da Tapada (tel. 066 744 620). Well located by the old town walls, this is a new hotel in the Ibis chain. Plenty of parking, comfortable rooms and buffet breakfast, an ideal base for exploring Évora.
Hotel Santa Clara, Travessa da Milheira, 19 (tel. 066 24 141). Good standard two-star hotel with some facilities for disabled, restaurant.
Pousada dos Lóios (tel. 066 22 618). Opened in 1965 in a restored 15th-century mansion, 32 rooms in a delightful setting with good restaurant.
Quinta da Nora (TR), Estrada dos Canaviais (tel. 066 29 810). Part of a farm 4km (2.5 miles) outside Évora, five rooms.
Quinta do Louredo (TR), Estrada do Igrejinha (tel. 066 22 813). Two rooms only in manor house just 5km (3 miles) outside Évora.

Eating in Évora is generally more expensive than in surrounding towns, and some of the overtly touristic restaurants are best avoided.
A Muralha, Rua Outubru, 21 (tel. 066 22 284). Fairly typical Portuguese restaurant, moderate cost.
Cozina de St Humberto, Rua da Moeda, 39 (tel. 066 24 251). A bit pretentious, avoid the house wine which is not as good as the food; moderate price.
O Fialho, Travessa do Mascarenhas, 14 (tel. 066 23 079). Widely regarded as the best restaurant in town, serves traditional dishes to the Portuguese. Expect to pay a little more.
O Lampião, Rua dos Mercadores, 72 (tel. 066 26 495). Award-winning soups, plenty of good pork dishes at reasonable cost.

ÉVORA MONTE
Monte da Fazenda (TR) (tel. 068 95 172). Rustic house on Alentejan farm producing olives and cork just outside Évora Monte. Five rooms with private sitting rooms.
Restaurant A Convenção (tel. 068 95 217). Next to castle, modern restaurant with good but limited range of dishes; on the expensive side.

MONSARAZ
Horta da Moura (tel. 066 55 206). Rural hotel on agricultural property delightfully situated just 3km (2 miles) outside Monsaraz. 13 rooms and one apartment with good on-site facilities including swimming and horse riding.
Restaurant O Alcaide (tel. 066 55 168). If the roast lamb has no appeal try the roast marinated snails, and very reasonable too.
Zé Lumumba (tel. 066 55 121). Plenty of game dishes in season; reasonable.

MOURÃO
Restaurant Adega Velha (tel. 066 56 443). Wine is made on the premises; good atmosphere and reasonable.

REDONDO
Quinta da Talha (AT), Estrada do Freixo (tel. 066 999 468). Peacefully located 3km (2 miles) outside Redondo on farm estate, a group of houses offering four rooms.
Vá Lá, on Vila Viçosa road (tel. 066 99 521). Restaurant behind small café, unpretentious, good food and very reasonable.

REGUENGOS DE MONSARAZ
Restaurant Central (tel. 066 52 219). On central square, has some interesting dishes on offer including baby shark soup, *sopa de cação*.

TERENA
Casa de Terena (TR), Rua Direita, 45 (tel. 068 45 132). Restored 18th-century house in centre, six rooms and lounge available.
Restaurant Migas (tel. 068 45 188). A little more expensive than most but good regional specialities.

VILA VIÇOSA
Casa de Peixinhos (TH) (tel. 068 98 472). 17th-century manor house forming part of a farm estate with six rooms.
Casa dos Arcos (TH), Paça de Matim Afonso de Sousa (tel. 068 98 518). Situated in 18th-century Renaissance-style manor house, with four rooms and two apartments.
Ouro Branco, Campo da Restauração (tel. 068 98 556). Typical Portuguese restaurant.
Restaurant Os Cuco, Mata Municipal (tel. 068 988 806). New restaurant near market square offering good regional specialities; reasonable.

Places of Interest

ESTREMOZ
Museu Rural, 62 Rossio, open 10am–1pm and 3pm–5.30pm, closed Mondays and holidays.
Museu Municipal, main square inside castle walls. Open 10am–12noon and 2–6pm.
ÉVORA
Museu Municipal, near cathedral, open 10am—12.30pm and 2pm–5pm, closed Mondays and holidays.
Museum of Sacred Art, within cathedral, open 9am–12noon and 2pm–5pm, closed Mondays and holidays.
VILA VIÇOSA
Ducal Palace, open 9.30am–1pm and 2pm–5pm, closed Mondays and holidays.
Museu da Caça (hunting), in castle, open 9.30am–1pm and 2pm–5pm, closed Mondays and holidays.

Tourist Offices

ALANDROAL Câmera Municipal, Praça da República (tel.068 44 150).
ARRAIOLOS Praça Lime de Brito (tel. 066 42 105).
BORBA Câmera Municipal, Praça da República (tel. 068 94 113).
ESTREMOZ Rossio Marquês de Pombal (tel. 068 332 071).
ÉVORA Praça do Giraldo (tel. 066 22 671).
MOURÃO Câmera Municipal, Praça da República (tel. 066 56 113).
MONSARAZ Largo D. Nuno Álvares Pereira (tel. 066 55 136).
REDONDO Câmera Municipal, Praça da República (tel. 066 99 112).
REGUENGOS DE MONSARAZ Rua 1 de Maio (tel. 066 51 315).
VIANA DO ALENTEJO Câmera Municipal, Praça da República (tel. 066 93 106).
VILA VIÇOSA Praça da República (tel. 068 98 305).

13. COSTA AZUL

This huge, pine-covered sand bank south of Lisbon and the Tagus would be infinitely more popular with visitors if it were not for the great industrial sprawl of Setúbal. Crossing the congested suspension bridge across the River Tagus is another deterrent which prevents many heading south from Lisbon to explore the Costa Azul, yet discerning Lisboans, who declare that there is no finer place to live, are willing to face the journey over the bridge twice a day. Choose a time outside rush hour and crossing this toll bridge is usually not difficult. The projected new bridge just a little further upstream should soon help to relieve the congestion.

Faced with image and access problems, the tourist authorities elect to promote the area under the glamorous name of the Blue Coast and work harder at its promotion than they do for other areas. The quality of their information is second to none in the country. Costa Azul, which extends down the Atlantic coast as far as Sines, has many outstanding natural features including the Serra da Arrábida Natural Park, the Natural Reserve of the Sado Estuary, the Natural Reserve of the Tagus Estuary and the Arrábida Fossil Area of the Costa Caparica (see the feature below). There are some very fine beaches including the remarkable Tróia peninsula, which is nothing more than a narrow finger of sand running for almost 17km (10.5 miles).

Costa Azul has a number of small resorts but lacks a major centre. Costa da Caparica, on the west coast just below Lisbon, has fine white sandy beaches and a number of small resorts, the haunt of day trippers out from the capital. Further south, the fishing port of Sesimbra, with good stretches of golden sand, doubles as a resort and is perhaps the most colourful place to stay. But there is no escaping the fact that Setúbal is the hub of the area and the most convenient base for exploring the region. The Novotel just off the EN10 on the outskirts of Setúbal is a convenient location with good access for getting around the area without the problems of Setúbal traffic. The tours described in this chapter all start from Setúbal. Tiny Tróia, on the very tip of the sand spit opposite Setúbal, is well connected by ferry and might suit visitors looking for something quieter with good beaches to hand, or those with an eye on the golf course nearby.

Natural Reserves of the Costa Azul

1. Serra da Arrábida. This natural park encompasses the scenic range of limestone mountains which track the coastline west of Setúbal as far as Sesimbra. Cloaked in green and set in a temperate climate, these mountains have a rich vegetation which is valued scientifically and enjoys protection within the European Biogenic Reserve Network. The diversity of the plants within such a confined area means that visitors barely have to travel any distance to see a whole spectrum of Mediterranean species from strawberry trees, mastic, myrtle, rosemary, lavender and thyme to the more transient delights of *Fritillaria lusitanica*, *Tulipa australis* and a host of wild orchids. These days the fauna is not as rich as it was but it still boasts a good number of small animals including genet, badger, polecat, fox, weasel, hare and rabbit, while the bird life is also diverse.

    2. Sado Estuary. This extensive reserve of 23,200 ha protects the area around the mouth of the River Sado, just to the east of Setúbal. Apart from protecting the diverse bird life – over 100 species appear throughout the year – the reserve also sets out to preserve the rich diversity of the wetlands' molluscs and crustaceans as well as traditional economic activities like the production of salt and resin. The zone has been occupied at least from Neolithic times (3500–2800 BC), and it was particularly important to the Romans who left plenty of evidence of their fishing activities in the form of *garum* tanks as seen on Tróia peninsula, detailed on page 238.

    Birdwatchers should have no trouble seeing white storks (*Ciconia ciconia*) and black-winged stilts (*Himantopus himantopus*) which are frequent visitors, but the marsh harrier (*Circus aeruginosus*) and the kingfisher (*Alcedo atthis*) may require more patience.

    3. The Arrábida Fossil Area of the Costa Caparica. Located on the west coast between Trafaria and Lagoa de Albufeira, the sedimentary rocks which form the river bank in this protected area have special geological significance. Formed over 15 million years, they are rich in fossils of flora, bivalves, gastropods and traces of fish from the Miocene period.

    4. Tagus (Tejo) Estuary. Covering the water surface and the banks around the Tagus estuary, this huge reserve is regarded as the most important in the country. A survey in 1990 counted more than 50,000 mud-living birds, representing 563 species apart from ducks, which constituted around one fifth of the total population. Discounting ducks, the most common species was avocet (*Recurvirostra avosetta*) which totalled 12,662 – reckoned to be half the entire population in Europe. Apart from providing nesting sites and a migratory resting place for birds, the reserve represents an awareness of the need to protect the whole ecosystem, involving molluscs, reptiles, amphibians and mammals, from the effects of agriculture, urban development and pollution.

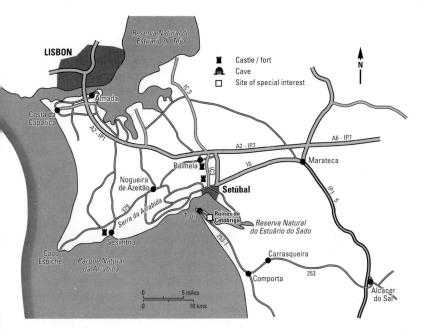

Setúbal

Looking on the dark side, Setúbal is a busy industrial town and the country's third port. However, it would be a mistake to be deterred by this as the attractive old centre is a different world, with narrow pedestrianised streets to wander and one or two interesting monuments and museums to visit.

The town is believed to have started life as a Celtic village sometime in the 7th century BC, but the Romans who occupied the area between the 1st and 5th centuries AD left far more tangible remains, both here and around the Tagus and Sado estuaries. This is where the Romans built a significant export industry based on the easily accessible and abundant supply of fish. Salted fish was one important product but there was also a number of condiments and pastes made from the maceration and fermentation of fish to which herbs were then added. *Garum* was the best known of such products; *Liquamen* and *muria* were two others which, like *garum,* were packed into amphorae for export to other Mediterranean regions. *Garum* tanks can be seen below the glass floor of the tourist office in Setúbal and again at Cetobriga on the Tróia peninsula. In Moorish times, Setúbal was gradually deserted as it increasingly became a battleground between the Moors and the Portuguese. By the time the area was reconquered for Portugal in the 12th century, the town was virtually abandoned and in ruins. It was resettled by moving people there from nearby Palmela, and by the middle of the 13th century it was enjoying rapid growth. Only then were its territorial limits defined and

An example of early Manueline architecture is seen in Igreja de Jesus, Setúbal

Serra de Arrabida scenery at its most alluring

protected by a wall, strengthened by towers, with four gates and 16 doors. Several parts of the old wall (*cerca velha*) still remain, some unfortunately hidden by modern buildings. It was only in 1846, during a period of industrial and commercial growth, that it was given a charter and granted the status of a town, and in 1926 it became capital of the region.

Praça do Bocage, in the heart of town, is named after the 18th-century poet Manuel Maria de Barbosa du Bocage, described by William Beckford as 'perhaps the most original poet ever created by God'. It is a good place to start a walking tour. Follow the narrow pedestrianised shopping streets east to reach Largo de Misercórdia and the tourist office just to the south. Apart from picking up a town street plan, it is a chance to see the old Roman *garum* tanks beneath the glass floor. Close by here is also the **Archaeological and Ethnographical museum** which features the fishing industry very strongly, with working models of fishing boats and dredgers. Fish scales seem an unlikely material for the artist but collages made of these became popular in the 19th century and there is an excellent example exhibited in the museum. The archaeological part exhibits artefacts largely from the Roman period of occupation. Further east still from here is **Casa do Bocage**, the house where the poet was born in 1765 which is now used as the museum of visual arts.

Igreja de Jesus, lying north-west of Praça do Bocage, is Setúbal's most important monument. Designed by Diogo Boitac and built in 1494 as part of the Convent of Jesus, it is an early example of Manueline architecture. The beautiful flamboyant doorway leads into a three-aisled church full of columns twisted like petrified rope and ribs crossing the vaulted ceiling. The best view is from the balcony at the rear reached by a spiral staircase. Next door to the church is the **Museum of Setúbal** which houses a fine collection of 15th- to 16th-century paintings mainly by Portuguese artists, as well as jewellery and some archaeological bits and pieces.

Located at the western end of town, in the foothills of Serra da Arrábida, is the **São Filipe fort**. It has been converted into a *pousada*, but part of the fort is still available to visitors. Although its construction was underway before the 60 years of Spanish rule, its enlargement and completion was ordered by Philip II of Spain in 1590 to protect both the land and the sea from pirate raids and similar irritations by the English. The climb up to the fort is worth it for the views across the Sado estuary towards the tip of the sandy finger which is Tróia. If the caretaker is around, it is possible to enter the chapel to see the *azulejo* scenes of the life of São Filipe created by Policarpo de Oliveira Bernardes in 1736.

Serra da Arrábida tour

This full-day tour extends beyond the natural park to Cabo Espichel at the very western tip and takes in all the places of interest along this section of the coastline. Fonseca's winery at Vila Nogueira de Azeitão is visited on the return run as well as the castle at Palmela.

Following the coast road west out of Setúbal, industrial scenery dominates until beyond the cement works at Outão, when the green-cloaked hills of Serra da Arrábida and a sand-fringed coastline immediately changes the mood. Slip roads occasionally lead down to the sandy beaches but the first one of any size is at **Praia da Figueirinha**, where there is space for water sports as well as a restaurant. There is another beach at **Galapos**, arguably the best along this coast, before the tiny harbour of **Portinho da Arrábida** is reached. Here there is a fine area of beach, a restaurant and, on the western point of the harbour, the Fort of Nossa Senhora da Arrábida, built in 1670 by the Infante Dom Pedro, later Dom Pedro II. It now belongs to the natural park and houses the Oceanographic and Marine museum.

Shortly turning inland, take the road that doubles back along the coast, now at a higher level. Park scenery at its most alluring lies ahead, with spectacular views down through the broom and the oak of the mountainside into tiny coves skirted by azure blue sea and across the same blue water to the Tróia peninsula. Take full advantage of the pull-offs when they occur, to enjoy the views. The first is overlooking the **Convent of Arrábida**, seen as a cluster of white buildings on the hillside which includes hermitages and chapels. It was built for the Franciscan monks in 1542 by the first Duke of Aveiro and extended by the third Duke to include inns and lookout posts. The monks left the monastery in 1834. It has had other owners but now belongs to a minority Oriental sect and there is strictly no admission. More breathtaking views are in store before this corniche road leads off the mountain. Before the cement works are reached again, turn around and enjoy the road over the Serra da Arrábida from the opposite direction. Turn inland on reaching the end and follow on to the next destination, Sesimbra.

Sesimbra

Perched high above the town is the Moorish **castle** – although it has little Moorish influence about it apart from some of the foundations. It was captured from the Moors by Dom Afonso Henriques in 1165 but lost back to the Moors for a time before it was eventually recovered by Dom Sancho I at the end of the 12th century. In facing ultimate defeat, the Moors operated a scorched earth policy in areas hard to defend, as here, and destroyed the castle before departing. Rebuilding started immediately and in 1236 it was granted to the Order of Santiago. There were various phases of modification and improvement up to the 17th century. The castle, which has open access, provides an excellent viewpoint down onto the town and shelters the 18th-century church of Santa Maria do Castelo. Those still with energy to spare can clamber around the walls, which are stepped in parts.

From here a steep road descends, through the rash of apartment blocks and modern buildings mushrooming on the outskirts, down to the sea front. Colourful fishing boats fill the harbour to the west while a blossoming tourist industry targets the old village. Sunbathers and swimmers might find the beach crowded in high season but there is plenty of atmosphere in the

Brightly painted fishing boats in Sesimbra harbour

narrow streets. Although there is not too much to see in town it is an enjoyable walk along the front, passing the 17th-century Santiago Fort, out to the harbour where the fish auctions are held in the mornings as soon as the fishing boats return. There are plenty of seafood restaurants around, and the two fish regarded as local specialities in the Setúbal area, *corvinha* and *cherne*, can be tried perhaps at Sesimbrense in Largo do Município.

Cabo Espichel

It is just a short drive from Sesimbra out to remote, windswept Cabo Espichel. Few will be impressed by the local claim that this desolate cape ranks amongst the most beautiful promontories in Portugal. Probably believing it to be the end of the world, people made pilgrimages in early days to the shrine of Nossa Senhora do Cabo and stayed in the two long arcaded wings flanking the church and facing into the courtyard. Abandoned years ago, this accommodation is now largely restored and used by weekenders. Fossilised dinosaur footprints were discovered at the north and south ends of Lagosteiros beach here, which was at one time a lagoon.

Follow the EN379 all the way back to Vila Nogueira de Azeitão.

Vila Nogueira de Azeitão

This charming town in the heart of muscatel country is home to the somewhat dilapidated 16th-century Távora Palace which belonged to the dukes of Aveiro. It also hosts a bustling regional fair on the first Sunday of every month, selling anything from goats and cows to belts and bowls. Attractions these may be, but the coachloads of visitors who roll up daily head straight for José Maria da Fonseca's **wine factory** with taste buds already tingling in anticipation. Fonseca produce some of Portugal's best known wines, including the full-bodied Periquita red which is produced from locally grown Castelão Francês and Espadeiro grape varieties. Their speciality, however, is the highly aromatic dessert wine Setúbal, made from the Moscatel de Setúbal grape. Free tours are laid on for visitors, with English guides, starting with the small museum in the waiting room. After visiting some of the earth-floor cellars stacked with oak barrels which remain at a constant 16–17°C and seeing some of the stages in the wine production, the tour ends in the bar for a tasting session. If there is an opportunity, try the new Albis, a dry white wine which is for export only but can be purchased at the factory.

Wine tours are also available at the more modern wine factory of J. M. da Fonseca Internacional, which split from the original Fonseca company some time ago and now has no connection apart from the name.

On leaving Vila Nogueira de Azeitão, join the main EN10 Setúbal road briefly before forking left to continue on to Palmela.

Palmela

Interest in Palmela is centred around its rather fine castle which now houses a *pousada*, craft shops and a café.

Archaeological evidence suggests that Palmela attracted a variety of cultures from the end of the Neolithic period up to the arrival of the Romans, but its history only comes clearly into focus with the recapture of the town from the Moors by Dom Afonso Henriques in 1148. This was one of the king's more remarkable feats, since he attended Palmela with only a small band of armed men merely to reconnoitre the situation. The Moorish ruler of Badajoz (in Spain), who was there to attend a reception fled, fearing for his life, and was promptly followed by the massively superior force defending the castle. These deeds are recounted in Camões' epic poem *The Lusiads*. Dom Afonso Henriques reinforced the castle and founded a monastery which he donated to the Order of St James (São Tiago), but the Almohads were back in strength in 1191 and the castle was ruined in the invasion. Don Sancho I rebuilt the castle in 1205 and by 1210 the Order of St James was again installed, since it was busy rendering invaluable service – and continued to do so – in the reconquest of the southern part of the country from the Moors. The castle was maintained and enlarged by successive kings, and in 1443, following a royal edict by Dom João I that the headquarters of the Order of St James be established at Palmela, the construction of a monastery was begun, to be completed around 1470. The massive earthquake of 1755 seriously damaged the castle and the church, but it was only on the abolition of religious orders and the confiscation of their property in 1834 that the monks left the ruins. The castle and church have both now been restored.

It doesn't take too long to wander around the castle, especially since the monastery has now been transformed into a *pousada*. The views from the walls are excellent on a clear day, encompassing Lisbon and the Tagus estuary in the north and the Sado estuary and Tróia to the south. Lying within the castle is the 15th-century church of St James which contains the remains of Jorge de Lencastre, son of Dom João II and last Grand Master of the Order of St James.

Tróia Peninsula

A frequent and regular car ferry service departs from the port at Setúbal and reaches Tróia just 15 minutes later, but long queues build up in summer. Although the return ferries are just as frequent, it is as convenient to complete the circuit and return via Alcácer do Sal taking in a number of places of interest on the peninsula, including Roman Cetobriga and one or two of the small towns at the southern end, like Carrasqueira. It makes a convenient day tour involving around 120km (75 miles) of driving.

Tróia itself is a compact holiday resort known as the Torralta Tourist Development and is full of discos, restaurants, high-rise buildings and superb sandy beaches. Fortunately, it clings to the very tip of the peninsula, so it is easy to leave behind for those searching for peace and quiet.

Cetobriga

As the crow flies, Roman Cetobriga is very close to Tróia, but by road it takes time and the way is not signposted. Head south from the tip of the peninsula and turn left fairly soon into a road signposted to a military installation. As the wide road sweeps right towards the gates of the military camp, keep ahead on a narrow strip of tarmac. Take the first left onto a narrow, stony and sandy track (which gets particularly sandy in parts) and follow it for around 2km (1 mile) until the River Sado and the area of the ruins is reached.

Cetobriga was an industrial complex for the salting of fish and the preparation of pastes such as *garum*. A paved footpath leads around the sandy site and there are information boards in English to explain the uses of a vast number of well preserved tanks. Thermal spas with still recognisable hot and cold areas and houses which originally had two storeys occupy a separate part of the site. The chronology of Cetobriga is not known for certain but it is believed that it continued in operation until the 6th century AD.

Carrasqueira

Follow the same route back to the main road to proceed south down the peninsula. Sand dunes and pines decorate the route all the way to the expanding village of Comporta where a left turns sets a course to Alcácer do Sal. Carrasqueira, passed along the way, is a village like no other and makes an interesting diversion. It sits alongside the ill-defined banks of the Sado estuary and divides its labours between fishing and farming as it has done for

Festivals

Not a summer weekend passes without a festival taking place some-where in Portugal. They are deeply bound up with religion and are usually held to celebrate a saint's day (a *festas*) or a religious pilgrimage (a *romario*). In addition there are popular festivals, like music festivals, but even these may have a religious connection.

Every village in the country has at least one celebration to look forward to in the season while bigger villages and towns may have a number. Months are spent in the planning and organising committees work hard to raise money to decorate the village and the route of the procession. On the day, the villagers gather for mass then walk in procession, carrying images of their patron saint, often to music provided by the local brass band. Do not for one moment think that these are entirely solemn occasions for, once the church procession is over, the folks let their hair down and really go to town, especially in the evening. Often dressed in local costume, the villagers dance and drink the evening away to music, blared through speakers, performed by brass bands or groups of folk singers. Some of the larger festivals are attended by street vendors and travelling funfairs creating a lively market atmosphere. Firecrackers add to the noise as celebrations move towards a climax.

Apart from these local celebrations, there are also big events in the calendar, like Easter and May Day, which are celebrated nationally. Some dates to look for include:

MARCH/APRIL

Easter weekend is celebrated everywhere; Lisbon's Graça district cele-brates with a procession dedicated to '**Senhor dos Passos**' (the Way of the Cross) on the second Sunday of Lent.

MAY

Festas de 'Senhor das Chagas' is held first week in May at Sesimbra to celebrate the miraculous vision of Christ which appeared four centuries ago.

Fátima: the country's most famous pilgrimage, 12/13 May.

Queima das Feitas, in Coimbra, when students burn their college ribbons at the end of the academic year.

JUNE

Festas dos Santos Populares, the feasts of St Anthony (12/13 June), St John (23/24 June) and St Peter (29 June) are all celebrated in many towns throughout the country. The **Festas de Santo António** is one of Lisbon's traditional celebrations.

Festas de São Pedro and **São João**, end of June, Castelo de Vide.

JULY

Festas da Rainha Santa Isabel, Coimbra.

Pilgrimage dedicated to **St Tomé and St James** with parade of horses, 25 July, Ança near Coimbra.
AUGUST
Festas de Nossa Senhora das Salvas, 15 August, Sines.
Festas de Bernardo, Alcobaça.
SEPTEMBER
Festas de N. S. da Nazaré, 8 September and the following weekend, Nazaré.
Romario ao Senhor do Bom Fim, end of September, Portalegre.
Feira de São Mateus, end of September, Elvas.

centuries, scarcely without change. Many of the houses are made from thatched reed with the side and end walls strengthened by spaced wooden planks painted white. White storks take the place of free-range chickens, picking over the fields here.

Alcácer do Sal

Next stop along here is Alcácer do Sal, on a well defined bank of the River Sado. This town can look back on 5000 years of history. It was known as Eviom in the Iron Age and Salatia Urles Imperatoria under the Romans, who collected and traded in salt and fish. Important enough in this period to mint its own coins, it continued in importance to became an episcopal town under the Visigoths. The Moors too valued this port and fortified it with a strong castle which, when back in Portuguese hands, was constantly rebuilt and strengthened throughout the Middle Ages.

Free of hustle and bustle, life goes on at a sedate pace here, but things do change slowly and over the years the dominance of salt has declined in favour of agriculture and cattle breeding. The wide promenade along the river front, where women in black sit beneath their sunshades selling prawns, is the place to rest and watch the world go by, perhaps at the café bar-restaurant Sado where you can actually try the fresh prawns. Wandering the narrow streets is interesting enough but the partially ruined **castle** makes a focal point to head for. The municipal museum, with a collection of archaeological arte-facts from the region, is housed in the **Espirito Santo** church.

Join the IP1 from here for a quick run back to Setúbal or onwards to Lisbon.

Palmela castle now serves as a twenty-six-roomed pousada

Practical Information

Hotels and Restaurants

PALMELA

Pousada da Palmela (tel. 01 235 12 26). Delightfully situated in Palmela castle, this 26-roomed *pousada* uses the monks' refectory of the former monastery as the dining room.

Quinta do Chaparro (tel. 01 235 04 31). Just 2km (1 mile) outside Palmela, this *quinta* offers just one apartment.

SESIMBRA

Hotel Apartamento Vilas de Sesimbra, Alto de S. João (tel. 01 223 27 75). This is a large four-star establishment offering apartments. Good facilities including a swimming pool and a restaurant.

Hotel do Mar, Rua General Humberto Delgardo, 10 (tel. 01 223 33 88). Built on hillside terraces, this two-star hotel with 120 rooms offers magnificent sea views. Facilities include a swimming pool and restaurant.

Residencial Espadarte, Av. 25 Abril, 10 (tel. 01 223 10 11). Situated on the promenade, it is fairly moderately priced. Of the 80 rooms on offer, the newer ones are the best.

Chez Nous, Largo do Município (tel. 01 223 01 41). French dishes on the menu make a change from seafood; moderate.

Restaurant Sesimbrense, Largo do Município. Excellent seafood restaurant, moderately expensive.

SETÚBAL

Hotel Bonfim, Av. Alexandre Herculano (tel. 065 534 111). This four-star hotel is centrally situated overlooking the park of the same name.

Hotel Ibis, Estrada Nacional EN10 (tel. 065 772 200). About 3km (2 miles) from the outskirts of Setúbal, this two-star hotel offers a modern standard of comfort, restaurant and swimming pool on site.

Hotel Novotel, Estrada Nacional EN10, Monte Belo (tel. 065 522 809). Part of the Novotel chain, this three-star hotel with 105 rooms offers a good modern standard of comfort. Facilities include bar, restaurant and swimming pool.

Pousada de S. Filipe, Castelo de S. Filipe (tel. 065 523 844). Delightful situation in the fortress of S. Filipe overlooking Setúbal and the Sado estuary. Opened in 1965, it offers 14 rooms, some of which were originally dungeons of the castle.

There are plenty of eating places in town and the dock area is particularly good for fish restaurants. Others to try include:

Beco, Rua Misericórdia, 24 (tel. 065 24 617). Typical Portuguese dishes figure strongly on the menu; reasonable.

O Caseiro, Av. Luisa Todi (tel. 065 29 268). Good menu but expensive.

O Bago de Arroz, Rua António Granjo, 22 (tel. 065 31 4888). This is one for the vegetarians.

VILA NOGUEIRA DE AZEITÃO
Quinta da Piedade, Casal da Portela, 1 (tel. 01 218 93 81). Delightfully situated just south of Vila Nogueira de Azeitão in the heart of Serra da Arrábida Natural Park. Four rooms are offered with the benefit of a swimming pool.
Quinta de Santo Amaro, Aldeia da Piedade (tel. 01 218 92 30). In the lovely setting of the Serra da Arrábida Natural Park, eight rooms in an 18th-century house; swimming pool.

Places of Interest

Museum of Setúbal, 9am–12noon and 2pm–5pm, closed Sundays and Mondays.
Cetobriga, 9am–1pm and 3pm–6pm.
Alcácer do Sal castle, 10am–12noon and 2pm–5pm.

Tourist Offices

Regional Office of Costa Azul
Travessa Frei Gaspar, 10, 2901 Setúbal (tel. 065 527 033).
TOURISM POSTS
PALMELA Largo do Chafariz (tel. 01 235 00 89).
SESIMBRA Largo da Marinha (tel 01. 223 57 43).
SETÚBAL Praça do Quebedo (tel. 065 534 222).

Metric and Conversion Tables

All measurements are given in metric units. For readers more familiar with the imperial system, the accompanying tables are design to facilitate quick conversion to imperial units. Bold figures in the central column can be read as either imperial or metric, e.g.: 1kg = 2.20lb or 1lb = 0.45kg.

mm		in	cm		in	m		yds
25.4	1	.039	2.54	1	0.39	0.91	1	1.09
50.8	2	.079	5.08	2	0.79	1.83	2	2.19
76.2	3	.118	7.62	3	1.18	2.74	3	3.28
101.6	4	.157	10.16	4	1.57	3.66	4	4.37
127.0	5	.197	12.70	5	1.97	4.57	5	5.47
152.4	6	.236	15.24	6	2.36	5.49	6	6.56
177.8	7	.276	17.78	7	2.76	6.40	7	7.66
203.2	8	.315	20.32	8	3.15	7.32	8	8.75
228.6	9	.354	22.86	9	3.54	8.23	9	9.84

g		oz	kg		lb	km		miles
28.35	1	.04	0.45	1	2.20	1.61	1	0.62
56.70	2	.07	0.91	2	4.41	3.22	2	1.24
85.05	3	.11	1.36	3	6.61	4.83	3	1.86
113.40	4	.14	1.81	4	8.82	6.44	4	2.48
141.75	5	.18	2.27	5	11.02	8.05	5	3.11
170.10	6	.21	2.72	6	13.23	9.65	6	3.73
198.45	7	.25	3.18	7	15.43	11.26	7	4.35
226.80	8	.28	3.63	8	17.64	12.87	8	4.97
255.15	9	.32	4.08	9	19.84	14.48	9	5.59

ha		acres
0.40	1	2.47
0.81	2	4.94
1.21	3	7.41
1.62	4	9.88
2.02	5	12.36
2.43	6	14.83
2.83	7	17.30
3.24	8	19.77
3.64	9	22.24

Metric to imperial conversion formulae

cm to inches	0.3937	km^2 to square miles	0.3861
m to feet	3.281	ha to acres	2.471
m to yards	1.094	g to ounces	0.03527
km to miles	0.6214	kg to pounds	2.205

INDEX